DIGITAL DESIGN

DIGITAL DESIGN

Er. N.B.L. Mathur

ANMOL PUBLICATIONS PVT. LTD.
NEW DELHI-110 002 (INDIA)

ANMOL PUBLICATIONS PVT. LTD.

Regd. Office: 4360/4, Ansari Road, Daryaganj,
New Delhi-110002 (India)
Tel.: 23278000, 23261597, 23286875, 23255577
Fax: 91-11-23280289
Email: anmolpub@gmail.com
Visit us at: www.anmolpublications.com

Branch Office: No. 1015, Ist Main Road, BSK IIIrd Stage
IIIrd Phase, IIIrd Block, Bangalore-560 085 (India)
Tel.: 080-41723429 • Fax: 080-26723604
Email: anmolpublicationsbangalore@gmail.com

Digital Design

First Edition, 2011

ISBN 978-81-261-4502-7

PRINTED IN INDIA

Printed at Mehra Offset Press, Delhi.

Contents

Preface

In today's digital design environment, engineers must achieve quick turn-around time with ready accesses to circuit synthesis and simulation applications. This type of productivity relies on the principles and practices of computer aided design (CAD). The book Digital Design includes basic concepts and principles which addresses many challenging issues which are critical today's in digital design practices such as hazards and logic minimization, finite-state-machine synthesis, cycles and races, and testability theories while providing hands-on experience using one of the industry's most popular design application.

The book begins with discussion, conventional and unconventional number systems, binary coding theories, and arithmetic as well as logic functions and Boolean algebra. Building upon classic theories of digital systems, the book illustrates the importance of logic minimization using the Karnaugh map technique. It continues by discussing implementation options and examining the pros and cons of each method in addition to an assessment of tradeoffs that often accompany design practices. The book also covers testability, emphasizing that a good digital design must be easy to verify and test with the lowest cost possible. Throughout the text, the authors analyze combinational and sequential logic elements and illustrate the designs of these components in structural, hierarchical, and behavior VHDL descriptions.

Author

Chapter 1

Digital System and Binary Numbers

SIGNED BINARY NUMBERS

Binary representations of positive can be understood in the same way as their decimal counterparts. For example

$$86_{10} = 1*64 + 0*32 + 1*16 + 0*8 + 1*4 + 1*2 + 0*1$$

or

$$86_{10} = 1*\ 2^6 + 0*\ 2^5 + 1*\ 2^4 + 0*\ 2^3 + 1*\ 2^2 + 1*\ 2^1 + 0*\ 2^0$$

or

$$86_{10} = 1010110_2$$

The subscript 2 denotes a binary number. Each digit in a binary number is called a bit. The number 1010110 is represented by 7 bits. Any number can be broken down this way, by finding all of the powers of 2 that add up to the number in question (in this case 2^6, 2^4, 2^2 and 2^1). You can see this is exactly analagous to the decimal deconstruction of the number 125 that was done earlier. Likewise we can make a similar set of observations:

- To multiply a number by 2 you can simply shift it to the left by one digit, and fill in the rightmost digit with a 0. To divide a number by 2, simply shift the number to the right by one digit.
- To see how many digits a number needs, you can simply take the logarithm (base 2) of the number, and add 1 to it. The integer part of the result is the number of digits. For instance, $\log_2(86)+1=7.426$. The integer part of that is 7, so 7 digits are needed.

- With n digits, 2^n unique numbers (from 0 to 2^n-1) can be represented. If n=8, 256 (=2^8) numbers can be represented 0–255.

It is often convenient to handle groups of bits, rather than individually. The most common grouping is 8 bits, which forms a byte. A single byte can represent 256 (2^8) numbers. Memory capacity is usually referred to in bytes. Two bytes is usually called a word, or short word (though word-length depends on the application). A two-byte word is also the size that is usually used to represent integers in programming languages. A long word is usually twice as long as a word. A less common unit is the nibble which is 4 bits, or half of a byte. It is cumbersome for humans to deal with writing, reading and remembering individual bits, because it takes many of them to represent even fairly small numbers. A number of different ways have been developed to make the handling of binary data easier for us.

Decimal	Hexadecimal	Binary
0	0	0000
1	1	0001
2	2	0010
3	3	0011
4	4	0100
5	5	0101
6	6	0110
7	7	0111
8	8	1000
9	9	1001
10	A	1010
11	B	1011
12	C	1100
13	D	1101
14	E	1110
15	F	1111

The most common is hexadecimal. In hexadecimal notation, 4 bits (a nibble) are represented by a single digit. There is obviously a problem with this since 4 bits gives 16 possible combinations, and there are only 10 unique decimal digits, 0 to 9. This is solved by using the first 6 letters (A..F) of the alphabet as numbers. The table shows the relationship between decimal, hexadecimal and binary.

There are some significant advantages to using hexadecimal when dealing with electronic representations of numbers (if people had 16 fingers, we wouldn't be saddled with the awkward decimal system). Using hexadecimal makes it very easy to convert back and forth from binary because each hexadecimal digit corresponds to exactly 4 bits ($\log_2(16) = 4$) and each byte is two hexadecimal digit. In contrast, a decimal digit corresponds to $\log_2(10) = 3.322$ bits and a byte is 2.408 decimal digits. Clearly hexadecimal is better suited to the task of representing binary numbers than is decimal.

As an example, the number $CA3_{16} = 1100\ 1010\ 0011_2$ ($1100_2 = C_{16}$, $1010_2 = A_{16}$, $0011_2 = 3_{16}$). It is convenient to write the binary number with spaces after every fourth bit to make it easier to read. Converting back and forth to decimal is more difficult, but can be done in the same way as before.

$$3235_{10} = C_{16}*256 + A_{16}*16 + 3_{16}*1 = C_{16}*16^2 + A_{16}*16^1 + 3_{16}*16^0$$

or

$$3235_{10} = 12*256 + 10*16 + 3*1 = 12*16^2 + 10*16^1 + 3*16^0$$

Octal notation is yet another compact method for writing binary numbers. There are 8 octal characters, 0...7. Obviously this can be represented by exactly 3 bits. Two octal digits can represent numbers up to 64, and three octal digits up to 512. A byte requires 2.667 octal digits. Octal used to be quiete common, it was the primary way of doing low level I/O on some old DEC computers. It is much less common today but is still used occasionally (e.g., to set read, write and execute permissions on Unix systems)

In summary:

Bit: a single binary digit, either zero or one.

Byte: 8 bits, can represent positive numbers from 0 to 255.

Hexadecimal: A representation of 4 bits by a single digit 0..9,A..F. In this way a byte can be represented by two hexadecimal digits *long word*: A long word is usually twice as long as a word.

Nibble: 4 bits, half of a byte.

Octal: A representation of 3 bits by a single digit 0..7. This is used much less commonly than it once was (early DEC computers used octal for much of their I/O)

Word: Usually 16 bits, or two bytes. But a word can be almost any size, depending on the application being considered—32 and 64 bits are common sizes

SIGNED BINARY INTEGERS

It was noted previously that we will not be using a minus sign (–) to represent negative numbers. We would like to represent our binary numbers with only two symbols, 0 and 1.

There are a few ways to represent negative binary numbers. The simplest of these methods is called ones complement, where the sign of a binary number is changed by simply toggling each bit (0's become 1's and vice-versa).

This has some difficulties, among them the fact that zero can be represented in two different ways (for an eight bit number these would be 0000 0000 and 1111 1111)., we will use a method called two's complement notation which avoids the pitfalls of one's complement, but which is a bit more complicated. To represent an n bit signed binary number the leftmost bit, has a special significance. The difference between a signed and an unsigned number is given in the table below for an 8 bit number.

The value of bits in signed and unsigned binary numbers

	Bit 7	Bit 6	Bit 5	Bit 4	Bit 3	Bit 2	Bit 1	Bit 0
Unsigned	$2^7 = 128$	$2^6 = 64$	$2^5 = 32$	$2^4 = 16$	$2^3 = 8$	$2^2 = 4$	$2^1 = 2$	$2^0 = 1$
Signed	$-(2^7) = h128$	$2^6 = 64$	$2^5 = 32$	$2^4 = 16$	$2^3 = 8$	$2^2 = 4$	$2^1 = 2$	$2^0 = 1$

Let's look at how this changes the value of some binary numbers

Binary	Unsigned	Signed
0010 0011	35	35
1010 0011	163	–93
1111 1111	255	–1
1000 0000	128	–128

If Bit 7 is not set (as in the first example) the representation of signed and unsigned numbers is the same. However, when Bit 7 is set, the number is always negative. For this reason Bit 7 is sometimes called the sign bit. Signed numbers are added in the same way as unsigned numbers, the only difference is in the way they are interpreted. This is important for designers of arithmetic circuitry because it means that numbers can be added by the same circuitry regardless of whether or not they are signed.

To form a two's complement number that is negative you simply take the corresponding positive number, invert all the bits, and add 1. The example below illustrated this by forming the number negative 35 as a two's complement integer:

$35_{10} = 0010\ 0011_2$
invert $\rightarrow$ $1101\ 1100_2$
add 1 $\rightarrow$ $1101\ 1101_2$

So 1101 1101 is our two's complement representation of -35. We can check this by adding up the contributions from the individual bits

$1101\ 1101_2 = -128 + 64 + 0 + 16 + 8 + 4 + 0 + 1 = -35.$

The same procedure (invert and add 1) is used to convert the negative number to its positive equivalent. If we want to know what what number is represented by 1111 1101, we apply the procedure again

$?=1111\ 1101_2$
invert $\rightarrow$ $0000\ 0010_2$
add 1 $\rightarrow$ $0000\ 0011_2$

Since 0000 0011 represents the number 3, we know that 1111 1101 represents the number –3.

POSITIVE BINARY FRACTIONS

The representation of unsigned binary fractions proceeds in exactly the same way as decimal fractions. For example

$0.625_{10} = 1*0.5 + 0*0.25 + 1*0.125 = 1*2^{-1} + 0*2^{-2} + 1*2^{-3} = 0.101_2$

Each place to the right of the decimal point represents a negative power of 2, just as for decimals they represent a negative power of 10. Likewise, if there are m bits to the right of a decimal, the precision of the number is 2^{-m} (versus 10^{-m} for decimal). Though it is possible to represent numbers greater than one by having digits to the left of the decimal place we will restrict ourselves to numbers less than one. These are commonly used by Digital Signal Processors.

The largest number that can be represented by such a representation is $1–2^{-m}$, the smallest number is 2^{-m}. For a fraction with 15 bits of resolution this gives a range of approximately 0.99997 to 3.05E–5.

Note that this representationis easily extended to represent all positive numbers by having the digits to the left of the decimal point represent the integer part, and the digits to the right representing the fractional part. Thus

$6.625_{10} = 110.101_2$

SIGNED BINARY FRACTIONS

Signed binary fractions are formed much like signed integers. We will work with a single digit to the left of the decimal point, and this will represent the number –1 (= $-(2^0)$). The rest of the representation of the fraction remains unchanged. Therefore this leftmost bit represents a sign bit just as with two's complement integers. If this bit is set, the number is negative, otherwise the number is positive. The largest positive number that can be represented is still $1\text{-}2^{-m}$ but the largest negative number is -1. The resolution is still $1–2^{-m}$.

There is a terminology for naming the resolution of signed fractions. If there are m bits to the right of the decimal point, the number is said to be in Q*m*format. For a 16 bit number (15 bits to the right of the decimal point) this results in Q15 notation.

BINARY CODES

INTRODUCTION

It would be stretching our imagination to suggest that Sir Francis had digital audio on his minde (sic) when he wrote the prophetic words

Nonetheless, this basic idea forms the basis of everything we do in digital computing, digital communications, and digital audio/video. In 1832, Samuel F. B.

Morse used the very same idea to propose that telegram *words* be coded into *binary addresses* or *binary codes* that could be transmitted over telegraph lines and decoded at the receiving end to unravel the telegram. Morse abandoned his scheme, illustrated in Figure, as too complicated and, in 1838, proposed his fabled Morse code for coding letters (instead of words) into objects (dots, dashes, spaces) capable of a threefold difference onely (sic).

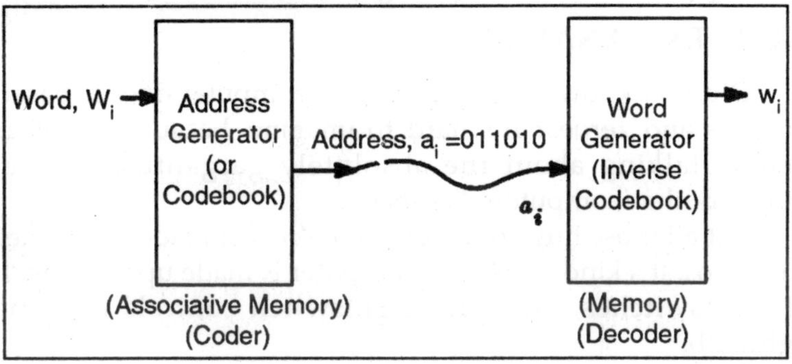

Fig. Generalized Coder-Decoder

The basic idea of Figure is used today in cryptographic systems, where the "address a_i" is an encyphered version of a messagew_i; in vector quantizers, where the "address a_i" is the address of a close approximation to data w_i; in coded satellite transmissions, where the "address a_i" is a data word w_i plus parity check bits for detecting and correcting errors; in digital audio systems, where the "address a_i" is a stretch of digitized and coded music; and in computer memories, where a_i is an address (a coded version of a word of memory) and w_i is a word in memory.

In this chapter we study three fundamental questions in the construction of binary addresses or binary codes. First, what are plausible schemes for mapping symbols (such as words, letters, computer instructions, voltages, pressures, etc.) into binary codes? Second, what are plausible schemes for coding likely symbols with short binary words and unlikely symbols with long words in order to minimize the number of binary digits (bits) required to represent a message?

Third, what are plausible schemes for "coding" binary words into longer binary words that contain "redundant bits" that may be used to detect and correct errors? These are not new questions.

They have occupied the minds of many great thinkers. Sir Francis recognized that arbitrary messages had binary representations. Alan Turing, Alonzo Church, and Kurt Goedel studied binary codes for computations in their study of computable numbers and algorithms.

BASIC EXPLANATION

Did you know that everything a computer does is based on ones and zeroes? It's hard to imagine, because you hear people talking about the absolutely gargantuan (huge) numbers that computers "crunch".

But all those huge numbers - they're just made up of ones and zeros. It's kind of like the computer is made up of a bunch of lightswitches, and each lightswitch controls just one lightbulb.

On or Off. One or Zero. But if you took *all* of those lightbulbs together, and said "Let's make each sequence of On-and-Off represent a different number!" Well then, you could get some pretty large numbers. What do I mean by sequence? Let's say you had two lightswitches.

There are four different ways we could flip those switches:

Both Off
First Off, Second On
First On, Second Off
Both On

Binary Code takes each of those combinations and assigns a num berto it, like this:

BothOff= 0
First Off, Second On = 1
First On, Second Off = 2
Both On = 3

Intermediate Explanation

Another way of thinking about it is this: let's give each lightbulb a point value. We'll say the first lightbulb is worth two points, and the second one is worth one point. Now take a look at the combinations:

Both Off = 0 + 0 = 0

First Off, Second On = 0 + 1 = 1

First On, Second Off = 2 + 0 = 2

Both On = 2 + 1 = 3

If we added in another lightbulb, we would make it worth twice as many points as the 2 pointer. Then, if all the bulbs were on, the point value would be 4 + 2 + 1 = 7. And if we added in *another* bulb, we would make it worth 8 points (twice as much as four). Now if they are all turned on, that's worth 8 + 4 + 2 + 1 = 15. As you can see, it's going to take a lot of lightbulbs to make a really big number!

Finally, even though we're giving point values to each of those lightbulbs, when we write them down we still only write them as ones and zeros. One means On, and Zero means Off.

So let's say we had 8 lightbulbs, and they were set up like this:

Off Off On On Off On Off Off.

The point values of those eight bulbs are: 0 + 0 + 32 + 16 + 0 + 4 + 0 + 0 (remember - we only give points if they're turned on!)

And that adds up to 52. So we would say the sequence of bulbs is worth 52. But how do we write it? We write it like this: 00110100

So now we can say $00110100_{binary} = 52$.

8421 BCD CODE

In the 8421 Binary Coded Decimal (BCD) representation each decimal digit is converted to its 4-bit pure binary equivalent.

For example: $57_{dec} = 0101\ 0111_{bcd}$

Addition is analogous to decimal addition with normal binary addition taking place from right to left. For example,

6	0110	BCD for 6	42	0100 0010	BCD for 42
+3	0011	BCD for 3	+27	0010 0111	BCD for 27
	1001	BCD for 9		0110 1001	BCD for 69

Where the result of any addition exceeds 9(1001) then six (0110) must be added to the sum to account for the six invalid BCD codes that are available with a 4-bit number. This is illustrated in the example below

8	1001	BCD for 8
+7	0111	BCD for 7
	1111	exceeds 9 (1001) so
	0110	add six (0110)
	0001 0101	BCD for 15

Note that in the last example the 1 that carried forward from the first group of 4 bits has made a new 4-bit number and so represents the "1" in "15". In the examples above the BCD numbers are split at every 4-bit boundary to make reading them easier. This is not necessary when writing a BCD number down. This coding is an example of a binary coded (each decimal number maps to four bits) weighted (each bit represents a number, 1, 2, 4, etc.) code.

4221 BCD CODE

The 4221 BCD code is another binary coded decimal code where each bit is weighted by 4, 2, 2 and 1 respectively. Unlike BCD coding there are no invalid representations. The decimal numbers 0 to 9 have the following 4221 equivalents

Decimal	4221	1's complement
0	0000	1111
1	0001	1110
2	0010	1101
3	0011	1100
4	1000	0111
5	0111	1000
6	1100	0011
7	1101	0010
8	1110	0001
9	1111	0000

the 1's complement of a 4221 representation is important in decimal arithmetic. In forming the code remember the following rules

- Below decimal 5 use the right-most bit representing 2 first.
- Above decimal 5 use the left-most bit representing 2 first.
- Decimal 5 = 2+2+1 and not 4+1.

GRAY CODE

Gray coding is an important code and is used for its speed, it is also relatively free from errors. In pure binary coding or 8421 BCD then counting from 7 (0111) to 8 (1000) requires 4 bits to be changed simultaneously. If this does not happen then various numbers could be momentarily generated during the transition so creating spurious numbers which could be read.

The first 16 Gray Coded Numbers are Indicated below.

Decimal	Gray Code
0	0000
1	0001
2	0011
3	0010
4	0110
5	0111
6	0101
7	0100
8	1100
9	1101
10	1111
11	1110
12	1010
13	1011
14	1001
15	1000

Gray coding avoids this since only one bit changes between subsequent numbers. To construct the code there are two simple rules. First start with all 0s and then proceed by changing the least significant bit (lsb) which will bring about a new state.

To convert a Gray-coded number to binary then follow this method:

- The binary number and the Gray-coded number will have the same number of bits
- The binary MSB (left-hand bit) and Gray code MSB will always be the same
- To get the binary next-to-MSB (i.e. next digit to the right) add the binary MSB and the gray code next-to-MSB. Record the sum, ignoring any carry.
- Continue in this manner right through to the end. Gray coding is a non-BCD, non-weighted reflected binary code.

CYCLIC CODES

Cyclic codes fall under the category of codes called linear codes. Definition 6 A linear code of dimension k and length n over a field $\mathbb{F}$ is a k-dimensional subspace of $\mathbb{F}^n$. Such a code is called an n,k code. If the minumum distance of the code is d, then the code is called an $[n,k,d]$ code.

The row-space of the following matrix forms a $[7,3,4]$ code.

$$\begin{pmatrix} 1 & 0 & 1 & 1 & 1 & 0 & 0 \\ 0 & 1 & 0 & 1 & 1 & 1 & 0 \\ 0 & 0 & 1 & 0 & 1 & 1 & 1 \end{pmatrix}$$

Notice that there are 4 ones in each row. Any binary n-vector can be thought of as the coeffiecients of an nth degree polynomial in $\mathbb{Z}_2$. Looking at the first row in the matrix we can relate it to the polynomial

$$g(x) = 1 + x^2 + x^3 + x^4$$

in the polynomial ring $\mathbb{Z}_2[x]$. Given a linear code the following proposition is clear.

Proposition 1 Let C be a linear code. Then $d(C)$ equals the smallest Hammming weight of all nonzero code vectors.

There are many different varieties of linear codes, such as the well known Hamming codes. We now want to consider a brand of linear codes called cyclic codes. Then we will define BCH codes, which are a specific type of cyclic code.

Definition 7 A linear code C is called cyclic if $(c_1, c_2, ..., n_c) \in C$ implies $(c_n, c_1, c-2, ..., n_{n-1}) \in C$

For example, if $(1,1,1,0,1,0)$ is in a cyclic code, then $(0,1,1,1,0,1)$ is also in the code. The definition is recursive and so every cyclic shift of the elements is in the code. In order to formalize the discussion we can use the following isomorphism

$$(a_0, a_1, ..., a_{n-1}) \in \mathbb{F}_q^n \rightleftharpoons a_0 + a_1 x + ... + a_{n-1} x^{n-1} \in \mathbb{F}_q[x]$$

between the n-dimensional vector space $\mathbb{F}_q^n$ and the residue class of polynomials $\mathbb{F}_q[x]/(x^n - 1)$. Recall from algebra that

$$\mathbb{F}_q[x]/(x^n - 1) = \{a_0 + a_1 x + ... + a_{n-1} x^{n-1} | a_i \in \mathbb{F}_q, 0 \le i \le n\}$$

We can now speak of codeword in C as the polynomials $c(x) | \mathbb{F}_q[x]/(x^n - 1)$, and the following theorem follows

Theorem 2 A linear code C in $\mathbb{F}_q^n$ is a cyclic code iff C is an ideal in $\mathbb{F}_q[x]/(x^n - 1)$.

Proof. $(\Rightarrow)$ If C is an ideal in $\mathbb{F}_q[x]/(x^n - 1)$ and $c(x) = c_0 + c_1 x + c_{n-1} x^{n-1}$ is any codeword, then $xc(x)$ is also a codeword. Thus

$$(c_{n-1}, c_0, c-1, ..., c_{n-2}) \in C \quad (\Leftarrow)$$

If C is cyclic, then for every codeword $c(x)$ the word $xc(x)$ is also a codeword. Therefore $x^i c(x)$ is in C for every i, and since C is linear $a(x)c(x)$ is in C for every polynomial $a(x)$. It follows that C is an ideal.

The next theorem states the general structure of cyclic codes.

Theorem 3 Let C be a cyclic code of length n over a finite field $\mathbb{F}$. To each codeword $(a_0, a_1, \ldots, a_n - 1) \in C$, associate the polynomial $a_0 + a_1 x + \ldots + a_{n-1} x^{n-1}$ in $\mathbb{F}[x]$. Among all the nonzero polynomials obtained from C in this way, let $g(x)$ have the smallest degree. We may assume that $g(x)$ is monic. This polynomial is called the generating polynomial for C. Then

- $g(x)$ is uniquely determined by C.
- $g(x)$ is a divisor of x^{n-1}.
- C is exactly the set of coefficients of the polynomials of the form $g(x)f(x)$ with deg $(f) \le n-1$.
- Write $x^n - 1 = g(x)h(x)$. Then $m(x) \in \mathbb{F}[x]/(x^n - 1)$ corresponds to an element of C iff $h(x)m(x) \equiv 0 \bmod (x^n - 1)$.

Proof:

1. The codespace is spanned by the rows of a matrix. Because the row space of the matrix is closed under subtraction the difference between any two vectors, or polynomials, in the space is still in the space. So if there was another monic generating polynomial $g_1(x)$ with minimum degree, then $g(x) - g_1(x)$ is

also in the space. But this is a contradiction since this new polynomial has smaller degree than both $g(x)$ and $g_1(x)$.

2. Divide $g(x)$ into $x^n - 1$. By the division algorithm we get $x^n - 1 = g(x)h(x) + r(x) \Rightarrow -r(x) \equiv g(x)h(x)$ mod $(x^n - 1)$ where deg $r(x) <$ deg $g(x)$.

But multiplying $g(x)$ by powers of x corresponds to a cyclic shift of the corresponding code vector and multiplication by a polynomial is thus a linear combination of the code vectors in the generating matrix and all of their cyclic shifts. So $r(x)$ is in the code space of C. Since deg $r(x) <$ deg $g(x) <$, $r(x)$ must be equal to zero. Thus $g(x) \mid x^n - 1$. Notice then that $\mathbb{F}[x]/(x^n - 1)$ is not a field since it has zero divisors.

3. Let $m(x)$ correspond to an element in C. Divide $g(x)$ into $m(x)$ $m(x) = g(x)f(x) + r_1(x)$ with deg $r(x) <$ deg $g(x)$. From (2) we know that $g(x)f(x)$ corresponds to a codeword and by assumption so does $m(x)$. So, since C is closed under subtraction, $m(x) - g(x)f(x)$ mod $(x^n - 1)$ is also a codeword. But this is just $r_1(x)$ and has degree less than $g(x)$. It follows that $r_1(x) \equiv 0$ and $m(x)$ is the product of the generating polynomial with another polynomial. Because each codeword has length n, deg $m(x) \leq n - 1$ so deg $f(x) \leq n - 1 -$ deg $g(x)$.

Conversely, we have shown that the product of any two polynomials $g(x)f(x)$ is in C. Thus, these polynomials yield all of the code words of C.

4. By (2) we can write $x^n - 1 = g(x)h(x)$. Let $m(x)$ correspond to an element in C. Then by (3) $h(x)m(x) = h(x)g(x)f(x) = (x^n - 1)f(x) \equiv 0 \mod (x^n - 1)$ Next suppose that $m(x)h(x) \equiv 0 \mod (x^n - 1)$.

Then $m(x)h(x) = (x^n - 1)q(x) = h(x)g(x)q(x)$ for some polynomial $q(x)$. We can now divide through by $h(x)$ and get $m(x) = g(x)q(x)$ and so $m(x)$ coresponds to a codeword of C.

Remark: There will be a unique polynomial $h(x)$ such that $g(x)h(x) = x^n - 1$. When thinking of the codespace as a product of polynomials with $g(x)$ instead of the row space of a binary matrix, this polynomial $h(x)$ will take the place of the check matrix in the decoding process.

Let $c(x) = b(x)g(x)$ be a codeword then

$$c(x) = h(x)g(x)h(x) = b(x)(x^n - 1)$$

Then if $m = \deg b(x)$ the coeffiecients of the m highest powers match the coeffiecients of the m lowest powers of x in the polynomial $c(x)h(x)$.

Further, if the generating polynomial

$g(x) = g_0 + g_1x + ... + g_{n-k}x^{n-k}$ has degree $n-k$, then the codewords $g(x), xg(x) + x^2g(x), ... + g_{n-k}x^{n-k}$ form a basis for the codespae C with a generating matrix

$$\begin{pmatrix} g_0 & g_1 & \cdots & g_{n-k} & 0 & 0 & ... & 0 \\ 0 & g_1 & ... & g_{n-k-1} & g_{n-k} & 0 & ... & 0 \\ 0 & 0 & ... & & & & ... & 0 \\ 0 & 0 & ... & & g_0 & g_1 & ... & g_{n-k} \end{pmatrix}$$

and we can Realise a code word as an information sequence $(a_0, a-1, ...a_{k-1})$ times the matrix $aG = \left(a_o + a_1x + ... + a_{k-1}x^{k-1}\right)g(x)$ mod $x^n - 1$ As stated before, we can treat the polynomial $h(x)$, having the condition that $g(x)h(x) \equiv 0$ mod $x^n - 1$, as the check polynomial of the code C. Knowing that we want $g_0h_i + g_1h_{i-1} + ... + g_{n-k}h_{i-n-k} = 0$ for $i = 0, 1, ..., n-1$, it follows that the check matrix for the code is

$$\begin{pmatrix} 0 & 0 & ... & 0 & h_k & ... & h_1 & h_0 \\ 0 & 0 & ... & h_k & ... & h_1 & h_0 & 0 \\ \vdots & & & & & & & \vdots \\ h_k & ... & h_1 & h_0 & 0 & ... & 0 & 0 \end{pmatrix}$$

Lets now consider an example using a 3×7 matrix of 0's and 1's.

$$\begin{pmatrix} 1 & 0 & 1 & 1 & 1 & 0 & 0 \\ 0 & 1 & 0 & 1 & 1 & 1 & 0 \\ 0 & 0 & 1 & 0 & 1 & 1 & 1 \end{pmatrix}$$

Because each of the three rows are linearly independent we know from linear algebra that the row space of the matrix is a 3-dimensional subspace of $\mathbb{F}^7$ where $\mathbb{F}$ is the field $\mathbb{Z}_2$.

In fact, since the algorithm is based on left multiplication by a code vector, the row space is the range of the matrix. In essence, because each code vector corresponds to a polynomial, the code space corresponds to cyclic shifts of the coefficients of polynomials, which is just all polynomial products $a(x)g(x)$ where $g(x)$ is the generating polynomial for the code C.

It turns out that in this case all the cyclic shifts of the first row vector account for every vector in the row space. Thus we have a cyclic code and the generating polynomial is

$$g(x) = 1 + x^2 + x^3 + x^4$$

which corresponds to the first row of the generating matrix.

Also, $(x^4 + x^3 + x^2 + 1)(x^3 + x^2 + 1) = x^7 - 1$ and so the check polynomial is

$$h(x) = x^3 + x^2 + 1$$

and we get the following check matrix

$$H = \begin{pmatrix} 0 & 0 & 0 & 1 & 1 & 0 & 1 \\ 0 & 0 & 1 & 1 & 0 & 1 & 0 \\ 0 & 1 & 1 & 0 & 1 & 0 & 0 \end{pmatrix}$$

Now taking the codeword c_g corresponding to $g(x)$ we get

$$Hc_g = \begin{pmatrix} 0 & 0 & 0 & 1 & 1 & 0 & 1 \\ 0 & 0 & 1 & 1 & 0 & 1 & 0 \\ 0 & 1 & 1 & 0 & 1 & 0 & 0 \end{pmatrix} \begin{pmatrix} 1 \\ 0 \\ 1 \\ 1 \\ 1 \\ 0 \\ 0 \end{pmatrix} = \begin{pmatrix} 0 \\ 0 \\ 0 \\ 0 \\ 0 \\ 0 \\ 0 \end{pmatrix}$$

mod 2

In fact, for every codeword c in the space C, the

product $\lfloor Hc$ will be the zero vector. This will be an extremely important detail when creating an algorithm for a single-error correcting BCH code

ERROR DETECTING AND CORRECTING CODES

ERROR-CORRECTING CODES

Introduction

The theory of error detecting and correcting codes is that branch of engineering and mathematics which deals with the reliable transmission and storage of data. Information media are not 100% reliable in practice, in the sense that noise (any form of interference) frequently causes data to be distorted. To deal with this undesirable but inevitable situation, some form of redundancy is incorporated in the original data.

With this redundancy, even if errors are introduced (up to some tolerance level), the original information can be recovered, or at least the presence of errors can be detected. We saw in class how adding to the original message the parity bit or the arithmetic sum allows the detection of a (certain type of) error.

However, that kind of redundancy doesn't allow for the correction of the error. Error-correcting codes do exactly this: they add redundancy to the original message in such a way that it is possible for the receiver to detect the error and correct it, recovering the original message.

This is crucial for certain applications where the re-sending of the message is not possible (for example, for interplanetary communications and storage of data). The crucial problem to be resolved then is how to add this redundancy in order to detect and correct as many errors as possible in the most efficient way.

This document starts with an overview of the applications of the error-correcting codes, followed by a session describing the fundamental concepts. It then addresses some of the issues involved in the design of the codes. The last session is a brief introduction of the very last discovery in the theory of error-correcting codes: the turbo codes. Most of us have used error-correcting codes, perhaps without knowing it.

The International Standard Book Number (ISBN) system identifies every book with a ten-digit number, such as 0-226-53420-0.

The first nine digits are the actual number but the tenth is added according to a mathematical formula based on the first nine. If a single one of the digits is changed, as in a misprint when ordering a book, a simple check verifies that something is wrong.

Other common numbers with check digits include the Chemical Abstracts Service (CAS) method of identifying chemical compounds and the United States Postal Service (USPS) nine-digit "zip+four" code, which when it is bar-coded includes a tenth check digit hidden to the human eye but visible to the bar code reader.

Some high-end computer memory chips, "ECC RAM," use extended nine-bit bytes. The ninth bit, or "check bit," is always set so that the total number of ones in the extended byte is even. (This rule is called a "checksum." Specifically, if the sum of the nine bits is not even, an error has been detected.) This ninth bit is not used or even seen by your software, but the computer hardware itself will signal an error if it ever reads an extended byte that contains an odd number of ones.

All these processes can *detect* a single error within a very short message: nine decimal digits for the ISBN and USPS codes, a varying number of decimal digits for the CAS numbers, eight binary digits for ECC RAM. However, they cannot *correct* any error that is detected. Furthermore, some combinations of two or more errors occurring within the message will not be detected.

Coding Theory

Coding theory deals with ways of extending the check-bit and checksum ideas to enable detection and even correction of large numbers of errors within messages. It builds on some beautiful mathematical ideas that we can hint at here. Let's focus on binary messages, the stuff of which computer communications is built.

The first thing is to break up the message into "words" of fixed size. We will focus on how to correct errors occurring within individual words.

If the words are n bits long, then there are 2^n possible messages each word can carry. The set of all such words has an interesting geometry based on the *Hamming distance.* The distance between two words is just the number of places in which they differ.

For example, let's consider the case n=7. The distance between 0100111 and 1100101 is two, because these words differ in the first and sixth places.Words can also be added to each other. This is done by the usual odd-even rules of addition, performed bit by bit. Specifically, 0+0=0, 0+1 = 1, 1+0 = 1, and 1+1 = 0. Thus 0100111 + 1100101 = 1000010.

Suppose you want to send a message in the form of a binary string, i.e., a string of 0's and 1's. Due to noise in the medium over which you are transmitting the message, be it a telephone line, a radio link or the Internet, it is possible that some of the 0's will be received as 1's and vice versa. Let us denote the probability that any one bit is garbled in transmission by *p*.

Typically, *p* will be small, say about one in a million, but that may still be too large for our purposes. If we are transferring a file that has 10 million bits, the chance that the file is incorrectly received is nearly 90%. How can we improve the reliability of the transmission? The simplest method is to repeat ourselves three times.

For example, if we want to send the string 010, we transmit 000111000. If a single error occurs in transmission, this may be received for instance as 001111000. At the receiver, we use what is called majority decoding. We look at each set of 3 bits and decode it as the bit which occurs most often. Thus, the received message above is correctly decoded as 010 even though an error occured in transmission. In the above example, it could have happened that two errors occured and we received the string 101111000. This would be decoded as

110, which is different from the original message. This shows that we cannot eliminate errors altogether, we can only make them less likely.

To see how much less likely, let us work out the probability that a single bit is incorrectly received. Since each bit is transmitted three times, it has to be incorrectly received at least twice in order for the decoder to get it wrong.

The probability of this is $3p^2+p^3$, which, for p equal to one in a million works out to about one in 330 billion. Thus, using the repetition code, a 10 Mbit file can be sent correctly with probability 99.997%. While this coding scheme dramatically reduces the likelihood of errors, it is rather inefficient. Can we do better?

Here's one way, using the famous (7,4) Hamming code. This works with a block of 4 bits at a time rather than with a single bit. Suppose we want to transmit the block 0011. Look at the picture below.

We write these bits in the intersections of the circles. Next, we fill in the part of each circle lying outside the intersection using the rule that the total number of 1's contained in each circle should be even.

The extra bits are called parity bits—they ensure even parity for the number of 1's in each circle. The message we transmit will consist of all seven bits, in a pre-arranged order so that the receiver can reconstruct the diagram. Suppose now that a single error occurs, so that the receiver gets a 1 in the intersection of the top two circles.

The receiver proceeds to work out the parity for each of the circles, and finds that the top two circles both have odd parity (odd number of 1's), while the bottom circle has even parity. This enables her to conclude that an error has occurred, and that the error is in the bit position common to the top two circles.

Therefore, the intended message can be decoded correctly. It is not hard to see that a similar approach works if the error is in some other bit position. However, if there are two errors, then the decoding procedure fails in that it yields a message different from the intended one.

Applications of Error Correcting Codes

The increasing reliance on digital communication and the emergence of the digital computer as an essential tool in a technological society have placed error-correcting codes in a most prominent position. We cite here a few specific applications, in an attempt to indicate their practicality and importance.

Many computers now have error-correcting capabilities built into their random access memories; it is less expensive to compensate for errors through the use of error-correcting codes than to build integrated circuits that are 100% reliable. The single error-correcting Hamming codes, and linear codes in general, are of use here.

Disk storage is another area of computing where error-coding is employed. Storage capacity has been greatly increased through the use of disks of higher and higher density. With this increase in density, error probability also increases, and therefore information is now stored on many disks using error-correcting codes.

In 1972, the *Mariner* space probe flew past Mars and transmitted pictures back to earth. The channel for such transmissions is space and the earth's atmosphere. Solar activity and atmospheric conditions can introduce errors into weak signals coming from the spacecraft. In order that most of the pictures sent could be correctly recovered here on earth, the following coding scheme was used. The source alphabet consisted of 64 shades of gray. The source encoder encoded each of these into binary 6-tuples and the channel encoder produced binary 32-tuples. The source decoder could correct up to 7 errors in any 32-tuple. This was done with the Reed-Muller codes.

In 1979, the *Voyager* probes began transmitting Colour pictures of Jupiter. For Colour pictures the source alphabet needed to be much larger and was chosen to have 4096 Colour shades. The source encoder produced binary 12-tuples for each Colour shade and the channel encoder produced 24-tuples (i.e. 24 dimensional vectors). This code would correct up to 3 errors in any 24-tuple, and is the Golay code.

The increasing popularity of digital audio is due in part to the powerful error-correcting codes that the digitization process facilitates. Information is typically stored on a small aluminized disk as a series of microscopic pits and smooth areas, the pattern representing a sequence of 0's and 1's.

A laser beam is used as the playback mechanism to retrieve stored data. Because the data is digital, error correction schemes can be easily incorporated into such a system. Given an error-coded digital recording, a digital audio system can on playback, correct errors introduced by fingerprints, scratches, or even imperfections originally present in the storage medium.

The compact disc system pioneered by Philips Corporation of the Netherlands in cooperation with Sony Corporation of Japan, allowing playback of pre-recorded digital audio disks, is an excellent example of the application of error-correcting codes to digital communication; *crossinterleaved Reed-Solomon* codes are used for error correction in this system. Digital audio tape (DAT) systems have also been developed, allowing digital recording as well as playback.

Error-correcting codes are particularly suited when the transmission channel is noisy. This is the case of wireless communication. Nowadays, all digital wireless communications use error-correcting codes.

Fundamental Concepts

We begin with a few definitions, in order to develop a working vocabulary.

Let A be an alphabet of q symbols. For example, A = {a,b,c,...,z) is the standard lower case alphabet for the English language, and A = (0,1) is the binary alphabet.

Definition A block code of length n containing M codewords over the alphabet A is a set of M n-tuples where each n-tuple takes its components from A. We refer to such a block code as an [n,M]-code over A.

In practice, we most frequently take A to be the binary alphabet.

Given a code C of block length n over an alphabet A, those specific n-tuples over A which are in C are referred to as codewords.

Note that while the channel encoder transmits codewords, the n-tuples received by the channel decoder may or may not be codewords, due to the possible occurrence of errors during transmission.

Example: Suppose the information we are to transmit comes from the set of symbols {A, B, C, D}. For practical considerations we associate sequences of 0's and l's with each of these symbols.

A → 00
B → 01
C → 10
D → 11

This is the source encoding.

Now we want to add some redundancy (channel encoding).

A → 00 → 00000
B → 01 → 10110
C → 10 → 01011
D → 11 → 11101

We have just constructed a [5,4]-code over a binary alphabet. That is, we constructed a code with 4 codewords, each being a 5-tuple (block length 5), with each component of the 5-tuple being O or 1. The code is the set of n-tuples produced by the channel encoder (as opposed to the source encoder). The source encoder transforms messages into k-tuples (k=2 in the example above) over the code alphabet A, and the channel encoder assigns to each of these information k-tuples a codeword of length n (n=5 in the example). Since the channel encoder is adding redundancy, we have n > k and hence we have message expansion. While the added redundancy is desirable from the point of view of error control, it decreases the efficiency of the communication channel by reducing its effective capacity. The ratio k to n is a measure of the fraction of information in the channel which is non-redundant.

Definition The rate of an [n,M]-code which encodes information k-tuples is

$$R = K/n$$

The rate of the simple code given in example 1 is 2/5.

The quantity r = n-k is sometimes called the redundancy of the code.

A fundamental parameter associated with an [n,M]-code C is the Hamming distance for C. Before we can define the Hamming distance for a code, we must define the Hamming distance between two codewords.

Definition The Hamming distance d(x,y) between two codewords x and y is the number of coordinate positions in which they differ.

Example: Over the alphabet A = (0,1}, the codewords x and y x=(10110) y=(11O11) have Hamming distance d(x,y) =3.

Example: The codewords u and v over the alphabet A = (0,1,2), given by u = (21002) v=(12001) have Hamming distance d(u,v) =3.

Definition Let C be an [n,M]-code.

The Hamming distance d of the code C is d= min {d(x,y): x,y belong to C, x != y}.

In other words, the Hamming distance of a code is the minimum distance between two distinct codewords, over all pairs of codewords.

Example: Consider C = $(c_0, c_1, c_2, c_3\}$ where c_0=(00000) c_1 =(10110) c_2= (01011) c_3= (11101) This code has distance d = 3. It is the [5,4] code constructed earlier.

Suppose we have an [n,M]-code C with distance d. We need to adopt a strategy for the channel decoder (or just decoder). When the decoder receives an n-tuple r it must make some decision. This decision may be one of

- *No errors have occurred*: Accept r as a codeword.
- *Errors have occurred*: Correct r to a codeword c.
- *Errors have occurred*: No correction is possible.

In general, the decoder will not always make the correct decision; for example, consider the possibility of an error pattern occurring which changes a transmitted codeword into another codeword. The goal is that the decoder take the course of action which has the greatest probability of being correct. One usually makes the assumption that errors are introduced by the channel at random, and that the probability of an error in one coordinate is independent of errors in adjacent coordinates.

The decoding strategy we shall adopt, called nearest neighbour decoding, can then be specified as follows.

Nearest Neighbour Decoding If an n-tuple r is received, and there is a unique codeword c that belongs to C such that d(r,c) is a minimun, then correct r to the c. If no such c exists, report that errors have been detected, but no correction is possible. By nearest neighbour decoding, a received vector is decoded to the codewords"closest" to it, with respect to Hamming distance.

The figure below illustrates the concept. The red dots are the codewords, the green ones are the received words that can be corrected to the closest codewords and the blue dot is a received word that is equidistant from 2 codewords and therefore cannot be corrected.

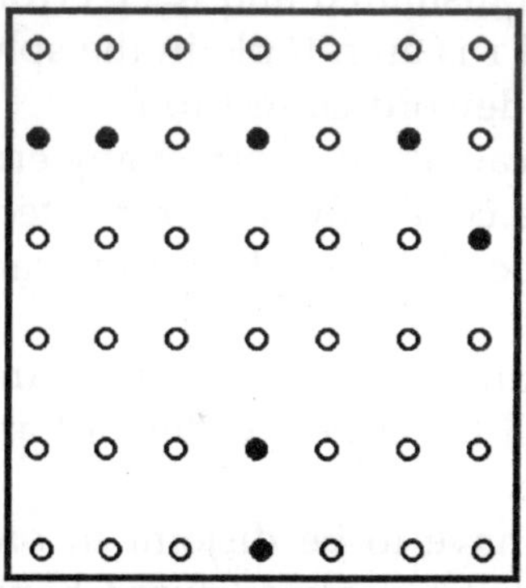

A code is said to correct e errors if a decoder using the above scheme is capable of correcting any pattern of e or fewer errors introduced by the channel. In this case, the decoder can correct any transmitted codeword which has been altered in e or fewer coordinate positions.

Theorem Let C be an [n,M]-code having distance d = 2e+1. Then C can correct e errors. If used for error detection only, C can detect 2e errors.

Let c be one codeword of C and S be the set of all n-tuples over the alphabet of C and define

S(c) = {x belongs to S: d(x,c) ⇐ e).

S(c) is called the sphere of radius e about the codeword c. It consists of all n-tuples within distance e of the codeword c, which we think of as being at the Centre of the sphere.

In the figure below, the"spheres" arount the codewords of the previous figure. The radius is in this case is 1.

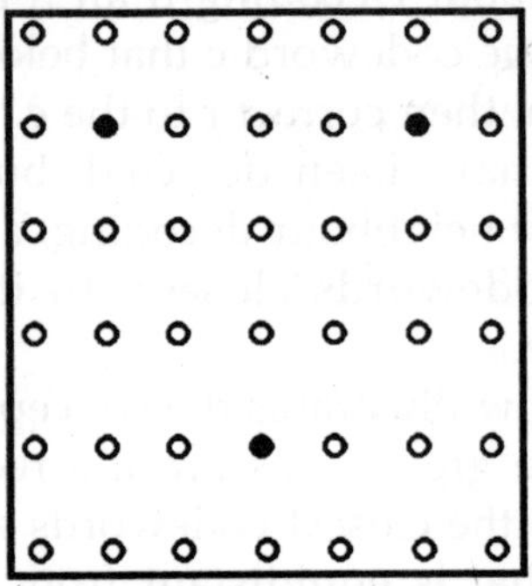

Given 2 codewords, their spheres don't intersect, hence if codeword c is transmitted and t⇐ e errors are introduced, the received word r is an n-tuple in the sphere S(c) and thus c is the unique codeword closest to r.

The decoder can always correct any error pattern of this type. If we use the code only for error detection, then at least 2e+1 errors must occur in a codeword to carry it into another codeword.

If at least 1 and at most 2e errors are introduced, the received word will never be a codeword and error detection is always possible.

The spheres have to be disjoint in order to be able to correct errors. But if a received word happens to be in the space between the spheres, correction is not possible: that space doesn't belong to any sphere, i.e. to any codeword: the error is detected but not corrected.

Therefore, we want to find codes such that the the spheres around the codewords are disjoint (to correctly correct the errors) but as close as possible to each other, to correct ALL the errors.

If all the space is taken by the sphere, all the words received will fall into the sphere of a codeword and therefore can be corrected to that codeword. These are the perfect codes. Lets give the formal definition of perfect codes.

Definition A perfect code is an e-error-correcting [n, M]-code over an alphabet A such that every n-tuple over A is in the sphere of radius e about some codework.

In a perfect code of block length n, the sphere of radiuse about codeworks are not only disjoint (since the code is e-error-correcting) but exhaust the entire space of n-tuples.

Issues in the Design of Error-correcting Codes

Designing a good code is a very hard problem. Also, lots of factors need to be taken in account. For instance, in practice the code should be designed appropriately depending on the expected rate of errors for the particular channel being employed.

If it is known that the probability that the channel will introduce 2 errors into any transmitted codeword is extremely small, then it is likely not necessary to construct a code that will correct all 2-bit error patterns.

A single error correcting code will likely suffice. Conversely, if double errors are frequent and a single error correcting code is being used, then decoding errors will be frequent. From this brief introduction, a number of questions arise.

- Given n, M and d, can we determine if an [n Al] code with distance d exists?
- Assuming such a code does exist, how would one be constructed in practice?
- How should information k-tuples be associated with codeword n-tuples to facilitate efficient channel encoding?
- How should channel decoding be performed?

Lets examine the issue of channel decoding in greater detail. When a word is received and it's not a codeword, finding the closest codeword involves computing the distance from the received word to each codeword, requiring M comparisons. While this might be acceptable for small M, in practice we usually find M quite large.

Suppose a code C is used with M = 2^50 codewords, which is not unrealistic. If we could carry out 1 million distance computations per second, it would take around 20 years to make a single correction.

Clearly, this is not tolerable and more efficient techniques are required. Wishing to retain the nearest neighbour decoding strategy, we seek more efficient techniques for its implementation.

The theory of error-correcting code is concerned with constructing codes for various values of n, M and d, and the consideration of appropriate encoding and decoding techniques.

Most of the best known codes are algebraic in nature like the linear codes. Linear codes are an important and general class of error-correcting codes.

For example, theBCH codes used for CDs are linear codes. They are heavily mathematical and an appropriate description here is not possible. The next session describes instead the last"discovery" in the theory of error correcting codes, the Turbo codes.

Turbo Codes

In session 3, when we introduced the Nearest Neighbour Decoding, we didn't mention the fact that what the decoding actually does is maximizing the probability P(r|c) that r is received, given that c is sent. i.e. choosing the nearest codeword is equivalent to choosing the most likely input message c given the received tuple r.

This decoding strategy is known as maximum likelihood decoding. We can then state the decoding problem in the following manner. Let U be the original message, X the encoded message and Y the message received after the noisy channel. This is schematized in the following figure.

The receiver knows Y and the model of the encoder, i.e. is has a knowledge of how the original message was originally encoded.

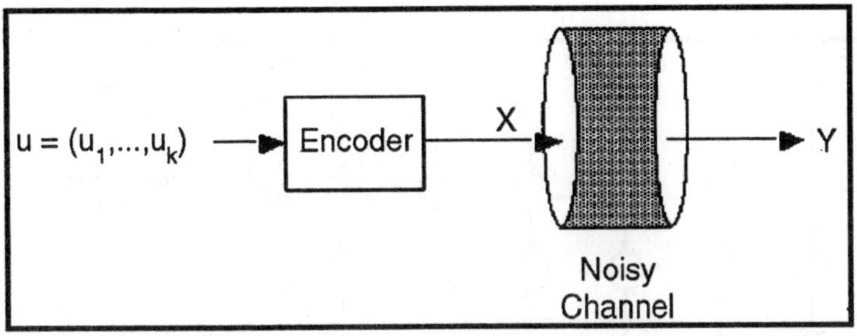

The problem now is finding the U that maximizes the probability that U was sent given that Y was received, i.e. the probability P(U | Y).

Having stated the decoding problem in probabilistic terms, we can take advantage of various methods that deal with probability estimations. A class of such methods is the class of graphical models.

The simplest graphical model:

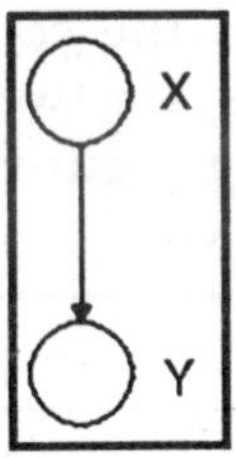

A classical problem of probability estimation is finding the probability distribution P(X | Y) where X and Y are 2 random variables.

The graphical model framework allows for such probability estimations to be calculated in an efficient way.

Note that the calculation of P(X | Y) from P(Y | X) and P(X) is just Bayes rule – P(X | Y) = P(Y | X)P(X)/P(Y) – and that graphical model inference algorithms can be viewed as generalizations of Bayes rule to arbitrary graphs.

Lets now see how we can view error correcting codes as graphical models. In the figure below, a convolution code as a graphical model.Let U be the original message, X the encoded message and Y the message received after the noisy channel.

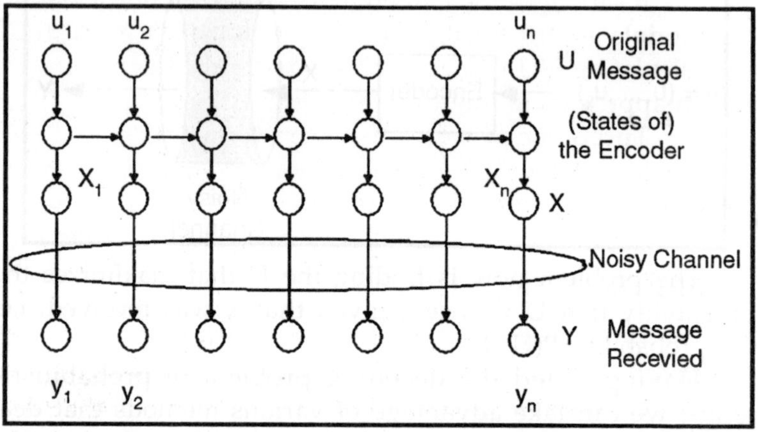

Now, the decoding problem of finding U that maximizes p(U|Y) can be tackled within the framework of graphical models.

We have introduced the convolutional codes mainly because the Turbo codes are two convolutional codes put together. The following figure illustrate the graphical representation of a turbo code.

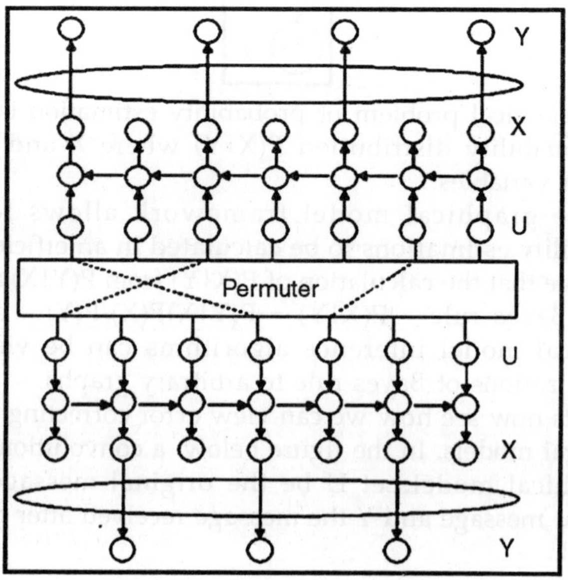

It should be mentioned that general inference in graphical models is NP-hard, and, in particular, exact inference, calculating P(U I Y), for turbo codes is infeasible and therefore an approximate inference algorithm is used.

Turbo codes were discovered very recently. There is much excitement about them. They outperform all other kinds of error-correcting codes in the case of long block lengths, although the reason why they do so is not yet clear.

ERROR DETECTING

R. W. Hamming wrote the paper that both opened and closed this field in 1950. His interest was in providing a means of self-checking in computers, which were just being developed at the time he wrote this. the paper appeared in the Bell System Technical Journal, April, 1950. Definitely worth tracking down in the library and reading.

Bit Strings as Addresses in Binary Hypercubes

The best starting point for understanding ECC codes is to consider bit strings as addresses in a binary hypercube. A hypercube is a generalization of a cube to various dimensions; we're probably most familiar with the notion of a four-dimensional hypercube. Here's a picture of binary hypercubes for several different dimensionalities:

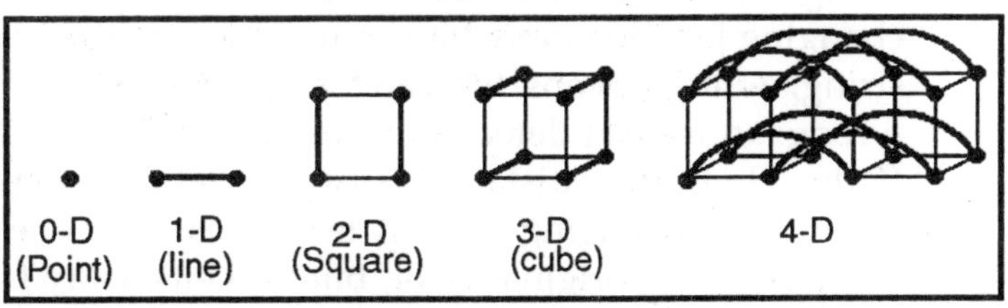

Each of them was created by copying the one to the left twice, and connecting corresponding vertices.

We can assign each vertex in a hypercube a location in a coordinate space determined by the dimensionality of the hypercube.

- A zero-dimensional hypercube requires no coordinates to know where you are

- A one-dimensional hypercube can use one bit to tell whether you're at the bottom or the top of the line segment.
- A two-dimensional hypercube can use two bits: first bit is left vs. right, second is inherited from the line.
- A three-dimensional hypercube can use a bit to tell front square from back, and inherit two bits from the square.
- A four-dimensional hypercube can use a bit to tell left cube from right, and inherits three bits from cube.

This can continue through as many dimensions as you want. The Hamming distance between two bit strings is the number of bits you have to change to convert one to the other: this is the same as the number of edges you have to traverse in a binary hypercube to get from one of the vertices to the other.

The basic idea of an error correcting code is to use extra bits to increase the dimensionality of the hypercube, and make sure the Hamming distance between any two valid points is greater than one.

- If the Hamming distance between valid strings is only one, a single-bit error results in another valid string. This means we can't detect an error.
- If it's two, then changing one bit results in an invalid string, and can be detected as an error. Unfortunately, changing just one more bit can result in another valid string, which means we can't know which bit was wrong: so we can detect an error but not correct it.
- If the Hamming distance between valid strings is three, then changing one bit leaves us only one bit away from the original error, but two bits away from any other valid string. This means if we have a one-bit error, we can figure out which bit is the error; but if we have a two-bit error, it looks like one bit from the other direction. So we can have single bit correction, but that's all.
- Finally, if the Hamming distance is four, then we can correct a single-bit error and detect a double-bit error.

This is frequently referred to as a SECDED (Single Error Correct, Double Error Detect) scheme.

Parity

The simplest case is by adding a parity bit. Suppose we have a three-bit word (so the bit strings define points in a cube). If we add a fourth bit, we can decree that any time we want to switch a bit in the original three-bit string, we also have to switch the parity bit.

If we start with 000 in the left cube, so the full string is 0000, changing any one of the original three bits requires us to change to the other cube: 1001, 1010, and 1100. Now if we change a second bit, we have to move back to the left cube: 0011, 0101, 0110. And if we change the third bit, we move back to the right cube: 0111.

So, there is a Hamming distance of two between any two valid strings. If we get a one-bit error, we know it is an error because it's on one of the invalid vertices.

This can be computed by counting the number of 1's, and making sure it's always even (so this is called even parity). We could have selected exactly the opposite set of vertices as the valid ones, which would have given us odd parity. We picked even parity because we'll be using it in the next step.

HAMMING CODES

Several Teletext packets contain information protected by hamming. This is a method for encoding data such that errors in reception can be detected, and if the error is sufficiently small, corrected. Teletext uses two hamming codes.

The simpler and more robust version encodes 4 bits of data in one 8-bit byte. This code is used extensively to protect the fields that have meaning to the Teletext system itself.

The more efficient code encodes 18 bits of data in three 8-bit bytes. It is used for to protect some of the data fields inside Teletext packets. Both codes are designed such that any one-bit error can be corrected, and any 2-bit error can be detected.There's an error correction code that separates the bits holding the original value (data bits) from the error correction bits (check bits), and the difference between the calculated and actual error correction bits is the position of the bit that's wrong. It's called a Hamming Code.

Error correction codes are a way to represent a set of symbols so that if any 1 bit of the representation is accidentally flipped, you can still tell which symbol it was. For example, you can represent two symbols x and y in 3 bits with the values x=111 and y=000.

If you flip any one of the bits of these values, you can still tell which symbol was intended. If more than 1 bit changes, you can't tell, and you probably get the wrong answer.

So it goes; 1-bit error correction codes can only correct 1-bit changes. If b bits are used to represent the symbols, then each symbol will own 1+b values: the value representing the symbol, and the values differing from it by 1 bit.

In the 3-bit example above, y owned 1+3 values: 000, 001, 010, and 100. Representing n symbols in b bits will consume n*(1+b) values. Hamming code is a set of error-correction code s that can be used to detect and correct bit errors that can occur when computer data is moved or stored.

Hamming code is named for R. W. Hamming of Bell Labs. Like other error-correction code, Hamming code makes use of the concept of parity and parity bit s, which are bits that are added to data so that the validity of the data can be checked when it is read or after it has been received in a data transmission. Using more than one parity bit, an error-correction code can not only identify a single bit error in the data unit, but also its location in the data unit.

In data transmission, the ability of a receiving station to correct errors in the received data is called forward error correction (FEC) and can increase throughput on a data link when there is a lot of noise present.

To enable this, a transmitting station must add extra data (called *error correction bits*) to the transmission. However, the correction may not always represent a cost saving over that of simply resending the information. Hamming codes make FEC less expensive to implement through the use of a *block parity* mechanism. Computing parity involves counting the number of ones in a unit of data, and adding either a zero or a one (called a *parity bit*) to make the count odd (for odd parity) or even (for even parity).

For example, 1001 is a 4-bit data unit containing two one bits; since that is an even number, a zero would be added to maintain even parity, or, if odd parity was being maintained, another one would be added.

To calculate even parity, the XOR operator is used; to calculate odd parity, the XNOR operator is used. Single bit errors are detected when the parity count indicates that the number of ones is incorrect, indicating that a data bit has been flipped by noise in the line. Hamming codes detect two bit errors by using more than one parity bit, each of which is computed on different combinations of bits in the data.

8/4 HAMMING

The 8/4 code is quite simple; if the input nibble is the 4-bit value:

```
b3, b2, b1, b0
```

with b3 being the most significant bit, then the output hammed byte is the 8-bit value:

```
b3, b3^b2^b1, b2, !b2^b1^b0, b1,
    !b3^b1^b0, b0, !b3^b2^b0
```

where ^ represents bitwise exclusive-or and ! is bitwise not.

This code has the property that every value is four bits different from all other such values. A one-bit error is therefore unambiguously correctable, being only one bit away from a valid code. A two-bit error is detectable but not correctable, being equidistant between two valid codes.

Here is the table of all 16 encoded nibbles:

Data nibble	Hammed byte
0 = 0 0 0 0	15 = 0 0 0 1 0 1 0 1
1 = 0 0 0 1	02 = 0 0 0 0 0 0 1 0
2 = 0 0 1 0	49 = 0 1 0 0 1 0 0 1
3 = 0 0 1 1	5E = 0 1 0 1 1 1 1 0
4 = 0 1 0 0	64 = 0 1 1 0 0 1 0 0
5 = 0 1 0 1	73 = 0 1 1 1 0 0 1 1

```
 6 = 0 1 1 0   38 = 0 0 1 1 1 0 0 0
 7 = 0 1 1 1   2F = 0 0 1 0 1 1 1 1
 8 = 1 0 0 0   D0 = 1 1 0 1 0 0 0 0
 9 = 1 0 0 1   C7 = 1 1 0 0 0 1 1 1
 A = 1 0 1 0   8C = 1 0 0 0 1 1 0 0
 B = 1 0 1 1   9B = 1 0 0 1 1 0 1 1
 C = 1 1 0 0   A1 = 1 0 1 0 0 0 0 1
 D = 1 1 0 1   B6 = 1 0 1 1 0 1 1 0
 E = 1 1 1 0   FD = 1 1 1 1 1 1 0 1
 F = 1 1 1 1   EA = 1 1 1 0 1 0 1 0
     | | | |        | | | | | | | |
b3b2b1b0 b3 |       b2 |b1 |b0      |
                    |    |    |     |
                    321 !210 !310 !320
```

Decoding a hammed byte back in to a 4-bit nibble can be done using the table below, or by a bit-twiddling algorithm. In the table, the hammed byte value is used to index the row (most significant 4 bits) and column (least significant four bits), and the decoded nibble is read out of the table. If a single bit error has been detected and corrected, the nibble is followed by ``!". If an uncorrecteable error has occurred, the table cell is ``.".

```
LSB
| 0 1 2 3 4 5 6 7 8 9 A B C D E F |
MSB+------------------------------------+---
0 | 1!. 1 1!. 0! 1!.. 2! 1!. A!.. 7!| 0
1 |. 0! 1!. 0! 0. 0! 6!.. B!. 0! 3!. | 1
2 |. C! 1!. 4!.. 7! 6!.. 7!. 7! 7! 7 | 2
3 | 6!.. 5!. 0! D!. 6 6! 6!. 6!.. 7!| 3
4 |. 2! 1!. 4!.. 9! 2! 2. 2!. 2! 3!. | 4
5 | 8!.. 5!. 0! 3!.. 2! 3!. 3!. 3 3!| 5
6 | 4!.. 5! 4 4! 4!.. 2! F!. 4!.. 7!| 6
7 |. 5! 5! 5 4!.. 5! 6!.. 5!. E! 3!. | 7
8 |. C! 1!. A!.. 9! A!.. B! A A! A!. | 8
9 | 8!.. B!. 0! D!.. B! B! B A!.. B!| 9
A | C! C. C!. C! D!.. C! F!. A!.. 7!| A
B |. C! D!. D!. D D! 6!.. B!. E! D!. | B
C | 8!.. 9!. 9! 9! 9. 2! F!. A!.. 9!| C
```

```
D | 8 8! 8!. 8!.. 9! 8!.. B!. E! 3!. | D
E |. C! F!. 4!.. 9! F!. F F!. E! F!. | E
F | 8!.. 5!. E! D!.. E! F!. E! E. E!| F
---+-------------------------------------+---
| 0 1 2 3 4 5 6 7 8 9 A B C D E F |
```

The algorithmic approach shows what is going on more clearly. Assuming the hammed byte is

```
h7, h6, h5, h4, h3, h2, h1, h0
```

with h7 being the most significant bit, we compute

```
p = h7 ^ h6 ^ h5 ^ h4 ^ h3 ^ h2 ^ h1 ^ h0
c0 = h7 ^ h5 ^ h1 ^ h0
c1 = h7 ^ h3 ^ h2 ^ h1
c2 = h5 ^ h4 ^ h3 ^ h1
```

If the parity, p, is correct (equal to 1) then either 0 or 2 errors occurred. If all the check bits, c0, c1, c2 are correct (equal to 1) then the byte was received intact, (no errors) otherwise it was damaged beyond repair (two errors).

If p is 0, then there was a single bit error which can be recovered:

```
c0 c1  c2 meaning
1 1 1  error in bit h6
1 1 0  error in bit h4
1 0 1  error in bit h2
0 1 1  error in bit h0
0 0 1  error in bit h7
0 1 0  error in bit h5
1 0 0  error in bit h3
0 0 0  error in bit h1
```

The erroneous bit should be flipped. Note that there is actually no need to fix errors in bits h6, h4, h2 and h0 since they are not used in the decoded byte.

After flipping bits if necessary, the decoded byte is then:

```
h7, h5, h3, h1
```

24/18 HAMMING

The more efficient 24/18 code is based on the same principle of interleaved check bits and an overall parity bit as the simpler 8/4 code.

Assuming the input bits are:

```
b17, b16, b15, b14, b13, b12, b11, b10, b9, b8,
            b7, b6, b5, b4, b3, b2, b1, b0
```

with b17 being the most significant bit, the six hamming check bits are:

```
c0 = ! b17 ^ b15 ^ b13 ^ b11 ^ b10 ^ b8 ^ b6 ^
b4 ^ b3 ^ b1 ^ b0
c1 = ! b17 ^ b16 ^ b13 ^ b12 ^ b10 ^ b9 ^ b6 ^
b5 ^ b3 ^ b2 ^ b0
c2 = ! b17 ^ b16 ^ b15 ^ b14 ^ b10 ^ b9 ^ b8 ^
b7 ^ b3 ^ b2 ^ b1
c3 = ! b10 ^ b9 ^ b8 ^ b7 ^ b6 ^ b5 ^ b4
c4 = ! b17 ^ b16 ^ b15 ^ b14 ^ b13 ^ b12 ^ b11
c5 = b17 ^ b14 ^ b12 ^ b11 ^ b10 ^ b7 ^ b5 ^ b4
^ b2 ^ b1 ^ b0
```

where ^ represents bitwise exclusive-or and ! is bitwise not.

c5 can alternatively and equivalently be computed as the odd parity of all the other data and check bits.

The output bytes are then:

```
c3, b3, b2, b1, c2, b0, c1, c0
c4, b10, b9, b8, b7, b6, b5, b4
c5, b17, b16, b15, b14, b13, b12, b11
```

in byte transmission order, with the most significant bit of each byte on the left.

To decode a hammed byte triplet:

```
h7, h6, h5, h4, h3, h2, h1, h0
h15, h14, h13, h12, h11, h10, h9, h8
h23, h22, h21, h20, h19, h18, h17, h16
```

with h0 being the least significant bit of the first byte and h23 being the most significant bit of the third byte, we compute

```
p = h23 ^ h22 ^ h21 ^ h20 ^... ^ h1 ^ h0
c0 = h0 ^ h2 ^ h4 ^ h6 ^ h8 ^ h10 ^ h12 ^
h14 ^ h16 ^ h18 ^ h20 ^ h22
c1 = h1 ^ h2 ^ h5 ^ h6 ^ h9 ^ h10 ^ h13 ^
h14 ^ h17 ^ h18 ^ h21 ^ h22
c2 = h3 ^ h4 ^ h5 ^ h6 ^ h11 ^ h12 ^ h13 ^
```

```
h14 ^ h19 ^ h20 ^ h21 ^ h22
    c3 = h7 ^ h8 ^ h9 ^ h10 ^ h11 ^ h12 ^ h13 ^
h14
    c4 = h15 ^ h16 ^ h17 ^ h18 ^ h19 ^ h20 ^ h21
^ h22
```

If the parity, p, is correct (equal to 1) then either 0 or 2 errors occurred. If all the check bits, c0, c1, c2, c3, c4, c5 are correct (equal to 1), then the byte was received intact, (no errors) otherwise it was damaged beyond repair (two errors).

If p is 0, then there was a single bit error which can be recovered. For the check bits which are incorrect (equal to 0), add the following powers of two together:

```
if c0 = 0 add 1
if c1 = 0 add 2
if c2 = 0 add 4
if c3 = 0 add 8
if c4 = 0 add 16
```

The sum gives the bit position 1--24 corresponding to h0--h23 which is in error. The erroneous bit should be flipped. Note that there is actually no need to fix errors in bits h23, h15, h7, h3, h1 and h0 since they are not used in the decoded byte.

The output data bits, d17--d0 are:

```
h22, h21, h20, h19, h18, h17, h16, h14, h13,
h12,
h11, h10, h9, h8, h6, h5, h4, h2
```

FLOATING POINT REPRESENTATION

There are several ways to represent real numbers on computers. Fixed point places a radix point somewhere in the middle of the digits, and is equivalent to using integers that represent portions of some unit. For example, one might represent 1/100ths of a unit; if you have four decimal digits, you could represent 10.82, or 00.01. Another approach is to use rationals, and represent every number as the ratio of two integers. Floating-point representation - the most common solution - basically represents reals in scientific notation. Scientific notation represents numbers as a base number and an exponent. For example, 123.456 could be represented as 1.23456×10^2. In hexadecimal, the number 123.abc might be represented as $1.23abc \times 16^2$.

Floating-point solves a number of representation problems. Fixed-point has a fixed window of representation, which limits it from representing very large or very small numbers. Also, fixed-point is prone to a loss of precision when two large numbers are divided. Floating-point, on the other hand, employs a sort of "sliding window" of precision appropriate to the scale of the number. This allows it to represent numbers from 1,000,000,000,000 to 0.0000000000000001 with ease.

Some of the greatest achievements of the 20th century would not have been possible without the floating point capabilities of digital computers. Nevertheless, this subject is not well understood by most programmers and is a regular source of confusion.

In a February keynote address entitled *Extensions to Java for Numerical Computing* James Gosling asserted "95% of folks out there are completely clueless about floating-point." However, the main ideas behind floating point are not difficult, and we will demystify the confusion that plagues most novices.

Precision vs. Accuracy

Precision = tightness of specification. Accuracy = correctness. Do not confuse precision with accuracy. 3.133333333 is an estimate of the mathematical constant À which is specified with 10 decimal digits of precision, but it only has two decimal digits of accuracy.

As John von Neumann once said "There's no sense in being precise when you don't even know what you're talking about." Java typically prints out floating point numbers with 16 or 17 decimal digits of precision, but do not blindly believe that this means there that many digits of accuracy!

Calculators typically display 10 digits, but compute with 13 digits of precision. Kahan: the mirror for the Hubble space telescope was ground with great precision, but to the wrong specification. Hence, it was initially a great failure since it couldn't produce high resolution images as expected. However, it's precision enabled an astronaut to install a corrective lens to counter-balance the error. Currency calculations are often defined in terms of a give precision, e.g., Euro exchange rates must be quoted to 6 digits.

Also, in some cases, the floating point formats of different sizes for some machines belonged to different groups. When this happened, all the formats for any one architecture were placed within the discussion of one of the groups of formats included.

Particularly unsusual formats discussed below include the single precision floating-point format for the PDP-4, 7, 9 and 15, which can be thought of as a rearranged Group II or Group III format, and the double precision floating-point format of the ICL 1900, which applies the principle of making a double-precision float out of two single-precision floats, usually used with hardware Group I formats, to a base floating-point format which belongs to Group III; this appears to be the result of either successive implementations of the architecture evolving from hardware multiply to full hardware floating-point or the availability of hardware floating-point as an option.

Another case where the same machine had floating point formats belonging to different groups is the Harris 800, which added a Group II quad-precision floating-point format to an existing architecture whose single and double precision floating-point formats belonged to Group III: here, the hardware level seems to have remained constant, and what happened was that the larger size of the quad-precision format made it reasonable to use a full word instead of a partial word for the exponent, and once that was done, a Group II format appeared more reasonable than a Group III format.

DECIMAL CASES

- 3.141592653589...
- 2.71828...

- 6.023×10^{23} (N_A)
- 6.626×10^{-32} ($\hbar$)

In programming, a floating point number—123.45×10^{-6} is expressed as—123.45E—6. In general, a floating-point number can be written as

$\pm M \times B^E$

where

- M is the fraction mantissa or significand.
- E is the exponent.
- B is the base, in decimal case B = 10.

BINARY CASES

As an example, a 32-bit word is used in MIPS computer to represent a floating-point number:

S	E	M

1 bit..... 8 bits.............. 23 bits

representing: $(-1)^S \times M \times 2^E$

- The implied base is 2 (not explicitly shown in the representation).
- The exponent can be represented in signed 2's complement (but also see biased notation later).
- The implied decimal point is between the exponent field E and the significand field M.
- More bits in field E mean larger range of values representable.
- More bits in field M mean higher precision.
- Zero is represented by all bits equal to 0: $0000...000_2$

NORMALIZATION

To efficiently use the bits available for the significand, it is shifted to the left until all leading 0's disappear (as they make no contribution to the precision).

The value can be kept unchanged by adjusting the exponent accordingly.

Moreover, as the MSB of the significand is always 1, it does not need to be shown explicitly. The significand could be further shifted to the left by 1 bit to gain one more bit for precision. The first bit 1 before the decimal point is implicit. The actual value represented is

$$(-1)^S \times (1.+M) \times 2^E$$

However, to avoid possible confusion, in the following the default normalization does not assume this implicit 1 unless otherwise specified.

Zero is represented by all 0's and is not (and cannot be) normalized.

Example

A binary number X = 0.0001101001101 can be represented in 14-bit floating-point form in the following ways (1 sign bit, a 4-bit exponent field and a 9-bit significand field):

- $x = 0.0001101001101 \times 2^0$ $\boxed{0}\boxed{000}\boxed{000110100}$
- $x = 0.001101001101 \times 2^{-1}$ $\boxed{0}\boxed{111}\boxed{001101001}$
- $x = 0.001101001101 \times 2^{-2}$ $\boxed{0}\boxed{1111}\boxed{001101001}$
- $x = 0.1101001101 \times 2^{-3}$ $\boxed{0}\boxed{1101}\boxed{110100110}$
- $x = 1.101001101 \times 2^{-4}$ $\boxed{0}\boxed{1100}\boxed{101001101}$ with an implied 1.0:

By normalization, highest precision can be achieved.

BIASED NOTATION FOR EXPONENT

To simplify the hardware for comparing two exponents (to use simpler integer sorting rather than subtraction), we may want to avoid 2's complement representation for the exponent.

This can be done by simply adding 1 (a bias) at the MSB of the exponent field and the resulting representation is called biased notation.

Consider a 5-bit exponent field (range of exponents: $-2^4 \sim 2^4 - 1$):

Decimal Exponent	Signed-2's Complement	Biased Noation (Excess-16)	Decimal Value of Biased Notation
15	01111	11111	31
14	01110	11110	30
...	...	...	...
1	00001	10001	17
0	00000	10000	16(bias)
–1	11111	01111	15
...	...	...	...
–15	10001	00001	1
–16	10000	00000	0

The bias depends on number of bits in the exponent field. If there are e bits in this field, the bias is Bias = 2^{c-1}, which lifts the representation (not the actual exponent) by half of the range to get rid of the negative parts represented by 2's complement. The range of actual exponents represented is still the same. With the biased exponent, the value represented by the notation is:

$$(-1)^S \times (1.+M) \times 2^{E-Bias}$$

FLOATING-POINT NOTATION OF IEEE 754

The IEEE 754 floating-point standard uses 32 bits to represent a floating-point number, including 1 sign bit, 8 exponent bits and 23 bits for the significand.

As the implied base is 2, an implied 1 is used, i.e., the significand has effectively 24 bits including 1 implied bit to the left of the decimal point not explicitly represented in the notation.

Note in particular that in IEEE 754 notation, the bias for the 8-bit exponent is $127_{10} = 01111111_2$ (instead of $2^{c-1} = 2^7 = 128$).

The 8-bit exponent field:

Decimal Exponent	Signed 2's Complement	Biased Notation	Decimal Value of Biased Noation
For Infinities			
127	01111111	11111111	255
...	...	...	...
2	00000010	10000001	129

1	00000001	10000000	128
0	00000000	01111111	127
–1	11111111	01111110	126
–2	11111110	01111101	125
...	...	...	...
–126	10000010	00000001	1
For Denorms	10000001	00000000	0

Note:

- Zero exponent is represented by 011111111_2 = $127_{10}$the bias of the notation;
- The range of exponents representable is from—126 to 127;
- The exponent 11111111 (with all zero significand) is reserved to represent infinities or not-a-number (NaN) which may occur when, e.g., a number is divided by zero;
- The smallest exponent 00000000 is reserved to represent denormalized numbers (smaller than 2^{-126} which cannot be normalized) and zero, e.g.,0.001 × 2^{-126} is represented by:

0	00000000	001000...0

OTHER IMPLIED BASES

Given e bits for the exponent field, the range of exponent values representable is $-2^{e-1} \sim 2^{e-1} - 1$ and the range of magnitudes representable is about

$$-2^{-2e-1} \sim 2^{2e-1} - 1$$

For example, if e = 4, the range of exponent values representable is

$$-2^3 = -8 \sim 2^3 - 1 = 7$$

and the range of magnitudes representable is

$$2^{-8} = -1/256 \sim 2^7 = 128$$

This range can be extended by (a) increasing number of bits for exponent, or (b) increasing the implied base from 2 to 4, 8, 16, etc. (or in general, 2^q). For example, when the implied base is $2^q = 2^2 = 4$, the range of magnitudes representable is

$$4^{-8} = 1/65536 \sim 4^7 = 16384$$

Normalization

If the implied base is $B = 2^q$, the significand must be shifted multiple of q bits at a time so that the exponent can be correspondingly adjusted to keep the value unchanged. If at least one of the first q bits of the significand is 1, the representation is normalized. Obviously, the implied 1 can no longer be used.

Examples

- Normalize 0.000000101×4^3. Note that the base is 4 (instead of 2)

$$0.00000101 \times 4^3 = 0.000101 \times 4^2 = 0.0101 \times 4^1$$

Note that the significand has to be shifted to the left two bits at a time during normalization, because the smallest reduction of the exponent necessary to keep the value represented unchanged is 1, corresponding to dividing the value by 4.

Similarly, if the implied base is $B = 2^3 = 8$, the significand has to be shifted 3 bits at a time. In general, if $B = 2^q$, normalization means to left shift the significand q bits at a time until there is at least one 1 in the highest q bits of the significand. Obviously the implied 1 can not be used.

- Represent –0.75 in biased notation with e = 5 bits for exponent field. The bias is $2^{5-1} = 2^4 = 16$ and implied base is 2.

$$-0.75_{10} = -0.11_2 = (-1.1 \times 2^{-1})_2$$

The biased exponent is –1 + 16 = 15, and the notation is (without implied 1):

$\boxed{1}\boxed{10000}\boxed{1100\cdots}$

or (with implied 1):

$\boxed{1}\boxed{01111}\boxed{1000\cdots}$

- Find the value represented in this biased notation:

$\boxed{1}\boxed{10001}\boxed{1100\cdots}$

The biased exponent is 17, the actual exponent is 17 – 16 = 1, the value is (without implied 1):

$-0.11_2 \times 2^1 = 1.1_2 = -1.1_2 = -1.5_{10}$

or (with implied 1):

$-1.11 \times 2^1 = -11.1_2 = -3.5_{10}$

Examples of IEEE 754:

- -0.3125

$-0.3125_{10} = -(0.25 + 0.0625)_{10} = -0.0101_2 = -1.01_2 \times 2^{-2} = 1.01_2 \times 2^{-2} = -1.01_2 \times 2^{125-127}$

The biased exponent is $-2 + 127 = 125$,

1	01111101	01000000000000000000000

- 1.0

$1.0 = 1.0 \times 2^0$

The biased exponent is 127,

0	01111111	00000000000000000000000

- 37.5

$$37.5_{10} = (100101.1)_2 = 1.001011 \times 2^5$$

The based exponent: $127 + 5 = 132 = (10000100)_2$,

0	00000100	00101100000000000000000

.

- -78.25

$$-78.25_{10} = -(1001110.01)_2 = -1.00111001 \times 2^6$$

The biased exponent: $127 + 6 = 133 = (10000101)_2$,

1	10000101	00111000000000000000000

- $0.01 \times 2^{-126} = 1.0 \times 2^{-128}$

As the most negative exponent representable is -126, this value is a denorm which cannot be normalized:

0	00000000	01000000000000000000000

Can you answer the following questions regarding 32–bit IEEE 754 floating-point representation and explain why?:

- What is the largest magnitude (absolute value) representable?

$$1.11\cdots1 \times 2^{127} = (2 - 2^{-23}) \times 2^{127} \approx 2^{128}$$

- What is the smallest magnitude (absolute value) representable?

$$0.00\cdots01\times2^{126}=2^{-23}\times2^{126}=2^{-149}$$

- What is the largest gap between two consecutive numbers?

$$2^{127}\times2^{-23}=2^{104}$$

- What is the smallest gap between two consecutive numbers?

$$2^{-126}\times2^{-23}=2^{-149}$$

Chapter 2

Gate-Level Minimization

DON'T CARE CONDITIONS

We now consider the use of K-Maps to simplify expressions that include the"d" or Don't-Care condition often generated when considering digital designs using flip-flops. We give a number of examples related to our previous designs of sequential circuits.

	X = 0	**X = 1**
Y_1Y_0	J_1	J_1
0 0	0	1
0 1	1	0
1 0	d	d
1 1	d	d

The general rule in considering a simplification with the Don't-Care conditions is to count the number of 0's and number of 1's in the table and to use SOP simplification when the number of 1's is greater and POS simplification when the number of 0's is greater. Again we admit that most students prefer the SOP simplification. With a two-two split, we try SOP simplification.

First we should explain the above table in some detail. The first thing to say about it is that we shall see similar tables again when we study flip-flops. For the moment, we call it a"folded over" truth table, equivalent to the full truth table at right. The function to be represented is J1. Lines 0, 1, 4, and 5 of the truth table seem to be standard, but what of the other rows in which J1 has a value of"d". This indicates that in these rows it is equally acceptable to have J1 = 0 or J1 = 1. We have four"Don't-Cares" or"d" in this table; each can be a 0 or 1 independently of the others - in other words we are not setting the value of d as a variable.

Y1	Y0	X	J1
0	0	0	0
0	0	1	1
0	1	0	d
0	1	1	d
1	0	0	1
1	0	1	0
1	1	0	d
1	1	1	d

Design with flip-flops is the subject of another course.

When attempting a K-Map for SOP simplification, we drop the 0's and plot the 1's and d's. We then attempt to group the 1's into 2-by-1, 2-by-2 groupings, etc. We use the d's as are convenient and have no requirement to cover any or all of them. Note that

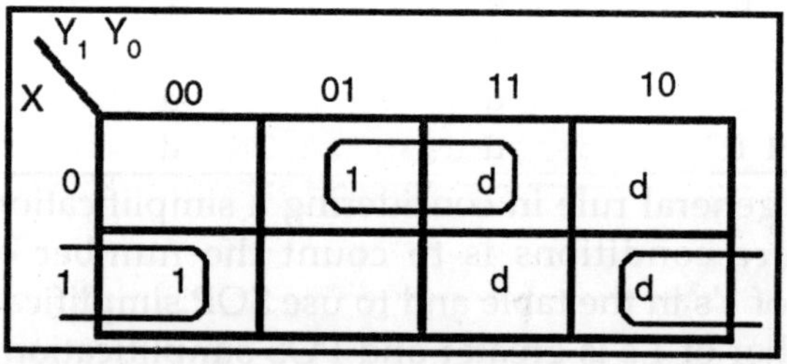

3-by-1 groupings are not valid and that the 2-by-2 grouping of d's does not add anything to the simplification, but only adds an extra useless term.

The terms in the top row, labeled 001 and 011 for $X'Y_1'Y_0$ and $X'Y_1Y_0$, simplify to 0-1 for $X'Y_0$, and the terms in the bottom row, labeled 100 and 110 for $XY_1'Y_0'$ and XY_1Y_0', simplify to 1-0 for XY_0', so the simplified expression is $X'\bullet Y_0 + X\bullet Y_0' = X\oplus Y_0$.

The sample at left, based on an earlier design shows a particularly simple problem. We find that using the d's to combine with the 1's to produce a

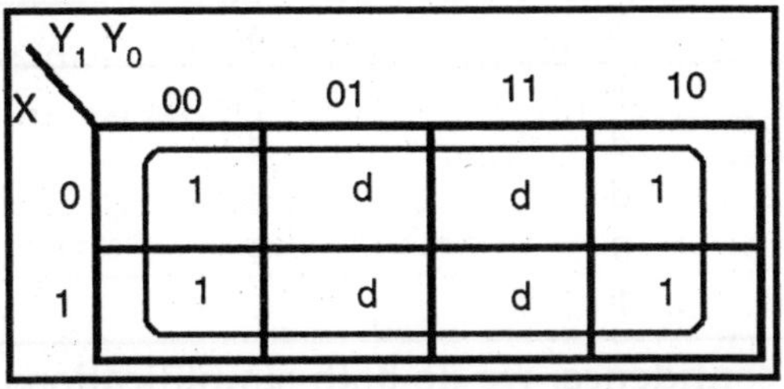

4-by-2 grouping of 1's. Since the entire K-Map is covered, the simplification is F = 1.

The K-Map at right corresponds to an input table with one 0 and three 1's. This immediately suggests a SOP approach to the K-Map; we plot the 1's and d's and drop the 0. The top row corresponds to X'. We then form the

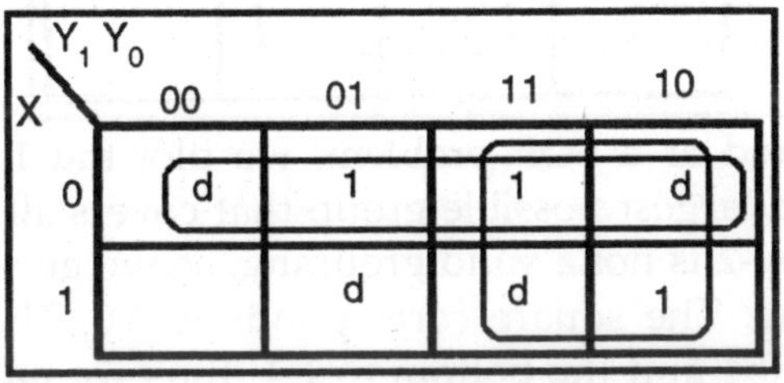

2-by-2 grouping at the right to obtain the term Y_1. Thus $F = X' + Y_1$. There is another simplification that should be considered. This corresponds to two 2-by-2 groupings.

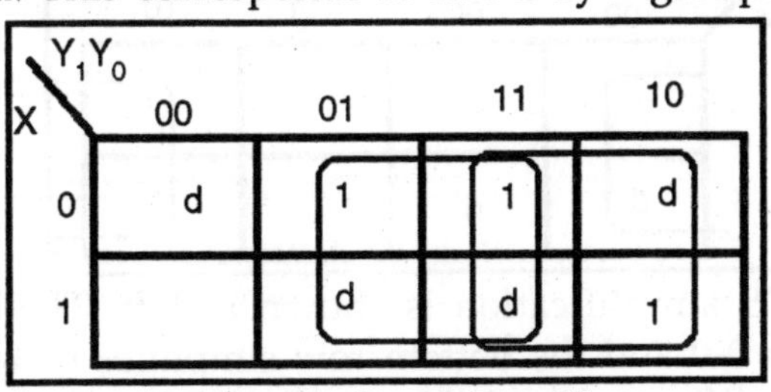

The 2-by-2 grouping at the right still corresponds to Y1. The new 2-by-2 grouping in the middle gives rise to Y0, so we get another simplification F = Y0 + Y1.

As a final example, we consider the input table, which contains two 0's and two 1's. According to the theory, this could be simplified equally well either as a SOP or POS expression.

	X = 0	X = 1
Y1Y0	K0	K0
0 0	d	d
0 1	d	d
1 0	0	0
1 1	1	1

To gain confidence, we do both simplifications, with the SOP first.

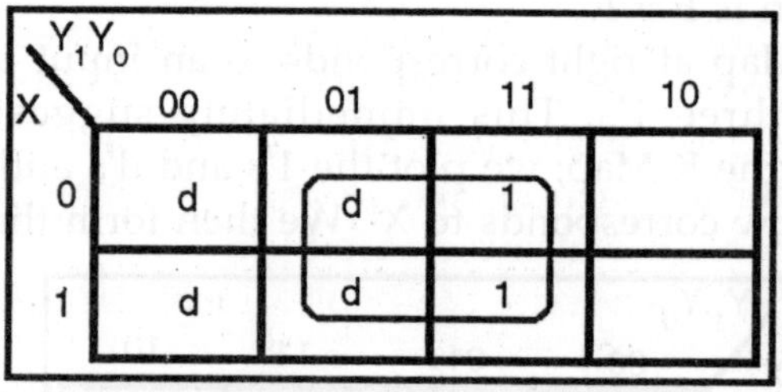

Considered as a SOP problem, we plot the 1's and d's, then form the largest possible group that covers all of the 1's. Note that 3-by-2 is not a valid grouping, so we go with the 2-by-2 grouping. The square corresponds to Y0. The top row simplifies to 0-1 and the bottom to 1-1, thus we have - - 1 or Y0.

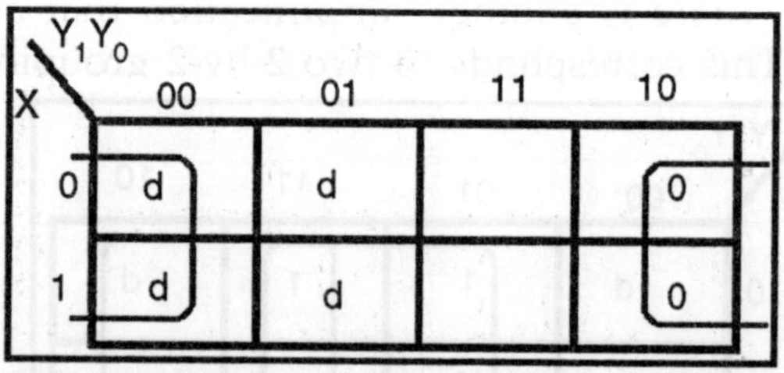

The POS simplification is shown at left. The top row simplifies to 0-0 and the bottom row simplifies to 1-0 so the K-Map simplifies to - - 0. Using the POS copy rule, this translates to Y0, as before. It's a good thing that the two methods agree.

A Diversion: Application of Simplification Techniques to Programming

This next section attempts to apply some of the Boolean simplification techniques to issues sometimes seen in software development, especially C++ programming. Consider the Boolean expressions in C++ that relate to equality. For variable x, we can have expressions such as (x = 0), (x = 0), and !(x == 0). The last two are logically identical, and all are distinct from the assignment statement (x = 0), which evaluates to False.

In our diversion, we consider three variables: x, y, and z. The only assumption made here is that each of the three is of a type that can validly be compared to 0; assuming that all are integer variables is one valid way to read these examples. Each of the expressions (x == 0), (y == 0), and (z == 0) evaluates to either T (True) or F (False).

Consider a function that is to be called conditionally based on the values of three variables:

x, y, and z. We write the Boolean expression as follows

```
if  (((x  !=  0)  &&  (y  !=  0)  &&  (z  !=  0))
||  ((x  !=  0)  &&  (y  !=  0)  &&  (z  ==  0))
||  ((x  !=  0)  &&  (y  ==  0)  &&  (z  ==  0))
||  ((x  ==  0)  &&  (y  !=  0)  &&  (z  !=  0))
||  ((x  ==  0)  &&  (y  !=  0)  &&  (z  ==  0))
||  ((x  ==  0)  &&  (y  ==  0)  &&  (z  ==  0)))  y  =
fzero()
```

We can apply the truth-table approach to analysis of the conditions under which the function fzero is invoked. The following table illustrates when the function is to be called.

(x == 0)	**(y == 0)**	**(z == 0)**	**Call fzero .**
F	F	F	Yes
F	F	T	Yes
F	T	F	No
F	T	T	Yes
T	F	F	Yes
T	F	T	Yes
T	T	F	No
T	T	T	Yes

If this looks a bit like a truth table, it is because it is equivalent to a truth table and can be converted to one. Consider the following definitions of Boolean variables A, B, and C.

A = (x = 0)
B = (y = 0)
C = (z = 0)

Consider the expression A = (x == 0) in the C++ programming language. It may seem a bit strange, but is perfectly legitimate. The expression (x == 0) is a Boolean expression - it evaluates to True or False.

The variable A is a Boolean variable, it also takes on one of the Boolean values. In order to translate the table above into a truth table that we recognize, we replace the expressions (x == 0), (y == 0), and (z == 0) by their equivalents - the Boolean variables A, B, and C. We are beginning to construct a Truth Table.

In order to apply the truth table approach to this problem, we must define a Boolean function. For our purpose, we define F(A, B, C) as follows

F(A, B, C) = 1 if fzero is called
= 0 if fzero is not called

Returning to our convention of 0 for False and 1 for True, we have the truth table.

A	B	C	F(A, B, C)
0	0	0	1
0	0	1	1
Q	1	0	0
0	1	1	1
1	0	0	1
1	0	1	1
1	1	0	0
1	1	1	1

This is a truth table that we have considered and simplified in an earlier section of the work. Using terminology we have already discussed, we see that this function F(A, B, C) can be expressed as either a SOP with six product terms or a POS with two sum terms. Reading this as a POS, we get

$F(A,B,C)=\left(A+\overline{B}+C\right)\cdot\left(\overline{A}+\overline{B}+C\right)$, which simplifies to $F(A,B,C)=\left(\overline{B}+C\right)$.

We now convert back to the original notation. Recalling that

B = (y == 0) and C = (z == 0), we note that B' = (y != 0) and the condition for calling the function fzero becomes ((y != 0) || (z == 0)). So the equivalent (and much simpler) expression is

```
if ((y != 0) || (z == 0)) y = fzero()
```

Consider now the Boolean expression ((x == 0) || ((x != 0) && (y == 0))). In an attempt to simplify this expression we define two Boolean variables

A = (x == 0)

B = (y == 0)

Recall that (x != 0) = !(x == 0) = $\overline{A}$. In our terminology, the expression is

F(A, B) = $A + \left(\overline{A} \bullet B\right)$

There are a number of ways to simplify this expression. The first, and least obvious, is to invoke the theorem of absorption, which states that the formula equals A + B.

To illustrate other options, we expand the above to canonical SOP and then examine it by means of both a truth table and a K-map. To expand the expression into canonical SOP, we need to have the first term contain a literal for the variable B.

$$A + \overline{A} \bullet B = A \bullet \left(\overline{B} + B\right) + \overline{A} + B = A \bullet \overline{B} + A \bullet B$$

The truth table for this expression is

A	B	F(A, B)
0	0	0
0	1	1
1	1	1
1	1	1

Representing this as a POS formula, we immediately get F(A, B) = (A + B), which translates to the C++ expression ((x == 0) || (y == 0)).

As a final example, consider the following Boolean expression in C++

((x == 0) || (y == 0) || (z == 0)) && ((x == 0) || (y == 0) || (z !=0)) &&

((x == 0) || (y != 0) || (z == 0)) && ((x != 0) || (y == 0) || (z == 0))

Define A = (x == 0)

B = (y == 0)

C = (z == 0)

With these definitions our expression becomes

$$F(A,B,C) = (A + B + C)\cdot(A + B + \overline{C})\cdot(A + \overline{B} + C)\cdot(\overline{A} + B + C)$$

This is known to simplify to

F(A, B, C) = (A + B) • (A + C) • (B + C)

So our Boolean expression in C++ simplifies to

((x == 0) || (y == 0)) && ((x == 0) || (z == 0)) && (y == 0) || (z == 0))

Inspection of the above shows that we want at least two of (x == 0), (y == 0), and (z == 0) to be true. Compare this with the original derivation of the function

F(A, B, C) = (A + B) • (A + C) • (B + C)

used for the carry-out of a Full-Adder, which is 1 if two or three of the inputs are 1.

POS SIMPLIFICATION

K-Maps for Product of Sums simplification are constructed similarly to those for Sum of Products simplification, except that the POS copy rule must be enforced: 1 for a negated variable and 0 for a non-negated (plain) variable.

As our first example we consider F(A, B, C) = (3, 5) = (A + B' + C')"(A' + B + C'). Recall that the term (A + B' + C') corresponds to 011 and that (A' + B + C') to 101.

C \ AB	00	01	11	10
0				
1		0		0

This is really somewhat of a trick question used only to illustrate placing of the terms for POS. Place a 0 at each location, rather than the 1 placed for SOP. Note that the two

0's placed are not adjacent, so we cannot simplify the expression.

For the next example consider F2 = (A + B + C)•(A + B + C')•(A + B' + C)•(A' + B + C). Using the POS copy rule, we translate this to 000, 001, 010, and 100.

Before we attempt to simplify F_2, we note that it is a very good candidate for simplification. Compare the first term 000 to each of the following three terms.

The term 000 differs from the term 001 in exactly one position. The same applies for comparison to the other two terms. Any two terms that differ in exactly one position can be combined in a simplification.

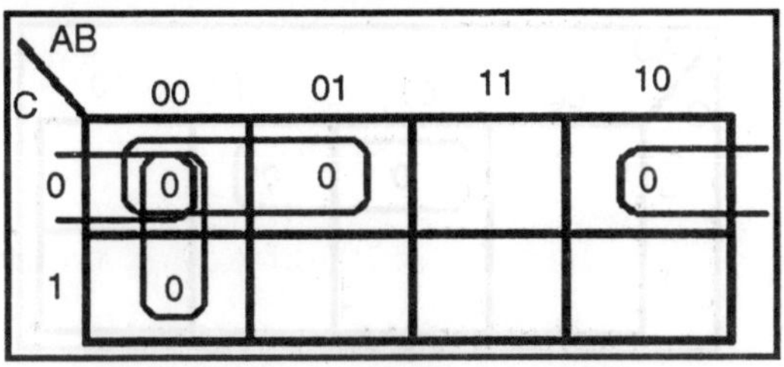

We begin the K-Map for POS simplification by placing a 0 in each of the four positions 000, 001, 010, 100. Noting that 000 is adjacent to 001, just below it, we combine to get 00- or (A + B). The term 000 is adjacent to 010 to its right to get 0-0 or (A + C).

The term 000 is adjacent to 100 to its"left" to get -00 or (B + C). As a result, we get the simplified form. F2 = (A + B)•(A + C)•(B + C)

Just for fun, we simplify this expression algebraically, using the derived Boolean identity

X•X•X = X for any Boolean expression X.

F2 = (A + B + C)•(A + B + C')•(A + B' + C)•(A' + B + C)

= (A + B + C)•(A + B + C')•(A + B + C)•(A + B' + C)•(A + B + C)•(A' + B + C)

= (A + B)•(A + C)•(B + C)

It is encouraging that we get the same answer.

We now consider simplification of a POS function specified by a truth table.

A	B	C	F
0	0	0	1
0	0	1	1
0	1	0	0
0	1	1	1
1	0	0	1
1	0	1	1
1	1	0	0
1	1	1	1

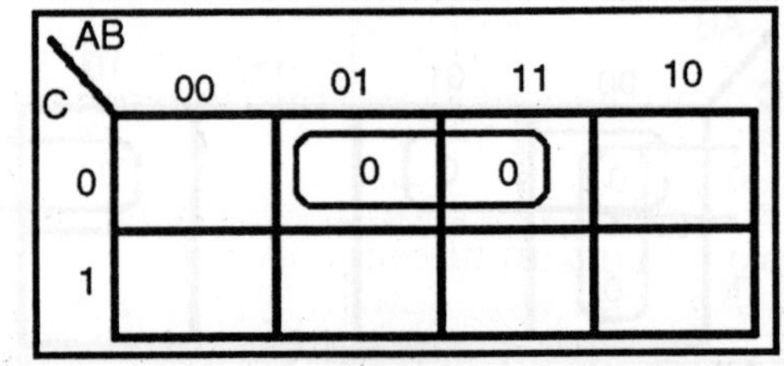

We plot two 0's for the POS representation of the function - one at 010 and one at 110. The two are combined to get -10, which translates to (B' + C).

More Examples of K-Maps

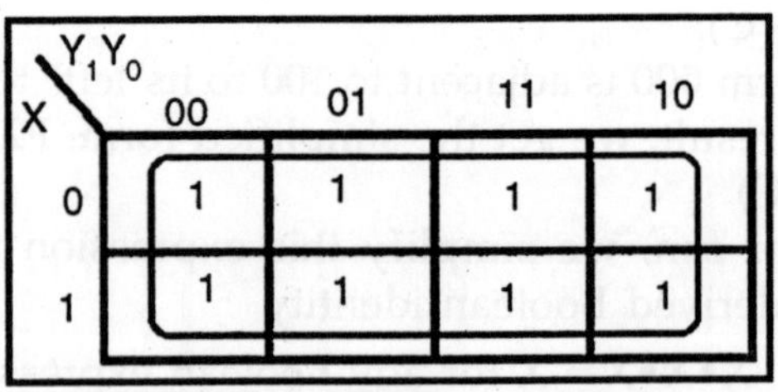

The sample at left, based on an earlier design shows a particularly simple problem. We find that all the entries in the K-Map are covered with a single grouping, thus removing all three variables. Since the entire K-Map is covered, the simplification is F = 1.

The K-Map at right shows an example with overlap of two groupings of 1's. All 1's in the map must be covered and some should be covered twice.

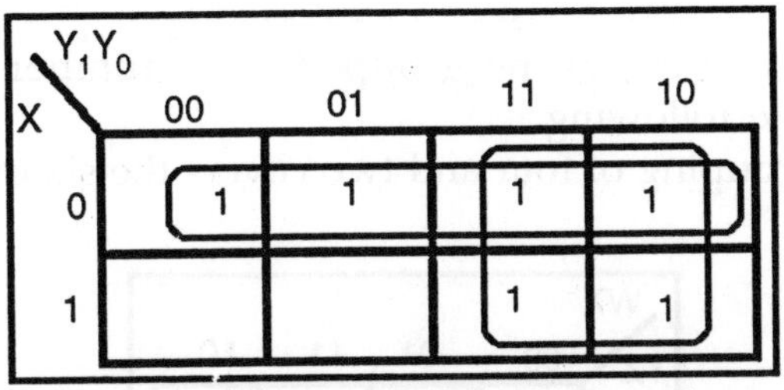

The top row corresponds to X'. We then form the 2–by–2 grouping at the right to obtain the term Y_1. Thus F = X' + Y_1.

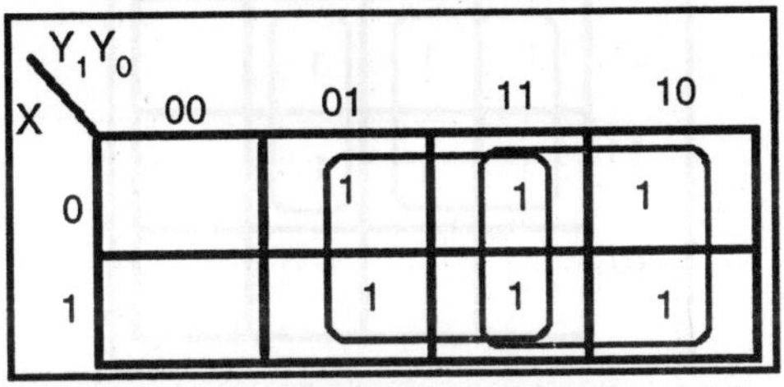

There is another simplification that should be considered. This corresponds to two 2–by–2 groupings. The 2–by–2 grouping at the right still corresponds to Y_1. The new 2–by–2 grouping in the middle gives rise to Y_0, so we get another simplification F = Y_0 + Y_1. *Just One More K-Map: Overlapping Circles:* We close the discussion of K-Maps with a technique that applies to both SOP and POS simplifications. We shall apply it to SOP simplification.

Consider the following K-Map.

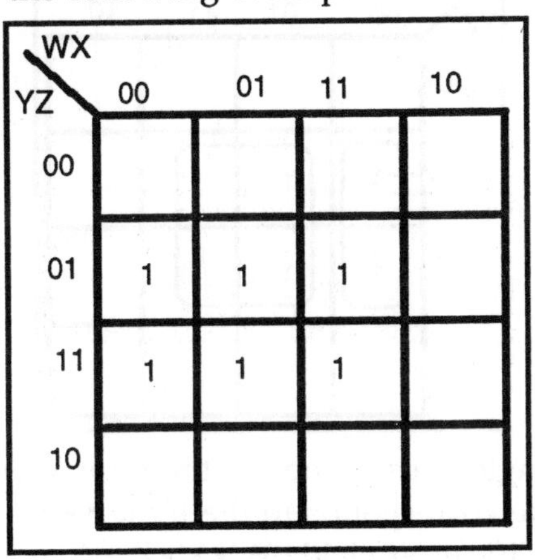

The six ones can be grouped in a number of ways. Consider the following.

This grouping of four and two covers the six one's in the K-Map.

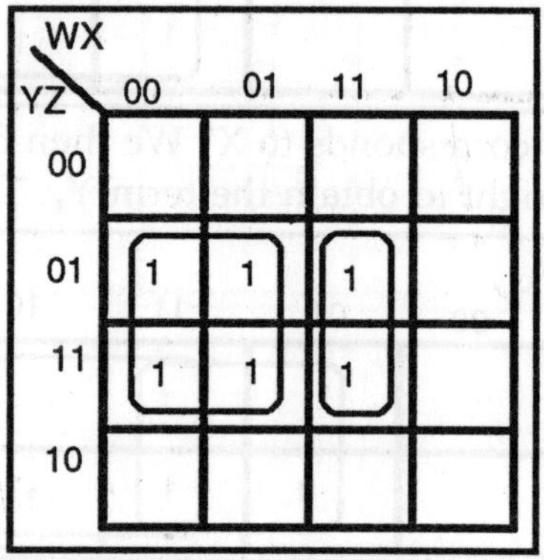

The four ones in the square form the term W'•Z. The two ones in the rectangle form the term

W•X•Z.

The K-Map simplifies to W•Z + W•X•Z.

Another way to consider the simplification of the K-Map is to group the rectangle and the square as in the figure at right.

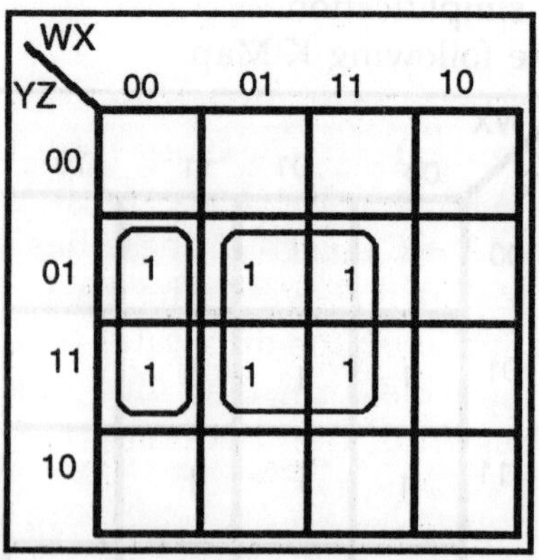

The rectangle corresponds to the term W'•X'•Z.

The square corresponds to the term X•Z.

This simplification yields W'•X'•Z + X•Z.

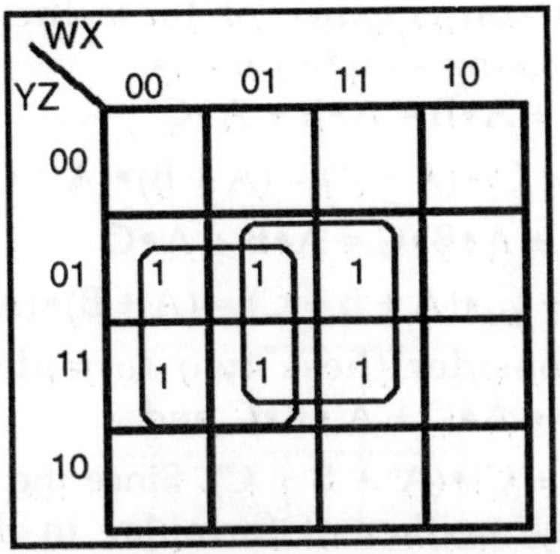

It is important to note that the groupings can overlap if this yields a simpler reduction.

Here we show two overlapping squares.

The square at left corresponds to the term W'•Z.

The square at right corresponds to the term X•Z.

This simplification yields W'•Z + X•Z, which is simpler than either of the other two forms validly produced by the K-Map method.

Try 1: W'•Z + W•X•Z

Try 2: W'•X'•Z + X•Z

Try 3: W'•Z + X•Z. This seems better.

Consider the POS formula (A + B)•(A + C)•(A + B + C). Again, the first term (A + B) is included in the third term (A + B + C), as is the second term.

An extreme form of inclusion is observed when the expression has identical terms. Examples of this would be the SOP expression A•B + A•C + A•B and the POS expression (A + B)•(A + C)•(A + C). Each of these has duplicate terms, so that the inclusion is 2-way. The basic idea is that an expression with included (or duplicate) terms is not written in the simplest possible form. The idea of simplifying such expressions arises from the theorems of Boolean algebra, specifically the following two.

T1 Idempotency a) X + X = X, for all X

b) X • X = X, for all X

T3 Absorption a) X + (X • Y) = X, for all X and Y

b) X • (X + Y) = X, for all X and Y

As a direct consequence of these theorems, we can perform the following simplifications.

A•B + A•C + A•B = A•B + A•C

(A + B)•(A + C)•(A + C) = (A + B)•(A + C)

A•B + A•C + A•B•C = A•B + A•C

(A + B)•(A + C)•(A + B + C) = (A + B)•(A + C)

We now consider these two formulae with slight alterations: A•B + A•C + A'•B•C and

(A + B)•(A + C)•(A' + B + C). Since the literal must be included exactly, neither of formulae in this second set contains included terms.

We now can produce the definitions of normal forms. A formula is in a normal form only if it contains no included terms; thus, a normal SOP form is a SOP form with no included terms and a normal POS form is a POS form with no included terms.

Sample Normal SOP: A + B•C A•B + A•C + B•C A'•B + A"C + B"C'

Sample Normal POS: A•(B + C) (A + B)•(A + C)•(B + C) (A' + B)•(A + C')

We now can define the canonical forms. A normal form over a number of variables is in canonical form if every term contains each variable in either the true or complemented form.

A canonical SOP form is a normal SOP form in which every product term contains a literal for every variable. A canonical POS form is a normal POS form in which every sum term in which every sum term contains a literal for every variable.

NAND AND NOR GATE IMPLEMENTATION

THE NAND

The NAND or Not AND function is a combination of two separate functions, the AND function and theNOT function connected together in series, and can be expressed by the Boolean expression of, A.B

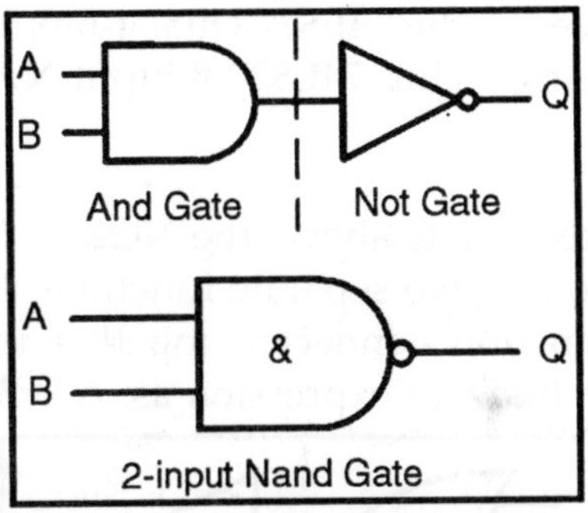

Switch Representation of the NAND Gate

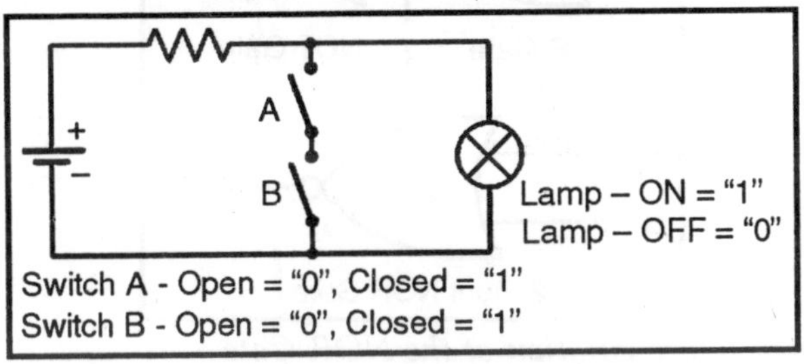

Table. Truth Table

Switch A	Switch B	Output	Description
0	0	1	A and B are both open, lamp ON
0	1	1	A is open and B is closed, lamp
ON			
1	0	1	A is closed and B is open, lamp
ON			
1	1	0	A is closed and B is closed, lamp
OFF			
Boolean Expression (A AND B)			A. B

The NAND Function is sometimes known as the Sheffer Stroke Function and is denoted by a vertical bar or upwards arrow operator, for example, A NAND B = A|B or A?B.

NAND Gates are used as the basic"building blocks" to construct other logic gate functions and are available in standard i.c. packages such as the very common TTL 74LS00 Quadruple 2-input NANDGates, the TTL 74LS10 Triple 3-

input NAND Gates or the 74LS20 Dual 4-input NAND Gates. There is even a single chip 74LS30 8-input NAND Gate.

THE NOR

Like the NAND Gate above, the NOR or Not OR Gate is also a combination of two separate functions, theOR function and the NOT function connected together in series and is expressed by the Boolean expression as, A + B

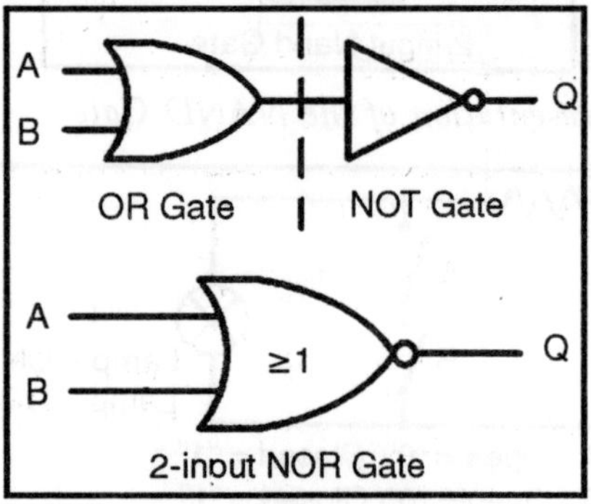

Switch Representation of the NOR Gate

Table. Truth Table

Switch A	Switch B	Output	Description
0	0	1	Both A and B are open, lamp ON
0	1	0	A is open and B is closed, lamp
OFF			
1	0	0	A is closed and B is open, lamp
OFF			
1	1	0	A is closed and B is closed, lamp
OFF			
Boolean Expression (A OR B)			A + B

The NOR Function is sometimes known as the Pierce Function and is denoted by a downwards arrow operator as shown, A NOR B = A↓B.

NOR Gates are available as standard i.c. packages such as the TTL 74LS0$_2$ Quadruple 2-input NORGate, the TTL 74LS$_{27}$ Triple 3-input NOR Gate or the 74LS260 Dual 5-input NOR Gate.

NAND and NOR Gates

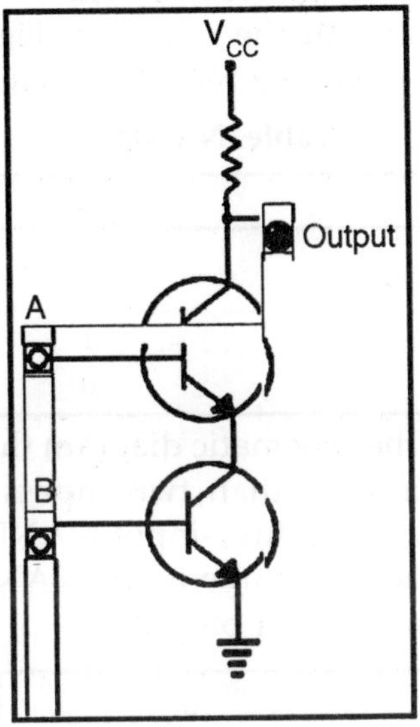

Fig. A NAND Gate.

The value of the output is controlled by the two inputs A and B.

The circuit of Figure illustrates some important concepts, but it isn't very interesting. We can do more if we build circuits with two or more inputs. Figure 4. shows a NAND gate. The name NAND is a contraction of not-and. Current can flow, and produce a voltage drop across the resistor, only if both transistors are conducting. Having either transistor switched off is enough to block current flow and hold the output high.

For purposes of this lecture we are going to define a"high" voltage – a voltage near Vcc – to indicate a logical 1, or true. A low voltage, near zero will indicate a logical 0, or false. (It is possible to reverse those definitions so long as one is consistent. We will not studynegative logic circuits here.)

Using 1 to represent a high voltage and 0 for low, we can write a truth table that describes the behaviour of the NAND gate. Columns A and B of the table represent the two inputs, A and B, of the NAND gate. The X column shows what the output will be for each combination of A and B. The truth table for the Boolean NAND function appears at the left. Experiment with the circuit in Figure 4 and verify that it actually computes the NAND function.

Table. NAND

A	B	X
0	0	1
0	1	1
1	0	1
1	1	0

It is clear from the schematic diagram that we could build a NAND gate with more than two inputs. Adding a third transistor in series gives a three-input NAND. As an exercise, write the truth table for a three-input NAND gate. You will have inputs A, B, and C and output X.

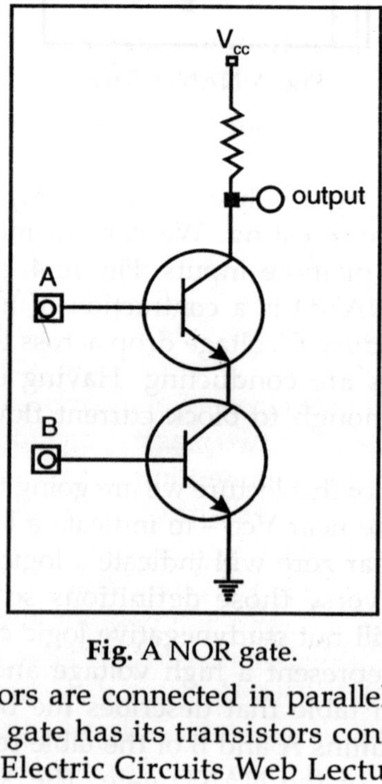

Fig. A NOR gate.

The transistors are connected in parallel.

The NAND gate has its transistors connected in series. Recall from the Electric Circuits Web Lecture that switches can be connected in series or parallel. If we connect transistors in parallel as shown in Figure above, applying a signal to the base of eithertransistor is sufficient to allow current to flow through the resistor and pull the output voltage to near zero. This is the NOR gate. The name NOR is a contraction of not-or.

Table. NOR

A	B	X
0	0	1
0	1	0
1	0	0
1	1	0

Let's look at the truth table for the NOR gate. Again we have inputs A and B and output X. This time, X is true, or 1, only when A and B are both 0. Another way of saying that is that X is 1 when neither A nor B is true. Experiment with the circuit to verify that it computes the function given in Table .

As with the Nand gate, the NOR gate can be extended to more than two inputs by adding more transistors, this time in parallel.

Figure makes it obvious why the power supply voltage is called Vcc. It is connected in parallel, or in common, through the resistor to the collectors of both transistors. In a complex digital logic circuit, the same power supply voltage will be connected in common to all the gates.

About now you may be wondering why we started with NAND and NOR gates instead of the more familiar AND and OR functions. There are two reasons, one founded in electrical engineering and one founded in logic.

Although the gates shown here are simplified by comparison to the actual construction of integrated circuits, you could go to an electrical engineering lab and build the circuits of Figures 3, 4, and 5. If you did, they would function just as the animations demonstrate. These three gates, NOT, NAND, and NOR are the simplest possible digital logic gates. Each has only one transistor per input. Any other gate, and in particular the non-inverting gates AND and OR require more transistors. Even more important is the fact that NAND and NOR are complete. This means that any other digital logic gate can be constructed using only NAND gates or only NORgates. A manufacturer of integrated circuits can lay down a pattern of one type of gate, and then implement any digital logic function by modifying how the gates are connected.

QUINE MC-CLUSKY METHOD

The Quine-McCluskey, or Tabular, method is an algorithmic method that finds prime implicants, necessary prime implicants, and minimum sum-of-products expressions for digital systems with any number of variables. The Quine-McCluskey method is an exact algorithm which finds a minimum-cost sum-of-products implementation of a Boolean function. This handout introduces the method and applies it to several examples.

There are 4 main steps in the Quine-McCluskey algorithm: Generate Prime Implicants Construct Prime Implicant Table Reduce Prime Implicant Table Remove Essential Prime Implicants Row Dominance Column Dominance Step #1, the prime implicants of a function are generated using an iterative procedure. In Step #2, a prime implicant table is constructed. The columns of the table are the prime implicants of the function. The rows are minterms of where the function is 1, called *ON-set minterms*. The goal of the method is to cover all the rows using a minimum-cost *cover* of prime implicants.

The reduction step (Step #3) is used to reduce the size of the table. This step has three sub-steps which are iterated until no further table reduction is possible! At this point, the reduced table is either (i) empty or (ii) non-empty. If the reduced table is empty, the removed essential prime implicants form a minimum-cost solution.

However, if the reduced table is *not* empty, the table must be "solved" (Step #4). The table can be solved using either "Petrick's method" or the "branching method". This handout focuses on Petrick's method.

The branching method is discussed in the books by

McCluskey, Roth, etc., but you will not be responsible for the branching method. The remainder of this handout illustrates the details of the Quine-McCluskey method.

RULES OF TABULAR METHOD

Consider a function of three variables f(A, B, C): $\overline{A}BC$ IS represented by 011 ← Binary notation, where A = 0, B = 1 and c = 1 $A\overline{B}\overline{C}$ is represented by 100

$A\,\overline{C}$ is represented by 1-0

B C is represented by –11

Consider the function:

$$f(A,B,C,D) = \Sigma(1110,1111) = ABC\overline{D} + ABCD = ABC$$

Listing the two minterms shows they can be combined

```
A B C D
1 1 1 0 ←┐
1 1 1 1 ←┘ Can combine (Differs in one digit position)
-------
1 1 1 –
```

Now consider the following:

$$f(A,B,C,D) = \Sigma(1101,1110) = AB\overline{C}D + ABC\overline{D}$$

Note that these variables cannot be combined

```
A B C D
1 1 0 1 ←┐
1 1 1 0 ←┘ Cannot Combine (Differs in more than one
-------      Digit Position)
   ?
-------
```

This is because the FIRST RULE of the Tabular method for two terms to combine, and thus eliminate one variable, is that they must differ in only one digit position.

Bear in mind that when two terms are combined, one of the combined terms has one digit more at logic 1 than the other combined term. This indicates that the number of 1's in a term is significant and is referred to as its index.

For example: f(A, B, C, D)

0000...................Index 0
0010, 1000.............Index 1
1010, 0011, 1001.......Index 2
1110, 1011.............Index 3
1111...................Index 4

The necessary condition for combining two terms is that the indices of the two terms must differ by one logic variable which must also be the same.

EXAMPLES

Example: Consider the function: Z = f(A,B,C) $= \overline{ABC} + A\overline{B}C + A\overline{BC} + A\overline{B}C$

To make things easier, change the function into binary notation with index value and decimal value.

$$f(A,B,C) = \Sigma(000,001,100,101) \text{ — } \textit{Binary notation}$$

$$0 \quad 1 \quad 1 \quad 2 \quad \text{— } \textit{Index}$$

$$0 \quad 1 \quad 4 \quad 5 \quad \text{— } \textit{Decimal value}$$

Tabulate the index groups in a colunm and insert the decimal value alongside.

		First List	Second List		Third List	
		A B C		A B C		A B C
Index 0 →	0	0 0 0 ✓	0,1	0 0 – ✓	0,1,4,5	– 0 –
Index 1 →	1	0 0 1 ✓	0,4	– 0 0 ✓	0,4,1,5	– 0 –
Index 1 →	4	1 0 0 ✓	1, 5	– 0 1 ✓		
Index 2 →	5	1 0 0 ✓	4, 5	1 0 – ✓		

From the first list, we combine terms that differ by 1 digit only from one index group to the next. These terms from the first list are then seperated into groups in the second list. Note that the ticks are just there to show that one term has been combined with another term. From the second list we can see that the expression is now reduced to: Z $= \overline{AB} + \overline{BC} + \overline{BC} + \overline{AB}$

From the second list note that the term having an index of 0 can be combined with the terms of index 1. Bear in mind that the dash indicates a missing variable andmust line up in order to get a third list. The final simplified expression is: Z $= \overline{B}$ Bear in mind that any unticked terms in any list must be included in the final expression (none occured here except from the last list). Note that the only prime implicant here is $Z = \overline{B}$.

The tabular method reduces the function to a set of prime implicants.

Note that the above solution can be derived algebracially. Attempt this in your notes.

Example: Consider the function f(A, B, C, D) = Σ (0,1,2,3,5,7,8,10,12,13,15), note that this is in decimal form.

Σ (0000,0001,0010,0011,0101,0111,1000,1010,1100,1101,1111) in binary form.

(0,1,1,2,2,3,1,2,2,3,4) in the index form.

First List

	A	B	C	D	
0	0	0	0	0	✓
1	0	0	0	1	✓
2	0	0	1	0	✓
8	1	0	0	0	✓
3	0	0	1	1	✓
5	0	1	0	1	✓
10	1	0	1	0	✓
12	1	1	0	0	✓
7	0	1	1	1	✓
13	1	1	1	1	✓
15	1	1	1	1	✓

Second List

	A	B	C	D	
0,1	0	0	0	–	✓
0,2	0	0	–	0	✓
0,8	–	0	0	0	✓
1,3	0	0	–	1	✓
1,5	0	–	0	1	✓
2,3	0	0	1	–	✓
2,10	–	0	1	0	✓
8,10	1	0	–	0	✓
8,12	1	–	0	0	$A\overline{C}\overline{D}$
3,7	0	–	1	1	✓
5,7	0	1	–	1	✓
5,13	–	1	0	1	✓
12,13	1	1	0	–	$AB\overline{C}$
7,15	–	1	1	1	✓
13,15	1	1	–	1	✓

Third List

	A	B	C	D	
0,1 2 3	0	0	–	–	$\overline{A}\overline{B}$
0,2 1 3	0	0	–	–	
0, 2, 8, 10	–	0	–	0	$\overline{B}\overline{D}$
0, 8, 2, 10	–	0	–	0	
1, 3, 5, 7	0	–	–	1	$\overline{A}D$
1, 5, 3, 7	0	–	–	1	
5, 7, 13, 15	–	1	–	1	BD
5, 13, 7, 15	–	1	–	1	

The prime implicants are: $\overline{AB} + \overline{BD} + \overline{AD}$ + BD + $A\overline{CD}$ + $AB\overline{C}$

The chart is used to remove redundant prime implicants. A grid is prepared having all the prime implicants listed at the left and all the minterms of the function along the top. Each minterm covered by a given prime implicant is marked in the appropriate position.

From the above chart, BD is an essential prime implicant. It is the only prime implicant that covers the minterm decimal 15 and it also includes 5, 7 and 13. $\overline{D}$ is also an essential prime implicant. It is the only prime implicant that covers the minterm denoted by decimal 10 and it also includes the terms 0, 2 and 8.

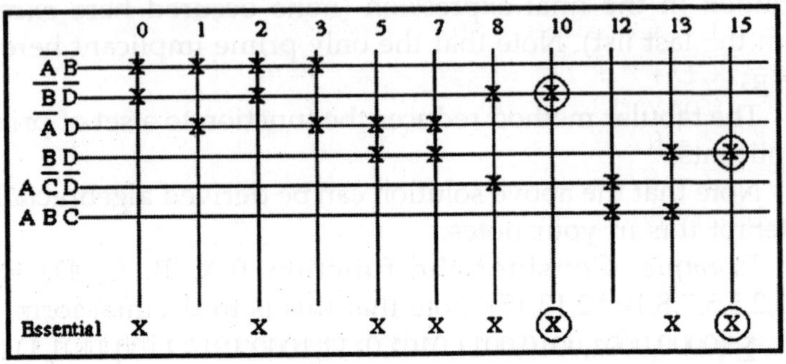

The other minterms of the function are 1, 3 and 12. Minterm 1 is present in $\overline{A}\overline{B}$ and $\overline{A}$D. Similarly for minterm 3. We can therefore use either of these prime implicants for these minterms. Minterm 12 is present in A$\overline{C}\overline{D}$ and AB$\overline{C}$, so again either can be used.

Thus, one minimal solution is: $Z = \overline{B}\overline{D} + BD + \overline{A}\overline{B} + A\overline{C}\overline{D}$

PROBLEMS

1. Minimise the function below using the tabular method of simplification:

$$Z = f(A,B,C,D) = A\overline{BCD} + \overline{ABCD} + \overline{AB}C\overline{D} + \overline{ABCD} + A\overline{BCD} + \overline{A}BCD + \overline{A}BC\overline{D} + \overline{AB}CD$$

2. Using the tabular method of simplification, find all equally minimal solutions for the function below.

	A	B	C	D	
0	0	0	0	0	✓
2	0	0	1	0	✓
4	0	1	0	0	✓
8	1	0	0	0	✓
5	0	1	0	1	✓
9	1	0	0	1	✓
12	1	1	0	0	✓

	A	B	C	D	
0, 2	0	0	–	0	$\overline{A}\,\overline{B}\,\overline{D}$
0, 4	0	–	0	0	✓
0, 8	–	0	0	0	✓
4, 5	0	1	0	–	$\overline{A}$ B $\overline{C}$
4, 12	–	1	0	0	✓
8, 9	1	0	0	–	A $\overline{B}\,\overline{C}$
8, 12	1	–	0	0	✓

	A	B	C	D	
0, 4, 8, 12	–	–	0	0	$\overline{C}\,\overline{D}$
0, 8, 4, 12	–	–	0	0	

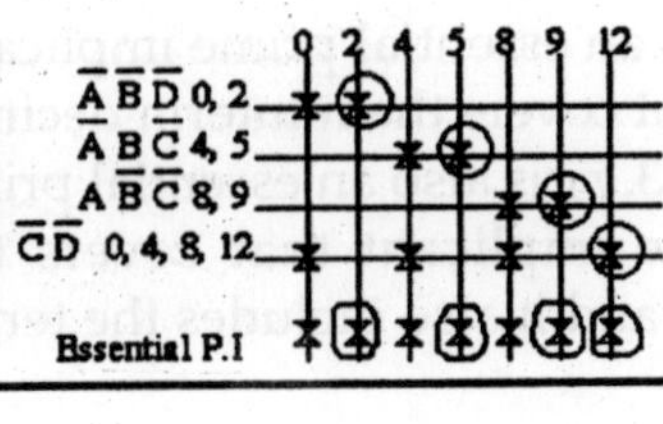

Z = f(A,B,C,D) = $\sum$ (1,4,5,10,12,14)

1. Consider the function: Z = f(A,B,C,D) $= A\overline{BCD} + \overline{ABCD} + A\overline{B}CD + A\overline{B}C\overline{D} + \overline{A}BC\overline{D} + \overline{A}\overline{B}CD$

Convert to decimal and binary equivalents:-

Z = f(A,B,C,D) = $\sum$ (0,2,4,5,8,9,12) - decimal equivalent

Z = f(A,B,C,D) = $\sum$ (0000,0010,0100,0101,1000,1001,1100) - binary equivalent (0, 1, 1, 2, 1, 2, 2) - index values

The simplified answer is: Z = $\overline{ABD} + \overline{A}B\overline{C} + A\overline{BC} + \overline{C}\,\overline{D}$

2. f(A, B, C, D)

$= \Sigma(0,1,4,5,10,12,14) \quad = \Sigma(000,0001,0100,0101,1010,1100,1110)$

$= \mathit{Index}: 0 \quad 1 \quad 1 \quad 2 \quad 2 \quad 2 \quad 3$

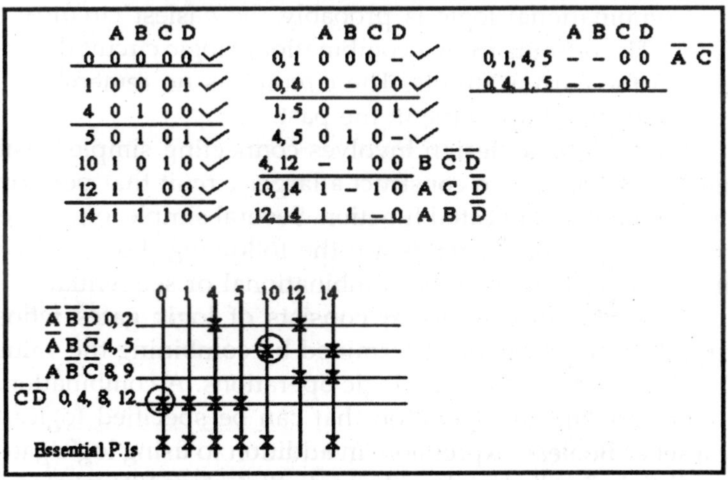

Note that the remaining term 12 is covered by and $AB\overline{D}$

One simplified answer is: Z = $\overline{AC} + AC\overline{D} + B\overline{CD}$

Another answer is: Z = $\overline{AC} + AC\overline{D} + AB\overline{D}$

Chapter 3

Combinational Logic

COMBINATIONAL CIRCUITS

Combinational logic is probably the easiest circuitry to design. The outputs from a combinational logic circuit depend only on the current inputs. The circuit has no remembrance of what it did at any time in the past.

Much of logic design involves connecting simple, easily understood circuits to construct a larger circuit that performs a much more complicated function. Several simple, often-used combinational logic circuits are the following: Logic circuits for digital systems may be combinational or sequential.

A combinational circuit consists of logic gates whose outputs at any time are determined by combining the values of the applied inputs using logic operations. A combinational circuit performs an operation that can be specified logically by a set of Boolean expression. In addition to using logic gates, sequential circuits employ elements that store bit values.

Sequential circuit outputs are a function of inputs and the bit value in storage elements. These values, in turn, are a function of previously applied inputs and stored values. As a consequence, the outputs of a sequential circuit depend not only on the presently applied values of the inputs, but also on pas inputs, and the behaviour of the circuit must be specified by a sequence in time of inputs and internal stored bit values.

A combinational circuit consists of input variables, output variables, logic gates and interconnections. The interconnected logic gates accept signals from the inputs and generate signals at the output. The n input variables come from the environment of the circuit, and the m output variables are available for use by the environment. Each input and output variable exists physically as a binary signal that represents logic 1 or logic 0.

For n input variables, there are 2^n possible binary input combinations. For each binary combination of the input variables, there is one possible binary value on each output. Thus, a combinational circuit can be specified by a truth table that lists the output values for each combination of the input variables.

A combinational circuit can also be described by m Boolean function, one for each output variable. Each such function is expressed as function of the n input variables.

A combinational circuit performs an operation that can be specified logically by a set of Boolean expression. In addition to using logic gates, sequential circuits employ elements that store bit values. Sequential circuit outputs are a function of inputs and the bit value in storage elements. These values, in turn, are a function of previously applied inputs and stored values.

As a consequence, the outputs of a sequential circuit depend not only on the presently applied values of the inputs, but also on pas inputs, and the behaviour of the circuit must be specified by a sequence in time of inputs and internal stored bit values.

A combinational circuit consists of input variables, output variables, logic gates and interconnections. The interconnected logic gates accept signals from the inputs and generate signals at the output. The n input variables come from the environment of the circuit, and the m output variables are available for use by the environment. Each input and output variable exists physically as a binary signal that represents logic 1 or logic 0.

ANALYSIS PROCEDURE

The bulk of the Combinational Analysis module is accessed through a single window of that name allowing you to view truth tables and Boolean expressions. This window can be opened in two ways.

VIA THE WINDOW MENU

Select Combinational Analysis, and the current Combinational Analysis window will appear. If you haven't viewed the window before, the opened window will represent no circuit at all.

Only one Combinational Analysis window exists within Logisim, no matter how many projects are open. There is no way to have two different analysis windows open at once.

VIA THE PROJECT MENU

From a window for editing circuits, you can also request that Logisim Analyse the current circuit by selecting the Analyse Circuit option from the Project menu. Before Logisim opens the window, it will compute Boolean expressions and a truth table corresponding to the circuit and place them there for you to view.

For the analysis to be successful, each input must be attached to an input pin, and each output must be attached to an output pin. Logisim will only Analyse circuits with at most eight of each type, and all should be single-bit pins. Otherwise, you will see an error message and the window will not open.

In constructing Boolean expressions corresponding to a circuit, Logisim will first attempt to construct a Boolean expressions corresponding exactly to the gates in the circuit.

But if the circuit uses some non-gate components (such as a multiplexer), or if the circuit is more than 100 levels deep (unlikely), then it will pop up a dialog box telling you that deriving Boolean expressions was impossible, and Logisim will instead derive the expressions based on the truth table, which will be derived by quietly trying each combination of inputs and reading the resulting outputs.

After analyzing a circuit, there is no continuing relationship between the circuit and the Combinational Analysis window. That is, changes to the circuit will not be reflected in the window, nor will changes to the Boolean expressions and/or truth table in the window be reflected in the circuit. Of course, you are always free to Analyse a circuit again; and, as we will see later, you can replace the circuit with a circuit corresponding to what appears in the Combinational Analysis window.

LIMITATIONS

Logisim will not attempt to detect sequential circuits: If you tell it to Analyse a sequential circuit, it will still create a truth table and corresponding Boolean expressions, although these will not accurately summarize the circuit behaviour. (In fact, detecting sequential circuits is provably impossible, as it would amount to solving the Halting Problem. Of course, you might hope that Logisim would make at least some attempt - perhaps look for flip-flops or cycles in the wires - but it does not.) As a result, the Combinational Analysis system should not be used indiscriminately: Only use it when you are indeed sure that the circuit you are analyzing is indeed combinational!

Logisim will make a change to the original circuit that is perhaps unexpected: The Combinational Analysis system requires that each input and output have a unique name that conforming to the rules for Java identifiers. (Roughly, each character must either a letter or a digit, and the first character must be a letter. No spaces allowed!) It attempts to use the pins' existing labels, and to use a list of defaults if no label exists. If an existing label doesn't follow the Java-identifier rule, then Logisim will attempt to extract a valid name from the label if at all possible.

Incidentally, the ordering of the inputs in the truth table will match their top-down ordering in the original circuit, with ties being broken in left-right order.

DESIGN PROCEDURE

Logic circuits for digital systems may be combinational or sequential. A combinational circuit consists of logic gates whose outputs at any time are determined by combining the values of the applied inputs using logic operations. A combinational circuit performs an operation that can be specified logically by a set of Boolean expression.

In addition to using logic gates, sequential circuits employ elements that store bit values. Sequential circuit outputs are a function of inputs and the bit value in storage elements.

These values, in turn, are a function of previously applied inputs and stored values. As a consequence, the outputs of a sequential circuit depend not only on the presently applied values of the inputs, but also on pas inputs, and the behaviour of the circuit must be specified by a sequence in time of inputs and internal stored bit values.

A combinational circuit consists of input variables, output variables, logic gates and interconnections. The interconnected logic gates accept signals from the inputs and generate signals at the output. The n input variables come from the environment of the circuit, and the m output variables are available for use by the environment. Each input and output variable exists physically as a binary signal that represents logic 1 or logic 0.

For n input variables, there are 2^n possible binary input combinations. For each binary combination of the input variables, there is one possible binary value on each output. Thus, a combinational circuit can be specified by a truth table that lists the output values for each combination of the input variables. A combinational circuit can also be described by m Boolean function, one for each output variable. Each such function is expressed as function of the n input variables.

Combinational Circuit Design

The design of combinational circuit starts from a specification of the problem and culminates in a logic diagram or set of Boolean equations from which the logic diagram can be obtained. The procedure involves the following steps:

- From the specifications of the circuit, determine the required number of inputs and outputs, and assign a letter symbol to each.

- Derive the truth table that defines the required relation ship between inputs and outputs.
- Obtain the simplified Boolean functions of each outputs as function of the input variables.
- Draw the logic diagram.
- Verify the correctness of the design.

BINARY ADDER-SUBTRACTOR

HALF ADDER/SUBTRACTOR

This figure shows the configuration for a Half Adder/ Subtractor. The first logic gate which is a XOR allows the circuit to do the complement of the binary bit when we want to do a subtraction. In the case that is needed to implement a addition the XOR keep the number the same.

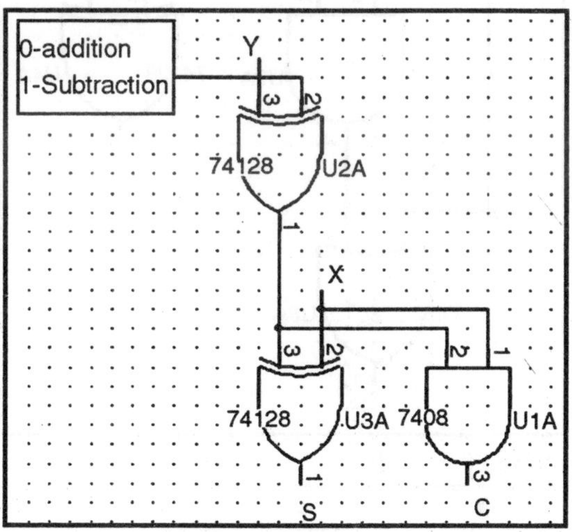

Truth Table

A	B	C	S
0	0	0	0
0	1	0	1
1	0	0	1
1	1	1	0

FULL ADDER/SUBTRACTOR

Full Adder Circuit

This circuit adds two binary one bit numbers. Also, it manages a carry that could come from another circuit.

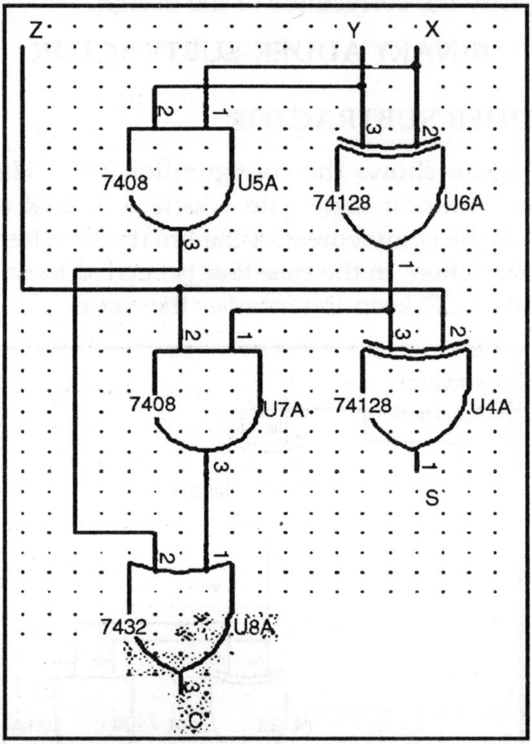

[(AA)'*(BB)']' = A+B

X	Y	Z	C	S
0	0	0	0	0
0	0	1	0	1
0	1	0	0	1
0	1	1	1	0
1	0	0	0	1
1	0	1	1	0
1	1	0	1	0
1	1	1	1	1

This figure shows the configuration for a Full Adder/ Subtractor. The box with the name of"Full Adder" has all the logic to do the addition and subtraction depending of the inputs that it receives. The XOR gate that is outside the box allows the circuit to do the complement of the binary bit when we want to do a subtraction. In the case that is needed to implement an addition the XOR keep the number the same. In the previous graph the internal logic for the box"Full Adder" is shown.

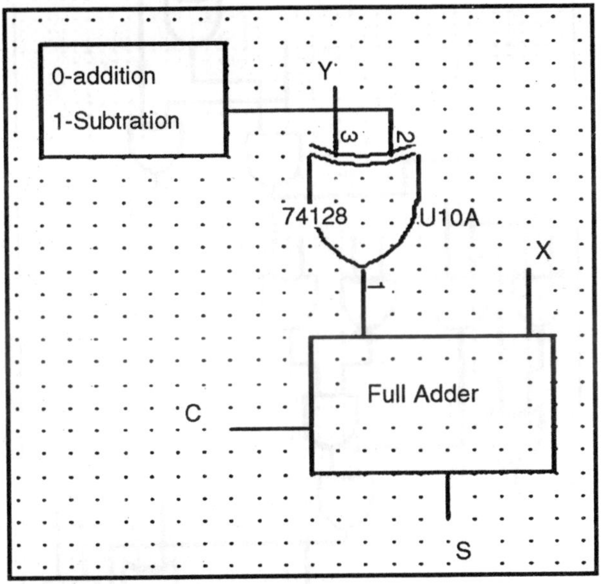

3-BIT ADDER/SUBTRACTOR

The 3-bit adder/Subtractor was implemented with three Full adder circuits and three XOR gates outside which implemented the operation (addition/subtraction) selected by the user. In this circuit, we have three inputs for the first three bits binary number and three inputs for the second three bits binary number.

When the addition is selected the XOR gates keep the binary numbers the same and add them together. On the other hand, when a subtraction is selected the XOR gates complement the second number which is represented with a"Y" and after that, the Full Adder circuit adds both numbers together.

The 3-bit Adder/Subtractor circuit has four outputs. The first three outputs represent the three bits that were the result of the subtraction or addition. The last bit represents a carry.

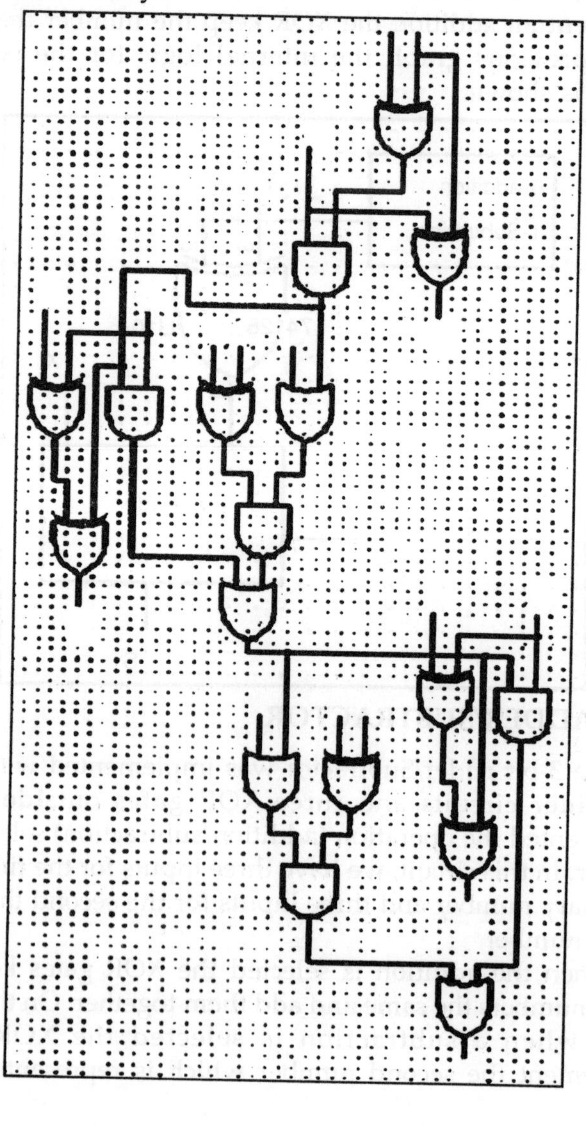

BINARY MULTIPLIER

Binary multiplication uses the same technique as decimal multiplication. In fact, binary multiplication is much easier because each digit we multiply by is either zero or one. Consider the simple problem of multiplying 1102 by 102. We can use this problem to review some terminology and illustrate the rules for binary multiplication.

- First, we note that 1102 is our multiplicand and 102 is our multiplier.

```
 110
× 10
────
```

- We begin by multiplying 1102 by the rightmost digit of our multiplier which is 0. Any number times zero is zero, so we just write zeros below. 110

```
 110
× 10
────
 000
```

- Now we multiply the multiplicand by the next digit of our multiplier which is 1. To perform this multiplication, we just need to copy the multiplicand and shift it one column to the left as we do in decimal multiplication.

```
 110
× 10
────
 000
110
```

- Now we add our results together. The product of our multiplication is 11002. 110

```
 110
× 10
────
 000
110
────
1100
```

When performing binary multiplication, remember the following rules:

- Copy the multiplicand when the multiplier digit is 1. Otherwise, write a row of zeros.
- Shift your results one column to the left as you move to a new multiplier digit.
- Add the results together using binary addition to find the product.

MAGNITUDE COMPARATOR

74L85 4-BIT MAGNITUDE COMPARATOR

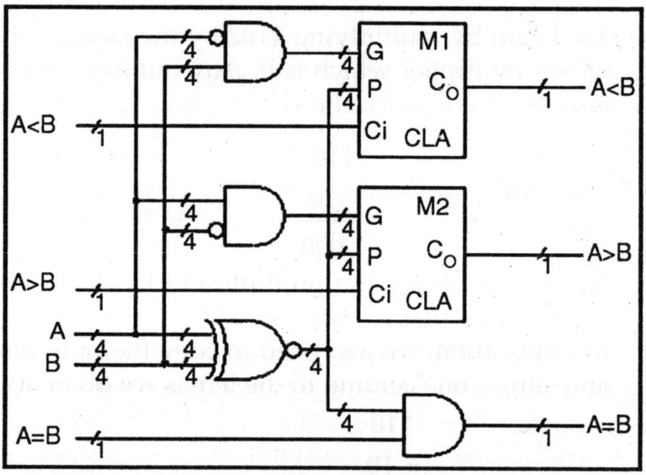

STATISTICS

11 inputs; 3 outputs; 33 gates;

FUNCTION

The 74L85 magnitude comparator can be functionally modeled as above. This is a simplification of implementing a magnitude comparator by a carry function with an inverted input bus as shown. Using this concept, common elements of the three comparator functions A < B, A > B, and A = B are combined to construct the model shown above, which maps directly onto the gate-level realization of the 74L85.

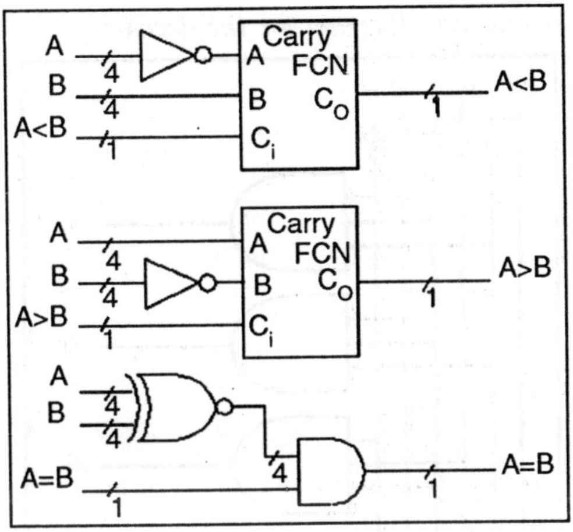

DECODERS

INTRODUCTION

In both the multiplexer and the demultiplexer, part of the circuits decode the address inputs, i.e. it translates a binary number of n digits to 2n outputs, one of which (the one that corresponds to the value of the binary number) is 1 and the others of which are 0.

It is sometimes advantageous to separate this function from the rest of the circuit, since it is useful in many other applications.

Thus, we obtain a new combinatorial circuit that we call the decoder. It has the following truth table (for n = 3):

a2	a1	a0	d7	d6	d5	d4	d3	d2	d1	d0
0	0	0	0	0	0	0	0	0	0	1
0	0	1	0	0	0	0	0	0	1	0
0	1	0	0	0	0	0	0	1	0	0
0	1	1	0	0	0	0	1	0	0	0
1	0	0	0	0	0	1	0	0	0	0
1	0	1	0	0	1	0	0	0	0	0
1	1	0	0	1	0	0	0	0	0	0
1	1	1	1	0	0	0	0	0	0	0

Here is the circuit diagram for the decoder:

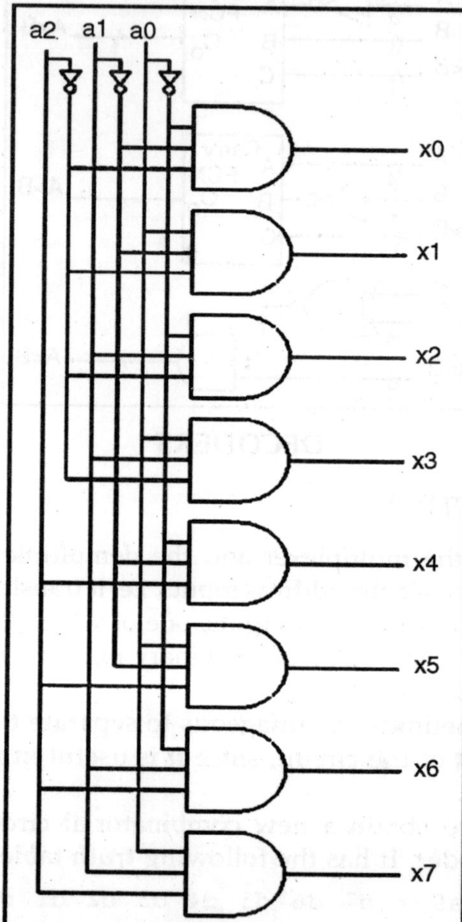

DECODER GENERATION

X86's decoder is generated using an ISA description like all the other ISAs, although how it does that is a bit different. Most of the instructions for most of the other ISAs are defined by passing chunks of code that perform the instruction into an instruction format.

The format is basically a template which puts wraps that bit of code in the structure needed to support it and you have your instruction object. Because almost all of the instructions in x86 are microcoded and many can be encoded in multiple ways and hence appear in the decoder more than once, and because the same non-trivial decoding rules apply to many different instructions, X86 uses the decoder as a layer of indirection and defines the majority of its instructions elsewhere.

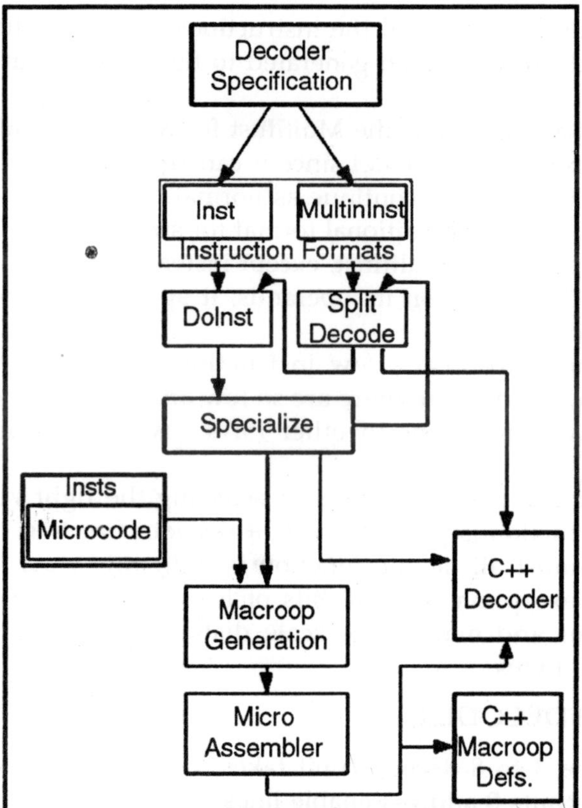

X86 almost exclusively uses only two different instruction formats, Inst and MultiInst. MultiInst is just a compact way of describing multiple related Insts. An Inst essentially selects an instruction like XOR and provides a specification for its operands.

Inside the instruction format, the instruction name and

operand specification are passed to a python function called"specializeInst" which figures out what to do with it. If the operand specification describes more than one version of the instruction, for instance one that uses memory and one that uses registers, the instruction's information is passed into another funciton,"doSplitDecode", which separates out those versions and passes each individually back through the same system.

This goes on until the instructions have been fully split out and code has been generated to figure out what version to use.

As a nice bonus, the MultiInst format doesn't add much complexity to this model since it can simply jump right into doSplitDecode and continue as normal.

There is one additional format for string instructions that works similar to MultiInst, except instead of specializing the instruction based on its operands, it specializes it based on its prefixes.

There are also a few instructions that don't use this system, but because there are so few and because they work like the instructions in other ISAs I won't describe them here.

At this point, the code for selecting the right version of an instruction is put into the C++ decoder function.

Almost all of this function is built this way, with the minor exception of small bits of logic that glue everything together and make large scale distinctions the number of opcode bytes.

3 TO 8 DECODER

The 3 to 8 decoder unit takes 3 address lines as input and outputs 8 address enable lines.

Which of the 8 output is enabled is dependant upon the configuration of the 3 address line.

If A0, A1, and A2 are all 0, then address 0 is enabled. If A0=0, A1=1, A2=0, then address 3 is enables. With 3 address lines, the number of words that can be addressed is 8 (2^3=8).

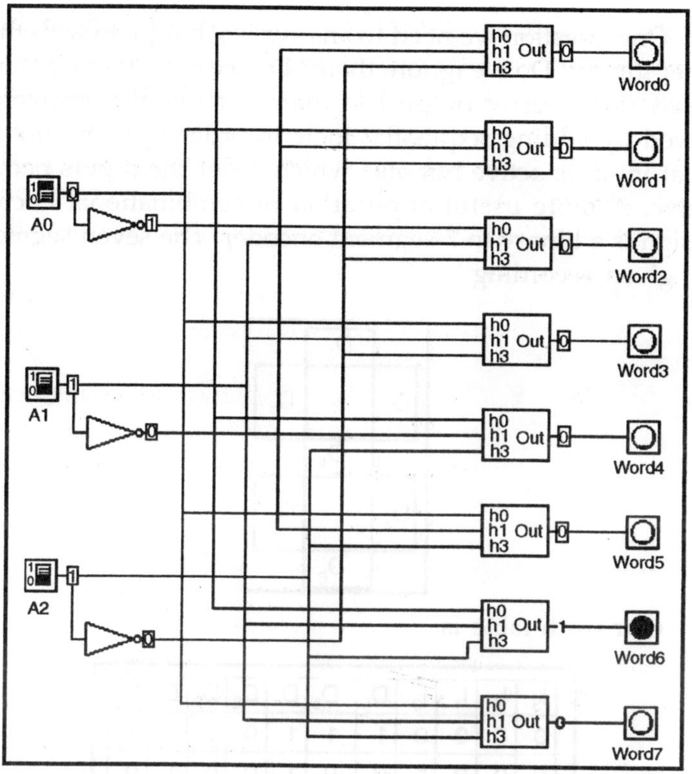

ENCODERS

An encoder is a circuit that changes a set of signals into a code. Lets begin making a 2-to-1 line encoder truth table by reversing the 1-to-2 decoder truth table.

D_1	D_0	A
0	1	0
1	0	1

This truth table is a little short. A complete truth table would be

D_1	D_0	A
0	0	
0	1	0
1	0	1
1	1	

One question we need to answer is what to do with those other inputs? Do we ignore them? Do we have them generate an additional error output? In many circuits this problem is solved by adding sequential logic in order to know not just what input is active but also which order the inputs became active. A more useful application of combinational encoder design is a binary to 7-segment encoder. The seven segments are given according

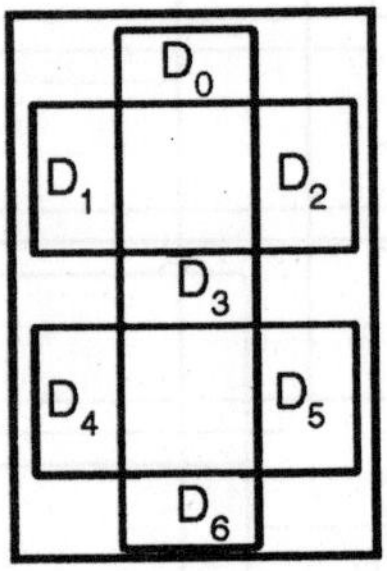

Our truth table is:

I_3	I_2	I_1	I_0	D_6	D_5	D_4	D_3	D_2	D_1	D_0
0	0	0	0	1	1	1	0	1	1	1
0	0	0	1	0	0	1	0	0	1	0
0	0	1	0	1	0	1	1	1	0	1
0	0	1	1	1	0	1	1	0	1	1
0	1	0	0	0	1	1	1	0	1	0
0	1	0	1	1	1	0	1	0	1	1
0	1	1	0	1	1	0	1	1	1	1
0	1	1	1	1	0	1	0	0	1	0
1	0	0	0	1	1	1	1	1	1	1
1	0	0	1	1	1	1	1	0	1	1

Deciding what to do with the remaining six entries of the truth table is easier with this circuit. This circuit should not be expected to encode an undefined combination of inputs, so we can leave them as"don't care" when we design the circuit. The boolean equations are

$$D_0 = l_3 + l_1 + \bar{l}_3\bar{l}_2\bar{l}_1\bar{l}_0 + \bar{l}_3\bar{l}_2\bar{l}_1\bar{l}_0$$

$$D_1 = l_3 + \bar{l}_2\bar{l}_1 + \bar{l}_2\bar{l}_1 + \bar{l}_2\bar{l}_0$$

$$D_2 = l_2 + \bar{l}_3\bar{l}_2\bar{l}_1\bar{l}_0 + \bar{l}_3\bar{l}_2\bar{l}_1\bar{l}_0$$

$$D_3 = l_3 + l_1\bar{l}_0 + l_2\bar{l}_1$$

$$D_4 = l_1\bar{l}_0 + \bar{l}_2\bar{l}_1\bar{l}_0$$

$$D_5 = l_3 + l_2 + l_0$$

$$D_6 = l_3 + l_1\bar{l}_0 + \bar{l}_3\bar{l}_2\bar{l}_1 + \bar{l}_3\bar{l}_2\bar{l}_1\bar{l}_0 + \bar{l}_3 l_2\bar{l}_1\bar{l}_0$$

and the circuit is

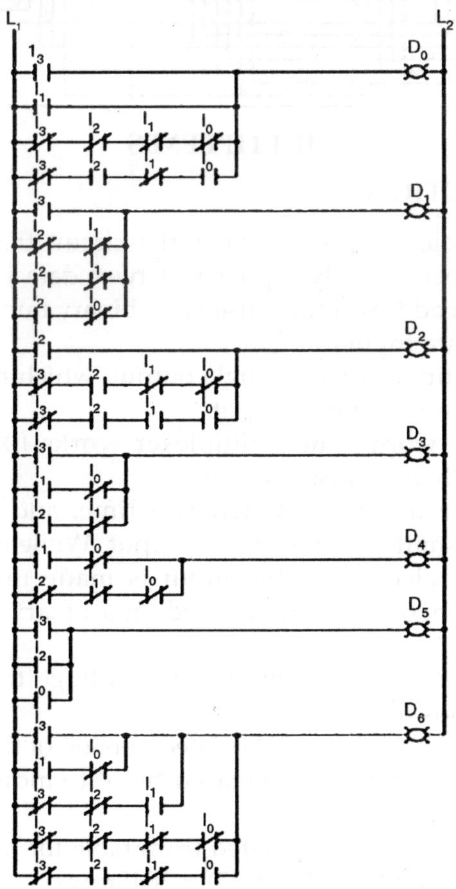

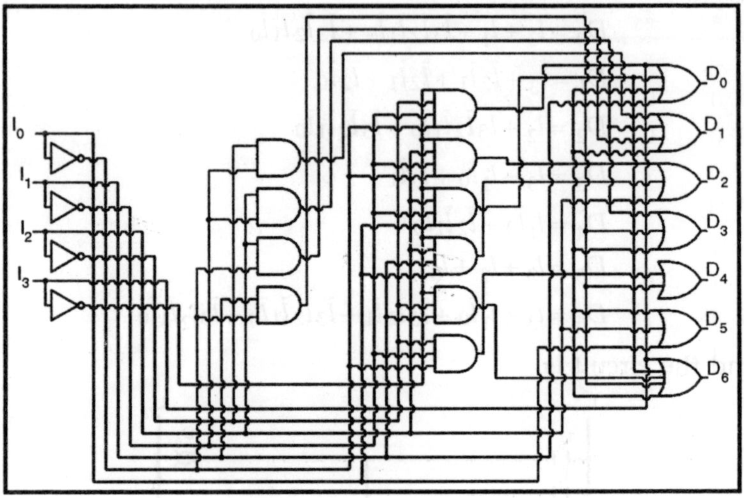

MULTIPLEXES

INTRODUCTION

A multiplexer is a combinatorial circuit that is given a certain number (usually a power of two) data inputs, let us say 2n, and n address inputs used as a binary number to select one of the data inputs.

The multiplexer has a single output, which has the same value as the selected data input.

In other words, the multiplexer works like the input selector of a home music system.

Only one input is selected at a time, and the selected input is transmitted to the single output. While on the music system, the selection of the input is made manually, the multiplexer chooses its input based on a binary number, the address input.

The truth table for a multiplexer is huge for all but the smallest values of n.

We therefore use an abbreviated version of the truth table in which some inputs are replaced by `-' to indicate that the input value does not matter.

Here is such an abbreviated truth table for n = 3. The full truth table would have 2(3 + 23) = 2048rows.

a_2	a_1	a_0	d_7	d_6	d_5	d_4	d_3	d_2	d_1	d_0	x
-	-	-	-	-	-	-	-	-	-	-	-
0	0	0	-	-	-	-	-	-	-	0	0
0	0	0	-	-	-	-	-	-	-	1	1
0	0	1	-	-	-	-	-	-	0	-	0
0	0	1	-	-	-	-	-	-	1	-	1
0	1	0	-	-	-	-	-	0	-	-	0
0	1	0	-	-	-	-	-	1	-	-	1
0	1	1	-	-	-	-	0	-	-	-	0
0	1	1	-	-	-	-	1	-	-	-	1
1	0	0	-	-	-	0	-	-	-	-	0
1	0	0	-	-	-	1	-	-	-	-	1
1	0	1	-	-	0	-	-	-	-	-	0
1	0	1	-	-	1	-	-	-	-	-	1
1	1	0	-	0	-	-	-	-	-	-	0
1	1	0	-	1	-	-	-	-	-	-	1
1	1	1	0	-	-	-	-	-	-	-	0
1	1	1	1	-	-	-	-	-	-	-	1

We can abbreviate this table even more by using a letter to indicate the value of the selected input, like this:

a_2	a_1	a_0	d_7	d_6	d_5	d_4	d_3	d_2	d_1	d_0	x
-	-	-	-	-	-	-	-	-	-	-	-
0	0	0	-	-	-	-	-	-	-	c	c
0	0	1	-	-	-	-	-	-	c	-	c
0	1	0	-	-	-	-	-	c	-	-	c
0	1	1	-	-	-	-	c	-	-	-	c
1	0	0	-	-	-	c	-	-	-	-	c
1	0	1	-	-	c	-	-	-	-	-	c
1	1	0	-	c	-	-	-	-	-	-	c
1	1	1	c	-	-	-	-	-	-	-	c

The same way we can simplify the truth table for the multiplexer, we can also simplify the corresponding circuit. Indeed, our simple design method would yield a very large circuit. The simplified circuit looks like this:

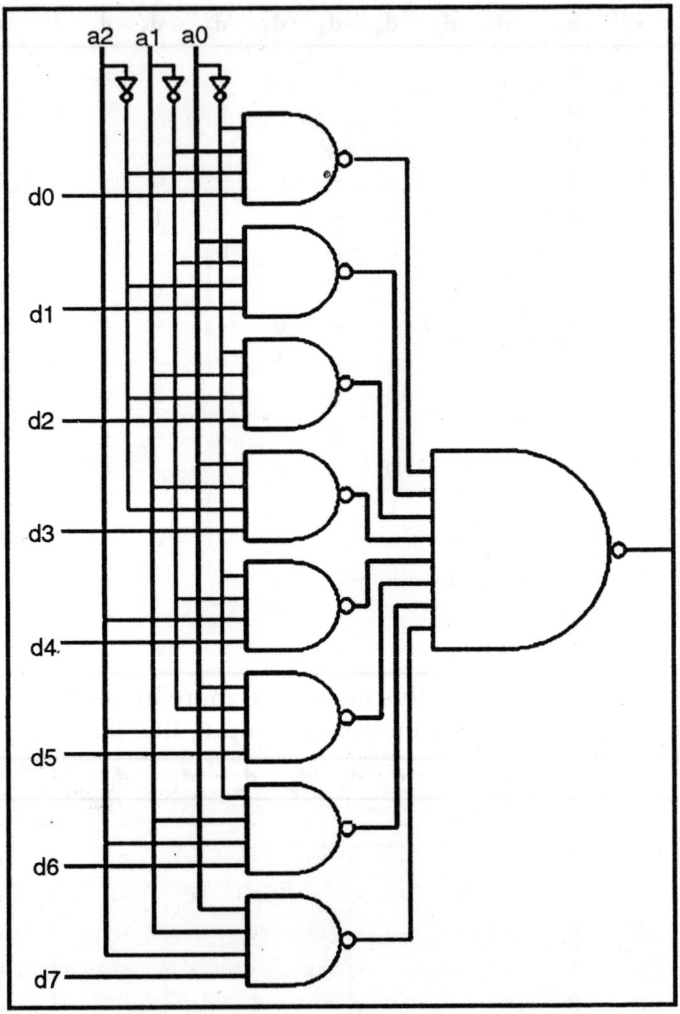

A multiplexer performs the function of selecting the input on any one of'n' input lines and feeding this input to one output line. Multiplexers are used as one method of reducing the number of integrated circuit packages required by a particular circuit design. This in turn reduces the cost of the system. Assume that we have four lines, C0, C1, C2 and C3, which are to be multiplexed on a single line, Output (f). The four input lines are also known as the Data Inputs. Since there are four inputs, we will need two additional inputs to the multiplexer, known as the Select Inputs, to select which of the C inputs is to appear at the output. Call these select lines A and B. The gate implementation of a 4-line to 1-line multiplexer is shown below:

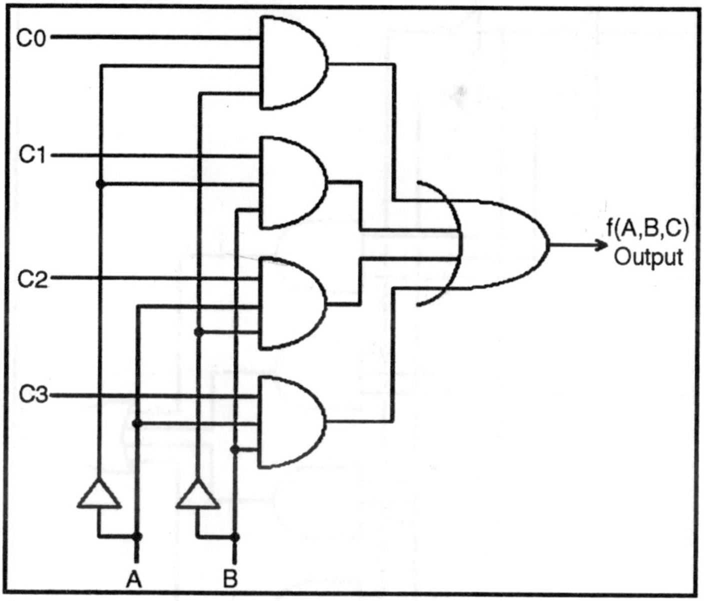

The circuit symbol for the above multiplexer is:

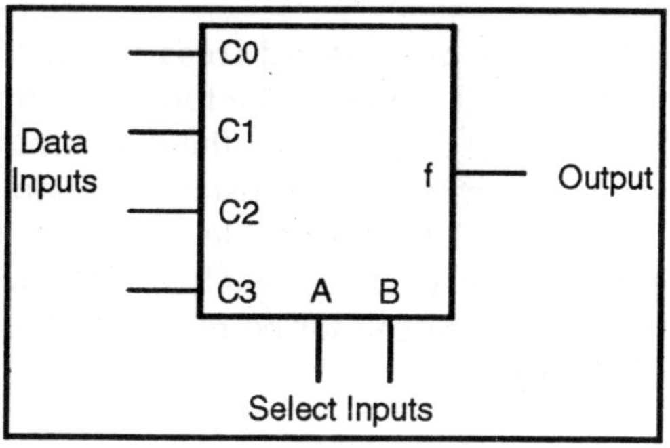

4 INPUT MULTIPLEXER

The multiplexer concept is not limited to two data inputs.

If we add a second addressing input, B, we can control as many as four data inputs, as shown to the left. A third and fourth addressing input will allow the multiplexer to control eight or sixteen inputs, respectively.

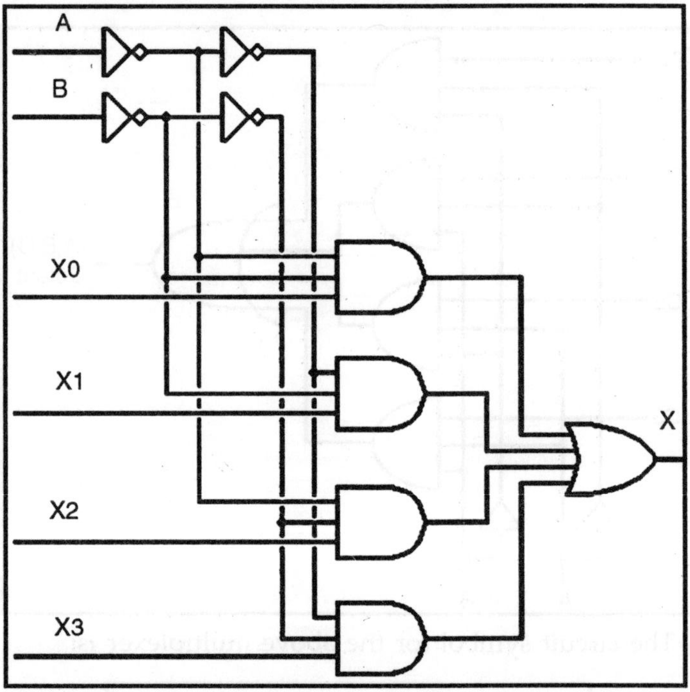

Inputs A and B are the addressing inputs to this multiplexer. They select which of the four data inputs will be transmitted to the final output, X. If the data inputs are to be multiplexed for transmission to a distant location, the inputs must cycle through all four possible addresses more than twice for each single cycle of each of the data inputs. Otherwise the input data cannot be reconstructed accurately at the receiving end.

Chapter 4

Synchronous Sequential Logic

SEQUENTIAL CIRCUITS

Digital electronics is classified into combinational logic and sequential logic. Combinational logic output depends on the inputs levels, whereas sequential logic output depends on stored levels and also the input levels.

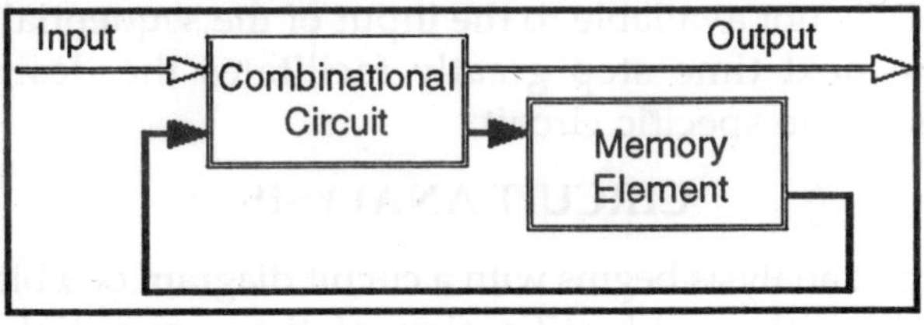

The following figure shows a way to consider sequential circuits.

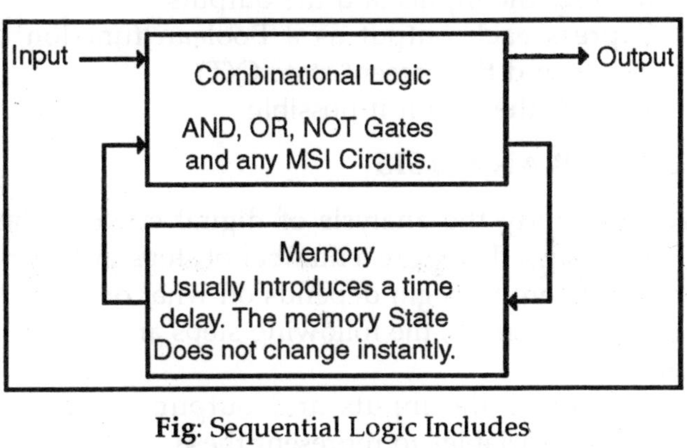

Fig: Sequential Logic Includes Combinational Logic and Memory

Sequential circuits can be characterized into two broad classes - synchronous and asynchronous. As a general rule, asynchronous circuits are faster, but much harder to design. We shall focus totally on synchronous circuits.

By Q(T) we denote the state of a sequential circuit at time T - this is basically its memory. We watch the state of the circuit change from Q(T) to Q(T + 1) as the clock ticks. The constraint on synchronous circuits is that the state of the circuit changes after the input, thus we have a typical sequence as follows:

- At time T, we have input (denoted by X) and state Q(T).
- As a result of the input X and state Q(T), a new state is computed,

This becomes available to the input only at time (T + 1) and so is called Q(T + 1).

The fact that the new state, computed as a result of X and Q(T), is not available to the input of the sequential circuit until the next time step greatly facilitates the design and analysis of the specific circuit.

CIRCUIT ANALYSIS

Circuit analysis begins with a circuit diagram or a black box and ends with an identification of the sequential circuit implemented by the device - normally a truth table. The steps are:

- Identify the inputs and the outputs
- Express each output as a Boolean function of the inputs and the present state Q(T)
- Identify the circuit if possible.

CIRCUIT FOR ANALYSIS

We first study the analysis of digital circuits, then we study their design. There are a number of steps in the analysis of a circuit. Where to begin depends on what one has. When given a circuit diagram, the following steps are used to begin the analysis.

- Determine the inputs and outputs of the circuit. Assign variables to represent these.

- Determine the inputs and outputs of the flip-flops.
- Construct the Next State and Output Tables.
- Construct the State Diagram.
- If possible, identify the circuit. There are no good rules for this step.

Consider the following circuit. We want to discover what it does.

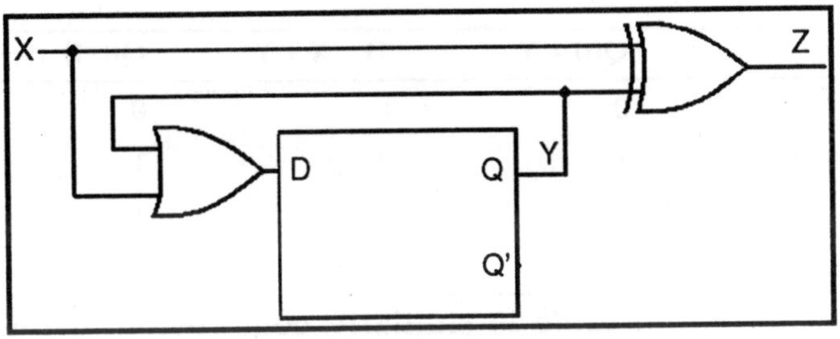

Fig: Circuit to Be Analysed

Step 1: Identify and Label the Inputs, Outputs, and Internal States

We use the following variables in the analysis of this circuit with a single flip-flop. X denotes the input, Y denotes the output of the flip-flop (Y' also), and Z the output of the circuit. If we had more than one flip-flop, we would label the flip-flop with a number beginning at 0 and use that as a subscript, so flip-flop 0 would have output Y0, etc.

Step 2: Determine the Inputs and Outputs of the Flip-flops

The next step is to determine the equations for Z, the output, and D, the input to the flip-flop. By inspection, we determine the following for the equations:

$$Z = X \oplus Y$$

$$D = X + Y$$

Step 3: Construct the Next State and Output Tables.

We begin this state by recalling the characteristic table of each flip-flop that is used in the design. Here we have only one flip-flip, a D with a very simple characteristic table that is better represented as an equation: Q(t+1) = D - the next state is what you put in now.

Noting that Q(t) = Y (the state of a flip-flop is also its

output) we construct the following Next-State diagram for the flip-flop, based on the characteristic table of a D flip-flop and the equation we derived for the D input: D = X + Y.

One simple caution here is that the input to a flip-flop is a function of the present state only, having nothing to do with the next state (as we have no crystal balls). Thus Y = Q(t).

Here is the present state (PS)/ next state (NS) diagram for the circuit.

X	Q(t) = Y	D = X + Y	Q(t+1)
0	0	0	0
0	1	1	1
1	0	1	1
1	1	1	1

The output table is similarly constructed, using the equation Z = X Y = Z = X Q(t). Again, note that the output is not a function of the next state.

X	Q(t)	Z
0	0	0
0	1	1
1	0	1
1	1	0

These two tables are combined to form the transition/ output table.

X	Q(t) = Y	D = X + Y	Q(t+1)/ Z
0	0	0	0/ 0
0	1	1	1/ 1
1	0	1	1/ 1
1	1	1	1/ 0

At this point, we should produce a state table in the standard format. This involves assigning labels to each of the two states, currently identified only as Q(t) = 0 and Q(t) = 1. For lack of anything more imaginative, we label the states 0 and 1.

Present State	Next State/Output	
	X = 0	X = 1
0	0/ 0	1/ 1
1	1/ 1	1/ 0

Step 4: Construct the State Diagram

The final step in the process may be the creation of the state diagram.

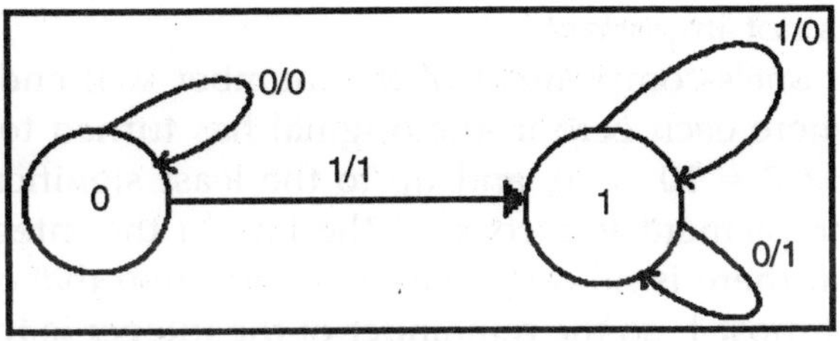

At this point, we have a complete description of the circuit. It may be possible to proceed from this diagram to obtain an understanding of what the circuit does.

Step 5: If possible, identify the circuit.

This circuit is a 2-state device, with memory represented by one bit. The circuit stays in state 0 from the start until a 1 is input at which time it transitions to state 1 and remains there.

Note the relation of the output to the input, depending on the state of the machine.

Input	Q(t)	Output	
0	0	0	For Q(t) = 0, the output is X
1	0	1	
0	1	1	For Q(t) = 1, the output is X'.
1	1	0	

A verbal description of the circuit is then that it copies its input to the output until the first 1 is encountered in the input stream. After that event, all input is output as complemented.

What this circuit does is take the two's-complement of a binary integer, presented to the circuit least-significant bit first. It is easy to prove that such a strategy produces the two's complement of a number. First, consider a number ending in 1, say $X_nX_n-1 \ldots X_2X_{11}$.

The one's complement of this number is Xn'Xn-1' .... $X_2'X_1'0$. Adding 1 to this produces the number $Xn'X_{n-1}'$ .... $X_2'X_1'1$, in which the least significant 1 is copied and the remaining bits are complemented. The proof is completed by supposing that the number terminates in a one or more zeroes; i.e., its least significant bits are 10 .... 0, where the count of zeroes is not important.

The one's-complement of this number will end with 01 .... 1, where each zero in the original has turned to a 1. But 01 .... 1 + 1 = 10 .... 0, and up to the least significant 1 the two's-complement is a copy of the bits in the integer itself. Note that there is no carry out of the addition that produced the right-most 1, so the remainder of the integer is formed by the one's-complement. Thus we have a complete description of the circuit.

It is a serial two's-complementer.

LATCHES

When showing either latches or flip-flops as circuit elements, it is undesirable to show the"internals" of the device.

Here are the symbols for SR and D latches.

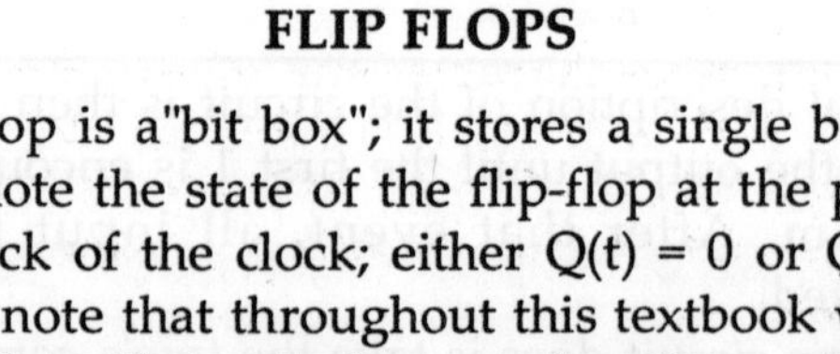

FLIP FLOPS

A flip-flop is a"bit box"; it stores a single binary bit. By Q(t), we denote the state of the flip-flop at the present time, or present tick of the clock; either Q(t) = 0 or Q(t) = 1. The student will note that throughout this textbook we make the assumption that all circuit elements function correctly, so that any binary device is assumed to have only two states.

A flip-flop must have an output; this is called either Q

or Q(t). This output indicates the current state of the flip-flop, and as such is either a binary 0 or a binary 1.

We shall see that, as a result of the way in which they are constructed, all flip-flops also output $\overline{Q(t)}$, the complement of the current state. Each flip-flop also has, as input, signals that specify how the next state, Q(t + 1), is to relate to the present state, Q(t).

Every flip-flop also has an input derived from the system clock, which allows it to function as a synchronous circuit. It also has connections to power and ground.

Here are the symbols for SR and D flip-flops, which we have not yet defined.

Note the small triangles on the clock input; this says"edge triggered".

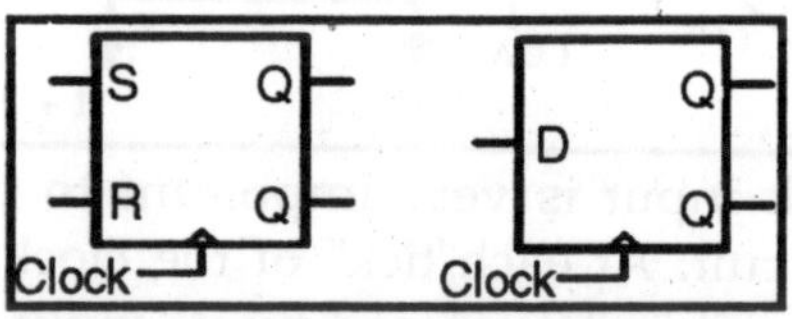

One should note that the more common symbols for flip-flops show the clock input coming in"from the side" as shown in the next figure.

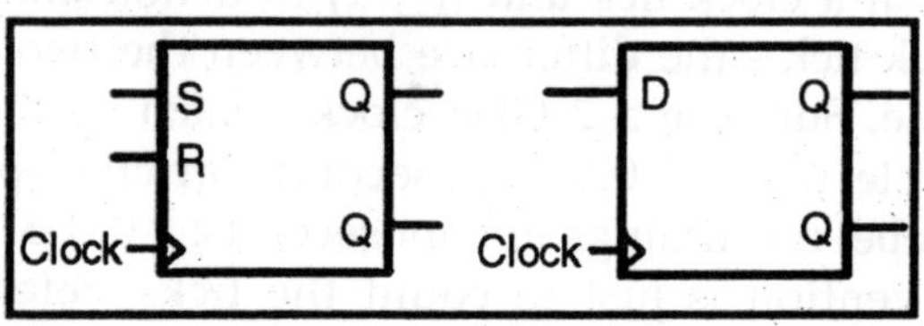

THE CLOCK

The most fundamental characteristic of synchronous sequential circuits is a system clock. This is an electronic circuit that produces a repetitive train of logic 1 and logic 0 at a regular rate, called the clock frequency. Most computer systems have a number of clocks, usually operating at related frequencies; for example - 2 GHz, 1GHz, 500MHz, and 125MHz. The inverse of the clock frequency is the clock cycle time. As an example, we consider a clock with a frequency of 2 GHz (2"109 Hertz). The cycle time is 1.0/ (2"109) seconds, or

0.5"10-9 seconds = 0.500 nanoseconds = 500 picoseconds.

Synchronous sequential circuits are sequential circuits that use a clock input to order events. Asynchronous sequential circuits do not use a common clock and, as hinted at above, are much harder to design and test. As we shall focus only on synchronous circuits, we immediately launch a discussion of the clock.

The following figure illustrates some of the terms commonly used for a clock.

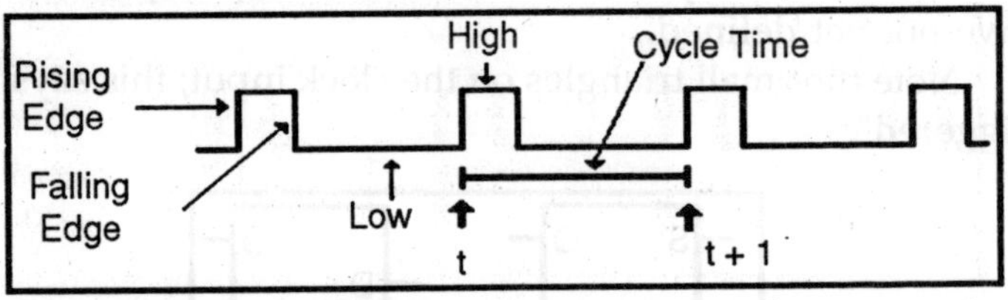

The clock input is very important to the concept of a sequential circuit. At each"tick" of the clock the output of a sequential circuit is determined by its input and by its state. We now provide a common definition of a"clock tick" - it occurs at the rising edge of each pulse. We use t to represent the time at a clock tick and (t + 1) to denote the time at the next clock tick - the difference between the two is the clock cycle time. Suppose a 2 GHz clock, which corresponds to a clock cycle time of 0.5 nanosecond. Strictly speaking, we should label our timings in nanoseconds: 1.0, 1.5. 2.0. 2.5, etc. The convention is just to count the ticks, referring to the present clock pulse as occurring at time t and the next one at time (t + 1).

DESCRIPTION

By definition, a flip-flop is an edge-triggered latch. We must now show how achieve edge triggering. In essence, what we shall do is take a level triggered latch and give it a clock pulse with a very short positive (logical 1) phase.

The key component of an edge-triggered flip-flop is a pulse generator that we studied in a previous chapter. This could be based on the gate delay of a NOT gate. More modern devices likely use a different circuit so as to generate a shorter pulse.

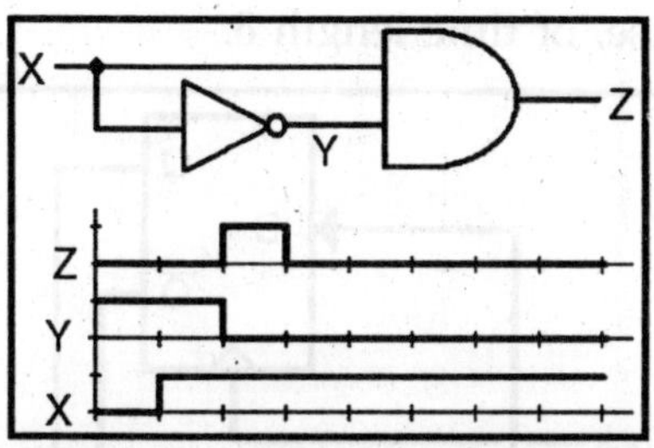

Now that we have a method to generate a short pulse, we can build an edge-triggered device. The following is a diagram of the components of two typical edge-triggered flip-flops. The top one is a SR flip-flop and the bottom one is a D flip-flop.

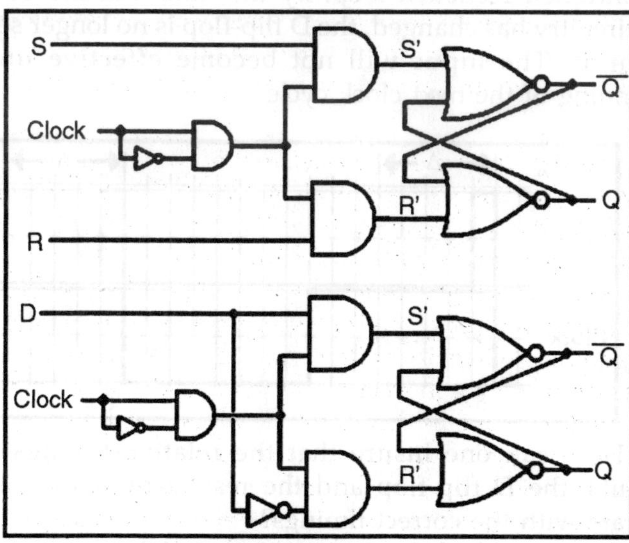

TYPES OF FLIP-FLOPS

In order to avoid the simple example, we shall examine the general case. Here is the circuit for consideration. We postulate a total of gate delays (including that of the D flip-flop) to be the time interval signified by Δ. Thus at time Δ after the D latch is first sensitive to its input, the circuitry has output a new value to become D. But the flip-flop is activated by a short pulse, of time length δ.

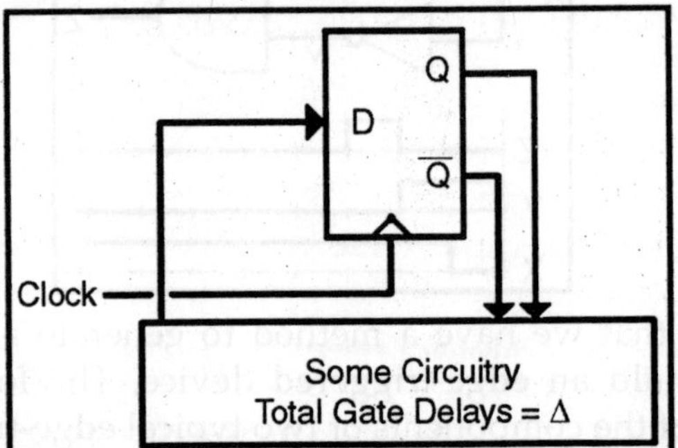

The timing diagram below shows the interruption of the uncontrolled feedback loop. By the time that the output of the circuitry has changed, the D flip-flop is no longer sensitive to input. The input will not become effective until the beginning of the next clock cycle.

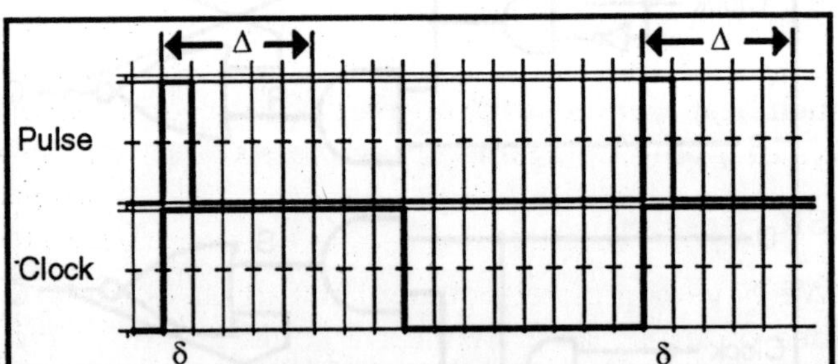

How can one insure that the relative timings of two circuits, the D flip-flop and the rest of the CPU circuitry, operate with the correct timings?

This is one of the issues of central importance in the design of a CPU; since we have stumbled into it, let's talk about it.

To be more precise, define two total gate delays: Δ_{MIN} and Δ_{MAX}. Δ_{MIN} is the total time delay for the fastest CPU operation and Δ_{MAX}. the delay for the slowest. We must haveΔ_{MIN} >, or the circuit would occasionally display uncontrolled feedback.

Conservatively, we might say Δ_{MIN} 1.5•. The next criterion is a bit more difficult to state precisely, but it might be stated something like T 1.5•δ Δ_{MAX}, where T denotes the clock period.

What we say here is that the clock period must be long enough for the CPU output to"settle". Note, however, that a value of T much larger than MAX is just wasted time.

Put another way, the value of MAX determines the fastest clock that can reasonably be applied to the CPU. A good part of the art of CPU design is based on this issue. When we study the RISC (Reduced Instruction Set Computer) movement, we shall see that one of the issues was to remove the more complex instructions, thus reducing MAX and allowing for a faster clock. There is a trade-off here that we shall explore in later chapters.

To be honest, the sum of CPU gate delays is not always the limiting factor in the clock speed. Some recent CPUs have been designed with a"hot clock" that is hot in both ways. It is very fast, being of the order of 4 to 5 GHz. It is also hot in the literal sense, in that the CPU, operating at that clock rate, emits so much heat that it overheats itself. The art of CPU design is always bumping up against those messy laws of physics.

The SR Flip-Flop

We have completely defined the SR flip-flop, based on the idea of an SR latch. While we could just leave the topic and proceed, it is appropriate at this time to review the subject and state, in one place, what the student is expected to know. We begin with a depiction of the SR flip-flop that will be used in all future discussions.

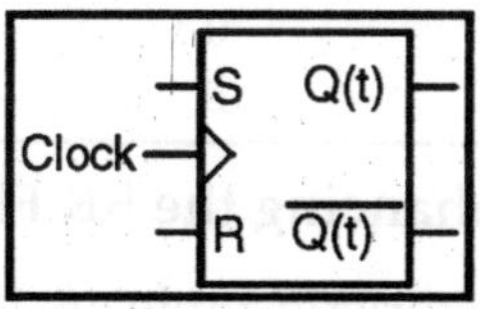

At this point we are no longer interested in the internal

construction of the flip-flop, but on its operational characteristics. These are given in the characteristic table.

S	R	Q(t + 1)
0	0	Q(t)
0	1	0
1	0	1
1	1	ERROR

We next address an issue that commonly arises in the use of flip-flops in circuit design. We have a number of scenarios.

For each, we know Q(t) and what Q(t + 1) should be. The question is how to achieve that change. For example, if Q(t) = 0 and we want Q(t + 1) = 0, we have two choices: either S = 0 and R = 0, or S = 0 and R = 1.

The first option, keeps the state unchanged at 0; the second forces it to 0. As S = 0 is sufficient to do this without regard to the value of R, we say that the input is S = 0 and R = d; the d standing for"don't care". On the other hand, if Q(t) = 0 and Q(t + 1) = 1, only S = 1 and R = 0 will do. This is the only combination that will give a next state of 1 when the present state is 0.

If we have Q(t) = 1 and want Q(t + 1) = 0, then our choice is simple: S = 0 and R = 1. If we have Q(t) = 1 and want Q(t + 1) = 1, then we can choose either S = 0 and R = 0, or

S = 1 and R = 0. This is denoted as S = d and R = 0.

The above discussions lead to the excitation table for the SR flip-flop.

Q(t)	Q(t + 1)	S	R
0	0	0	d
0	1	1	0
1	0	0	1
1	1	d	0

The JK Flip-Flop: Enhancing the SR Flip-Flop

Recall the characteristic table of the SR flip-flop. We repeat the table here for emphasis.

S	R	Q(t + 1)
0	0	Q(t)
0	1	0
1	0	1
1	1	ERROR

The theoretician examining this table would note two facts immediately.

- The input S = 1 and R = 1 is disallowed; we would like to do something with it.
- The values for Q(t + 1) are three of the possible four Boolean functions of 1 variable.

Considering Q as a Boolean variable, we now show that there are exactly four Boolean functions of this Boolean variable.

These are f(Q) = 0, f(Q) = 1, f(Q) = Q, and f(Q) = $\overline{Q}$. We do this by showing the truth table for each of these functions and noting that there are only four different ways to put 0's and 1's into the two row entries for a function..

Table: The Four Boolean Functions of Boolean Variable Q

Q	0	Q	$\overline{Q}$	1
0	0	0	1	1
1	0	1	0	1

Given this, our enhanced SR flip-flop would have Q(t + 1) = $\overline{Q}$(t) as one possible output. For maximal compatibility with the existing SR, we would want to leave the existing valid inputs alone and just make good use of the invalid one. What we get is a JK flip-flop.

Recalling that an SR flip-flop is so called because it is a Set-Reset device, we may ask for the meaning of JK. One is tempted to make up some story related to names in German, but the basic answer is that"I don't know".

In any case, we present the characteristic table for the JK flip-flop and then ask how one might modify an SR flip to achieve that goal.

Here is the desired characteristic table.

J	K	Q(t + 1)
0	0	Q(t)
0	1	0
1	0	1
1	1	$\overline{Q}$ (t)

Viewing this as a modification of the SR flip-flop, we ask how to generate each of S and R from the inputs J and K under the following constraints;

- Except when J = 1 and K = 1, we want to have S = J and R = K.

  Under these circumstances, the behaviour is identical.
- When J = 1, K = 1, and Q = 0, we want S = 1 and R = 0. This makes Q(t + 1) = 1.
- When J = 1, K = 1, and Q = 1, we want S = 0 and R = 1. This makes Q(t + 1) = 0.

When in doubt about how to create a circuit, we make a truth table. The inputs to the truth table are J, K, and Q (the present state). The outputs are S and R.

Row	Q	J	K	S	R
0	0	0	0	0	0
1	0	0	1	0	1
2	0	1	0	1	0
3	0	1	1	1	0
4	1	0	0	0	0
5	1	0	1	0	1
6	1	1	0	1	0
7	1	1	1	0	1

We have two patterns that almost work: $S = J \bullet \overline{Q}$ and R = K"Q. Let's examine each case.

$S = J \bullet \overline{Q}$ produces the expected result for all rows except row 6. In that row we have

Q = 1, J = 1, and K = 0. We want Q(t + 1) to be 1. But S = 0 and R = 0 will cause

Q(t + 1) = Q(t) = 1, exactly what we want. So this simple formula causes no trouble.

R = K•Q produces the expected result for all rows except row 1. In that row we have

Q = 0, J = 0, and K = 1. We want Q(t + 1) to be 0. But S = 0 and R = 0 will cause

Q(t + 1) = Q(t) = 0, exactly what we want. So again we have no trouble.

Here is the basic detailed circuit for the JK flip-flop.

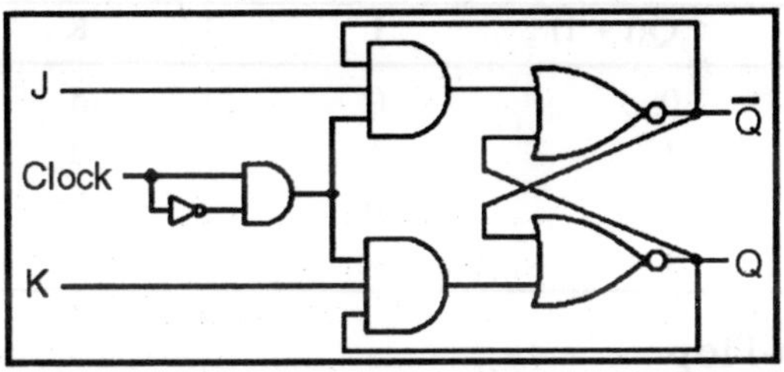

We now give the standard representation of the JK flip-flop as will be used in future discussions. Again, note the triangle symbol on the clock input, indicating edge triggering.

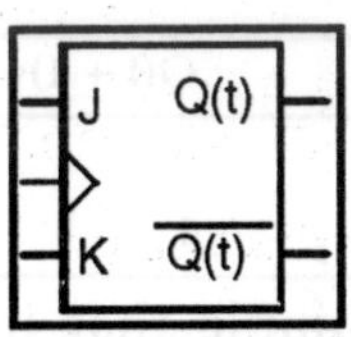

We have already presented the characteristic table for the JK flip-flop. Here it is again.

J	K	Q(t + 1)
0	0	Q(t)
0	1	0
1	0	1
1	1	$\overline{Q}$ (t)

We now create the excitation table for the JK.

If Q(t) = 0 and Q(t + 1) is to be 0, we can use either J = 0 and K = 0, or J = 0 and K = 1.

If Q(t) = 0 and Q(t + 1) is to be 1, we can use either J = 1 and K = 0, or J = 1 and K = 1.

Note that this is a new option, not available for an SR flip-flop.

If Q(t) = 1 and Q(t + 1) is to be 0, we can use either J = 0 and K = 1, or J = 1 and K = 1.

Note that this also is a new option, not available for an SR flip-flop.

If Q(t) = 1 and Q(t + 1) is to be 1, we can use either J = 0 and K = 0, or J = 1 and K = 0.

This gives the excitation table for the JK flip-flop.

Q(t)	Q(t + 1)	J	K
0	0	0	d
0	1	1	d
1	0	d	1
1	1	d	0

The D Flip-Flop

We have already examined the D latch. The input is labeled"D" for"Data". The D flip-flop has a characteristic table identical to that of a D latch.

D	Q(t + 1)
0	0
1	1

The device is so simple that it does not require an excitation equation. We just use an excitation equation, which simply states"Give it what you want".

D = Q(t + 1)

The T Flip-Flop

This is the fourth and last of the major types of flip-flops. The input to this flip-flop is labeled"T" for toggle. When T = 0, the state remains the same. When T = 1, the flip-flop changes state. This gives rise to the following characteristic table.

T	Q(t + 1)
0	Q(t)
1	$\overline{Q}$ (t)

The excitation table for this flip-flop is almost obvious.

Q(t)	Q(t + 1)	T
0	0	0
0	1	1
1	0	1
1	1	0

This gives rise to an excitation equation.

$T = Q(t) \oplus Q(t + 1)$

JK As a General Flip-Flop

We now take notice that the JK can be configured to function as any of the other 3 flip-flop types. In this, it is the most general type of flip-flop.

JK As a D Flip-Flop

To convert a JK to a D flip-flop, connect the inputs as follows.

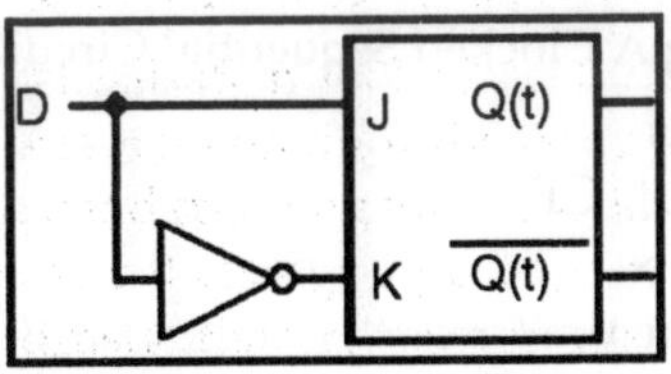

If D = 0, then J = 0, K = 1, and Q(t + 1) = 0, If D = 1, then J = 1, K = 0, and Q(t + 1) = 1.

The JK As A T Flip-Flop

To convert a JK to a T flip-flop, connect the inputs as follows.

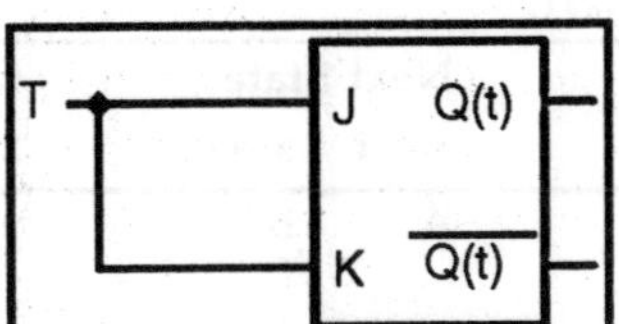

If T = 0, then J = 0, K = 0, and Q(t + 1) = Q(t).

If T = 1, then J = 1, K = 1, and $Q(t + 1) = \overline{Q}(t)$

ANALYSIS OF CLOCKED SEQUENTIAL CIRCUITS

Analysis consists of obtaining a state-table or a state-diagram from a given sequential circuit implementation. In other words analysis closes the loop by forming state-table from a given circuit-implementation. We will show the analysis procedure by deriving the state table of the example circuit we considered in synthesis. The circuit is shown in Figure.

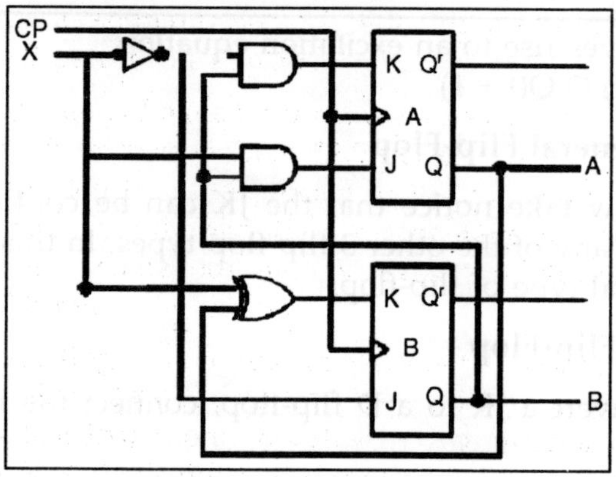

Fig. A Clocked Sequential Circuit

The circuit has

- Clock input, CP.
- One input x
- One output y
- One clocked JK flip-flop
- One clocked D flip-flop (the machine can be in maximum of 4 states)

A State table is representation of sequence of inputs, outputs, and flip-flop states in a tabular form. Two forms of state tables are shown.

Present State		**Next State**		**Output**	
	x = 0	**x = 1**	**x = 0**	**x = 1**	
A	B	A	B	y	y
0	0				
0	1				
1	0				
1	1				

Analysis is the generation of state table from the given sequential circuit.

The number of rows in the state table is equal to 2 (number of flip-flops+ number of inputs). For the circuit under consideration, number of rows = $2^{(2+1)} = 2^{(3)} = 8$

Present State		**Input**	**NextState**	**Output**
A(t)	B(t)	x	A(t+1)B(t+1)	y
0	0	0		
0	0	1		
0	1	0		
0	1	1		
1	0	0		
1	0	1		
1	1	0		
1	1	1		

In the present case there are two flip-flops and one input, thus a total of 8 rows as shown in the table.

Present State		**Input**	**NextState**		**Output**
A(t)	B(t)	x	A(t+1)B(t+1)		y
0	0	0	0	0	0
0	0	1	0	1	0
0	1	0	1	0	0
0	1	1	0	1	0
1	0	0	0	0	0
1	0	1	0	0	0
1	1	1	1	1	0
1	1	1	0	1	1

The analysis can start from any arbitrary state. Let us start deriving the state table from the initial state 00.

As a first step, the input equations to the flip-flops and to the combinational circuit must be obtained from the given logic diagram. These equations are:

$J_A = BX'$

$K_A = BX + B'X'$
$D_B = X$
$y = ABX$

The first row of the state-table is obtained as follows:

When input X = 0; and present states A = 0 and B = 0 (as in the first row); then, using the above equations we get:

$$y = 0,\ J_A = 0,\ K_A = 1, \text{ and } D_B = 0.$$

The resulting state table is exactly same from which we started our design example. Thus analysis is opposite to design and combined they act as a closed loop.

STATE REDUCTION

The problem of state reduction is to find ways of reducing the number of states in a sequential circuit without altering the input-output relationships. In other words, to reduce the number of states, redundant states should be eliminated. A redundant state Si is a state which is equivalent to another state Sj. Two states are said to be equivalent if, for each member of the set of inputs, they give exactly the same output and send the circuit either to the same state or to an equivalent state.

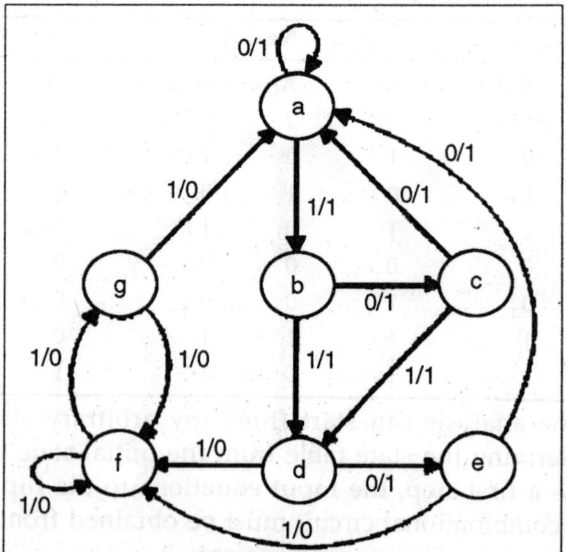

Fig. State Diagram

Since'm' flip-flops can describe a state machine of up to 2m states, reducing the number of states may (or may not) result in a reduction in the number of flip-flops. For example, if the number of states are reduced from 8 to 5, we still need 3 flip-flops. However, state reduction will result in more don't care states. The increased number of don't care states can help obtain a simplified circuit for the state machine.

The state reduction proceeds by first tabulating the information of the state diagram into its equivalent state-table form (as shown in the table) The problem of state reduction requires identifying equivalent states. Each N states is replaced by 1 state.

Consider the following state table.

Present State	**Next State**		**Output**	
	x = 0	x = 1	x = 0	x = 1
a	a	b	1	1
b	c	d	1	1
c	a	d	1	1
d	e	f d	1	0
e	a	f d	1	0
f	g e	f	1	0
g	a	f	1	0

States'g' and'e' produce the same outputs, i.e.'1' and'0', and take the state machine to same next-states,'a' and'f', on inputs'0' and'1' respectively. Thus, states'g' and'e' are equivalent states.

We can now remove state'g' and replace it with'e' as shown. We next note that the above change has caused the states'd' and'f' to be equivalent. Thus in the next step, we remove state'f' and replace it with'd'. There are no more equivalent states remaining. The reduced state table results in the following reduced state diagram.

STATES ASSIGNMENT

When constructing a state diagram, variable names are

used for states as the final number of states is not known a priori. Once the state diagram is constructed, prior to implementation (using gates and flip-flops), we need to perform the step of'state reduction'.

The step that follows state reduction is state assignment. In state assignment, binary patterns are assigned to state variables.

Table: Possible State Assignments

State	Assignment 1	Assignment 2	Assignment 3
a	001	000	000
b	010	010	100
c	011	011	010
d	100	101	101
e	101	111	011

For a given machine, there are several state assignments possible. Different state assignments may result in different combinational circuits of varying complexities.

State assignment procedures try to assign binary values to states such that the cost (complexity) of the combinational circuit is reduced.

There are several heuristics that attempt to choose good state assignments (also known as state encoding) that try to reduce the required combinational logic complexity, and hence cost.

As mentioned earlier, for the reduced state machine obtained in the previous example, there can be a number of possible assignments.

As an example, three different state assignments are shown in the table for the same machine.

DESIGN PROCEDURE

DESIGN WITH UNUSED STATES

There are occasions when a sequential circuit, implemented using m flip-flops, may not utilize all the possible 2m states

Table: Reduced Table with binary Assignment

Present State	Next State		Output	
	x = 0	x = 1	x = 0	x = 1
a	a	b	1	1
b	c	d	1	1
c	a	d	1	1
d	e	d	1	0
e	a	d	1	0

In the previous example of machine with 5 states, we need three flip-flops. Let us choose assignment 1, which is binary assignment for our sequential machine example (shown in the table).

The unspecified states can be used as don't-cares and will therefore help in simplifying the logic. The excitation table of previous example is shown. There are three states, 000, 110, and 111 that are not listed in the table under present state and input.

Fig. Exciation Table

Present State			Input	Next state			Flip-flop inputs						Output
A	B	C	X	A	B	C	SA	RA	SB	RB	SC	RC	Y
0	0	1	0	0	0	1	0	X	0	X	X	0	1
0	0	1	1	0	0	1	0	X	1	0	0	1	1
0	1	0	0	0	1	0	0	X	X	0	1	0	1
0	1	0	1	0	1	0	1	0	0	1	0	X	1
0	1	1	0	0	1	1	0	X	0	1	X	1	1
0	1	1	1	0	1	1	1	0	0	1	0	0	1
1	0	0	0	0	0	0	1	0	0	1	0	1	1
1	0	0	0	1	0	0	x	0	0	X	1	0	1
1	0	1	0	1	0	1	0	1	0	X	X	0	1
1	0	1	1	1	0	1	X	0	0	X	0	1	0

With the inclusion of input 1 or 0, we obtain six don't-care minterms: 0, 1, 12, 13, 14, and 15.

The K-maps of SA and RA is shown in the figure. Other

K-Maps can be obtained similarly and the equations derived are shown in the figure.

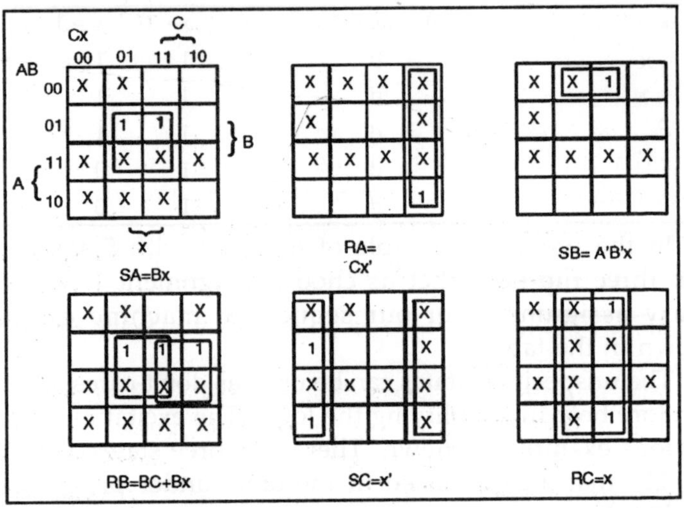

The logic diagram thus obtained is shown in the figure.

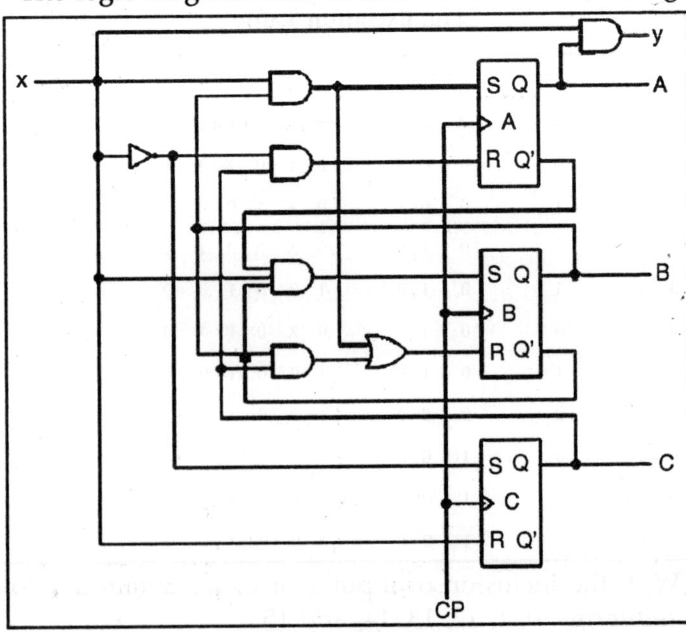

Fig. Logic Diagram

SA = BX
RA = Cx′
SB = A′B′X
RB = BC +Bx
SC = x′
RC = x
y = A′ + x′ = (Ax)′

Note that the design of the sequential circuit is dependent on binary codes for states. A different binary state codes set may have resulted in some different combinational circuit.

FINITE STATE MACHINES (FSM)

Strictly speaking a finite state machine (FSM) is a device that can exist in one of a finite number of states. Associated with an FSM is a memory that is used to store an identifier of the state, so that the machine may process its input (if any) and move to the next state. Due to this coincidence, finite state machines are often studied in conjunction with flip-flops.

We are all familiar with finite state machines, although we rarely think of them as such. Consider a washing machine. The states for this machine are: off, fill with water, wash, spin, and rinse. The control unit for the FSM is the knob on the washer that we turn to start it.

A traffic light is also a finite state machine. We normally think of a traffic light as having only three states: Green, Yellow, and Red. The truth is a bit more complex, in that the physical unit must display at least two sets of lights, one for each intersecting street. Nevertheless, a standard traffic light can be modeled with no more than eight states, although the introduction of advanced green lights and turn signals complicates things a bit.

A standard digital clock that displays only hour, minute, and second, can be said to have

24 • 60 • 60 = 86,400 states - still a finite number. Normally the FSM construct is used to model systems with far fewer states; in our work we shall normally limit a FSM to either eight or sixteen states; that is N 2^3 or N 2^4.

If a finite state machine does not have too many states,

we may represent its operation by a state diagram. The following is a state diagram for a circuit called a sequence detector. For those who are interested, this is the state diagram for a 11011 sequence detector; it has five states because it is detecting a five-bit sequence.

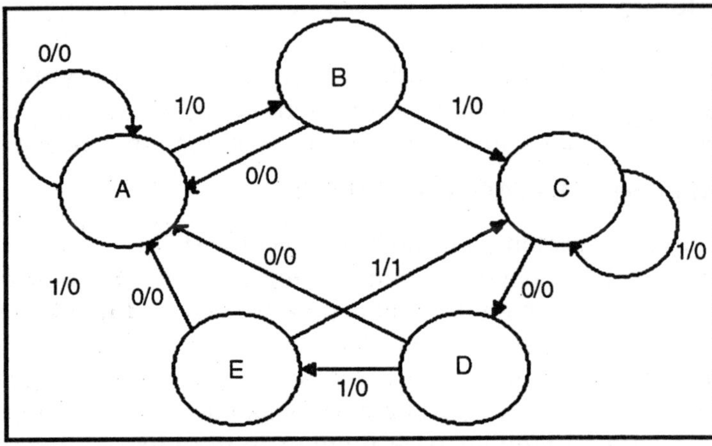

Fig. State Diagram for a 11011 Sequence Detector

At this stage of the presentation, we focus not on the details of generating the state diagram, but just use it as an example of a generic state diagram. What do we note about this one?

- In terms of discrete mathematics, it is a directed graph with loops. Thus, it is not a simple graph. In simple graphs, arcs do not connect any vertex with itself.
- The arcs each have direction and a label of the form X/Z. What we see here is the FSM reacting to input by moving between states and producing output. In the X/Z labeling scheme, X is the binary input (0 or 1) and Z is the binary output.
- There is output associated with the transitions. Not all FSM have output associated with the transitions between states. This one does.
- This and all typical FSM represents a synchronous machine; transitions between states and production

of output (if any) takes place at a fixed phase of the clock, depending on the flip-flops used to implement the circuit.

Not all finite state machines have such complex state diagrams. The figure at left is the state diagram for a modulo-4 up-counter. It just counts 0, 1, 2, 3 and repeats, continually counting up (modulo 4). There is no input (other than the clock, which we almost never mention) and no output directly associated with the transitions. For this type of FSM, the output is associated with the states and not with the transitions.

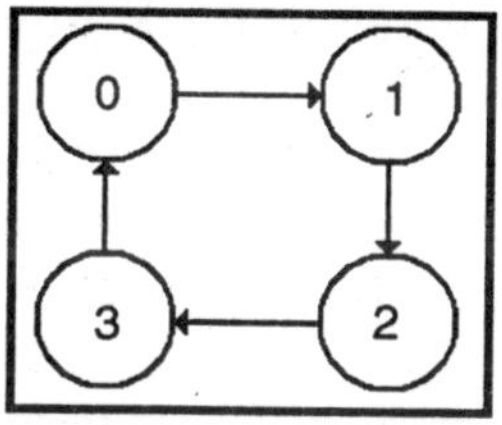

Fig. State Diagram for a Modulo-4 Up-Counter

Many mathematical models of FSM focus on the state diagram. For most of our work, it is more convenient to work with the state table of the FSM, a tabular representation of the state diagram. Translation between the state diagram and state table is automatic. The state table presents the data in terms of present state Q(t) and next state Q(t+1) using the labeling that most naturally fits the problem. Here are the state tables for the two FSM above. Note that eh state table contains exactly the same information as the state diagram.

Fig. State Table for 11011 Sequence Detector, Showing Output

Present State	Next State/ Output	
	X = 0	X = 1
A	A/ 0	B/ 0
B	A/ 0	C/ 0
C	D/ 0	C/ 0
D	A/ 0	E/ 0
E	A/ 0	C/ 1

Figure: State Table for a Modulo-Four Up-Counter

Present State	Next State
0	1
1	2
2	3
3	0

One notes immediately that the second state table is simpler than the first; this is expected it represents a simpler state diagram.

Specifically there is no input, so there is only one column for the next state. In general, for K inputs there are 2K next state columns in the table.

Another tool in the design and analysis of sequential circuits is the transition table. It contains the same information as the state table, except that all labels have been replaced by binary numbers.

There are many creative ways to assign binary numbers to state labels, here we just do the obvious. For the sequence detector, let A = 000, B = 001, C = 010, D = 011, and E = 100 (as there are five states). The following is the sequence detector transition table.

Table Transition/Output Table for the 11011 Sequence Detector

Present State	Next State/ Output	
	X = 0	X = 1
A = 000	000/ 0	001/ 0
B = 001	000/ 0	010/ 0
C = 010	011/ 0	010/ 0
D = 011	000/ 0	100/ 0
E = 100	000/ 0	010/ 1

What we have in the above figure is a special type of truth table. We shall now investigate the table in a bit more detail. Note that the state of the machine is represented by a 3-bit binary number. We shall use the notation Y2Y1Y0 for that number. Given this notation, we write the table as shown below.

Table: The Transition/Output Table as a Modified Truth-Table

Present State			Next State/Output							
			X = 0				X = 1			
Y_2	Y_1	Y_0	Y_2	Y_1	Y_0	Z	Y_2	Y_1	Y_0	Z
0	0	0	0	0	0	0	0	0	1	0
0	0	1	0	0	0	0	0	1	0	0
0	1	0	0	1	1	0	0	1	0	0
0	1	1	0	0	0	0	1	0	0	0
1	0	0	0	0	0	0	0	1	0	1

The table above can be viewed as a truth table that has been"folded over". Another way to represent this table is as a standard truth table depending on Y2, Y1, Y0, and X.

Table: The Transition/Output Table as a Standard Truth Table

Y2	Y1	Y0	X	Y2	Y1	Y0	Z
0	0	0	0	0	0	0	0
0	0	0	1	0	0	1	0
0	0	1	0	0	0	0	0
0	0	1	1	0	1	0	0
0	1	0	0	0	1	1	0
0	1	0	1	0	1	0	0
0	1	1	0	0	0	0	0
0	1	1	1	1	0	0	0
1	0	0	0	0	0	0	0
1	0	0	1	0	1	0	1

Students are invited to use either form of the transition/ output table that suit them. This instructor prefers to use the folded-over version, but that is not necessary.

We now have three equivalent representations of a FSM.

- The state diagram,
- The state table, and
- The transition/output table (probably not a standard name).

DESIGN OF SEQUENTIAL CIRCUITS

Having seen how to Analyse digital circuits, we now

investigate how to design digital circuits. We assume that we are given a complete and unambiguous description of the circuit to be designed as a starting point. At this level, most design problems focus on one of two topics: modulo-N counters and sequence detectors.

Here is an overview of the design procedure for a sequential circuit:

- Derive the state diagram and state table for the circuit.
- Count the number of states in the state diagram (call it N) and calculate the number of flip-flops needed (call it P) by solving the equation 2P-1 < N 2P. This is best solved by guessing the value of P.
- Assign a unique P-bit binary number (state vector) to each state.
  Often, the first state = 0, the next state = 1, etc.
- Derive the state transition table and the output table.
- Separate the state transition table into P tables, one for each flip-flop.
- Warning: Things can get messy here; neatness counts.
- Decide on the types of flip-flops to use. When in doubt, use all JK's.
- Derive the input table for each flip-flop using the excitation tables for the type.
- Derive the input equations for each flip-flop based as functions of the input and current state of all flip-flops.
- Summarize the equations by writing them in one place.
- Draw the circuit diagram. Most homework assignments will not go this far, as the circuit diagrams are hard to draw neatly.

Design Problem: A Modulo-4 Counter

As our first design problem, let's consider a modulo-four counter. When the direction is not specified, we usually intend to build a modulo-four up-counter: 0, 1, 2, 3, 0, 1, 2, 3, etc. We solve these design problems by using the step-wise procedure listed above.

Step 1: Derive the state diagram and state table for the circuit.

Here is the state diagram. Note that it is quite simple and involves no input.

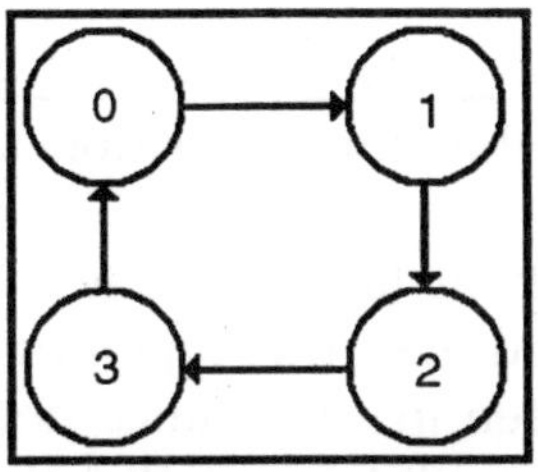

Fig. The State Diagram for a Modulo-4 Up Counter

The state table is simply a rearrangement of the state diagram into a tabular form.

Present State	Next State
0	1
1	2
2	3
3	0

Step 2: Count the number of states in the state diagram (call it N) and calculate the number of flip-flops needed (call it P) by solving the equation $2^{P-1} < N \leq 2^P$.

The number of states on a modulo-N counter is simply N; these are labeled 0 through (N - 1). Specifically, a modulo-4 counter has four states: labeled 0, 1, 2, and 3.

We solve the equation $2^{P-1} < 4 \leq 2^P$ by noting that $2^1 = 2$ and $2^2 = 4$, so we have determined that $2^1 < 4 \leq 22$, hence P = 2. We shall see later that there are valid solutions with more than two flip-flops, but there are none with fewer.

Step 3: Assign a unique P-bit binary number (state vector) to each state.

Often, the first state = 0, the next state = 1, etc.

Some sequential circuits suggest an innovative numbering system, but modulo-N counters never do. We go with the obvious labeling, generated by assigning each decimal number its two-bit binary equivalent as an unsigned integer in the range from 0 to 3.

State	2-bit Vector
0	0 0
1	0 1
2	1 0
3	1 1

Step 4: Derive the state transition table and the output table.

There is no output table for any modulo-N counter, as the output associated with this type of table is the output on a transition, as is seen in a sequence detector. The transition table is a direct translation of the state table, using the assignments from the previous step.

Present State		Next State
0	00	01
1	01	10
2	10	11
3	11	00

Step 5: Separate the state transition table into P tables, one for each flip-flop.

Here we separate the state transition table into 2 tables, one for each flip-flop. Note that the flip-flops will be numbered 0 and 1, with flip-flop 0 storing the least significant bit of the state information. Thus, we shall refer to the state information as Y1Y0.

Flip-Flop 1		Flip-Flop 0	
Present State	**Next State**	**Present State**	**Next State**
$Y_1\ Y_0$	$Y_1(T+1)$	$Y_1\ Y_0$	$Y_0(T+1)$
0 0	0	0 0	1
0 1	1	0 1	0
1 0	1	1 0	1
1 1	0	1 1	0

Step 6: Decide on the types of flip-flops to use. When in doubt, use all JK's.

Up to this point, we have made no assumptions about the type of flip-flop to use. In order to proceed any farther with the design, we must now commit to a specific type. In line with this author's preferences, he chooses to use two JK flip-flops.

Q(t)	Q(t+1)	J	K
0	0	0	d
0	1	1	d
1	0	d	1
1	1	d	0

The excitation table for a JK flip-flop is shown at right. Recall that the"d" stands for"Don't Care". For example, if we have Q(t) = 0 and want Q(t+1) = 0, we can use either J = 0, K = 0 or J = 0, K = 1. Similarly either J = 1 and K = 0 or J = 1 and K = 1 will take Q(t) = 0 to Q(t + 1) = 1.

Step 7: Derive the input table for each flip-flop using the excitation tables for the type.

First look at flip-flop 1, representing the high-order bit. Note that we compare the present state of Y1 to its next state in order to determine J1 and K1.

PS	NS	Input	
Y1 Y0	Y1	J1	K1
0 0	0	0	d
0 1	1	1	d
1 0	1	d	0
1 1	0	d	1

Note that in deciding on the input, we must match only the 0's and 1's. We ignore the don't-cares. Note that the"d" for"don't-care" is not a variable to be assigned a value. It is a value that does not need to be matched. At the moment, Y0 is included in the table for future use only. It plays no part in determining the values of J1 and K1.

Here is the table for Y0

PS	NS	Input	
Y1 Y0	Y0	J0	K0
0 0	1	1	d
0 1	0	d	1
1 0	1	1	d
1 1	0	d	1

Again, Y1 is included in the table for future use only. It plays no part in determining the values of J0 and K0.

Step 8 Derive the input equations for each flip-flop based as functions of the input and current state of all flip-flops.

At this point, we try to derive an expression that matches each column. Formal methods can be used, but generally are more trouble than they are worth. Here is this author's set of rules to match an expression to a given column.

- If a column does not have a 0 in it, match it to the constant value 1.

  If a column does not have a 1 in it, match it to the constant value 0.
- If the column has both 0's and 1's in it, try to match it to a single variable, which must be part of the present state. Only the 0's and 1's in a column must match the suggested function.
- If every 0 and 1 in the column is a mismatch, match to the complement of a function.
- If all the above fails, try for simple combinations of the present state.

Let's look at the input table for Y1.

PS	**NS**	**Input**	
Y_1 Y_0	Y_1	J_1	K_1
0 0	0	0	d
0 1	1	1	d
1 0	1	d	0
1 1	0	d	1

Note that the column for J1 has a 0 and a 1 in it as does the column for K1. Each column has two"don't cares" in it, but we ignore these. Because each column has both a 0 and a 1 in it, neither is a match for a constant function. We now try to match J1.

J1 does not match Y1, because Y1 is 0 in the same row (0 1) as J1 is 1. J1 matches Y0. In row 0 0, both Y0 and J1 are 1. In row 0 1, both Y0 and J1 are 1.

In rows 1 0 and 1 1, J1 is a"don't care", so we do not need to match it.

Similar logic shows that K1 matches Y0 also.

So now we have the following matches for J1 and K1.

PS	NS	Input	
$Y_1\ Y_0$	Y_1	J_1	K_1
0 0	0	0	d
0 1	1	1	d
1 0	1	d	0
1 1	0	d	1

$J_1 = Y_0 \qquad K_1 = Y_0$

We now examine Y_0

PS	NS	Input	
$Y_1\ Y_0$	Y_0	J_0	K_0
0 0	1	1	d
0 1	0	d	1
1 0	1	1	d
1 1	0	d	1

Note that there are no 0's in either the J0 or K0 column. The simplest (and best) match is

J0 = 1 and K0 = 1.

Step 9: Summarize the equations by writing them in one place.

Here they are.

J1 = Y0 K1 = Y0

J0 = 1 K0 = 1

This is a counter, so there is no Z output.

Step 10 Draw the circuit diagram.

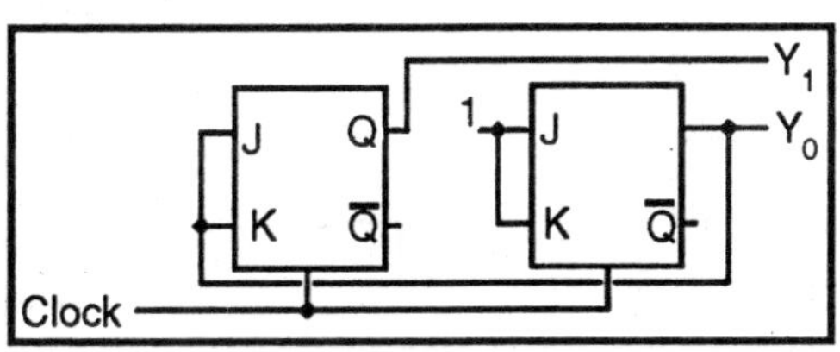

But wait - there is another solution hidden here. Recall that a JK flip-flop can be used to emulate a T flip-flop by setting the J input equal to the K input. Note that the design has the following interesting property.

J1 = K1 = Y0
J0 = K0 = 1

Given this, we can replace each JK flip-flop with a T flip-flop, arriving at this design.

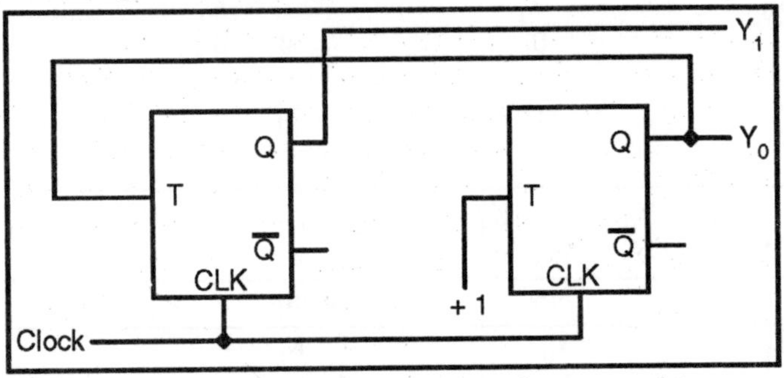

The modulo-4 counter just designed outputs binary codes for the time pulses. Specifically, we assume that it is initialized to Y1Y0 = 00 and then outputs 01, 10, 11, 00, 01, 10, 11, etc. A more realistic circuit would output discrete pulses corresponding to the decoded output, so that first T0 = 1 and all others are 0, then T1 = 1 and all others are 0, etc. In order to produce the discrete signals T0, T1, T2, and T3, we need to add a decoding phase to the counter.

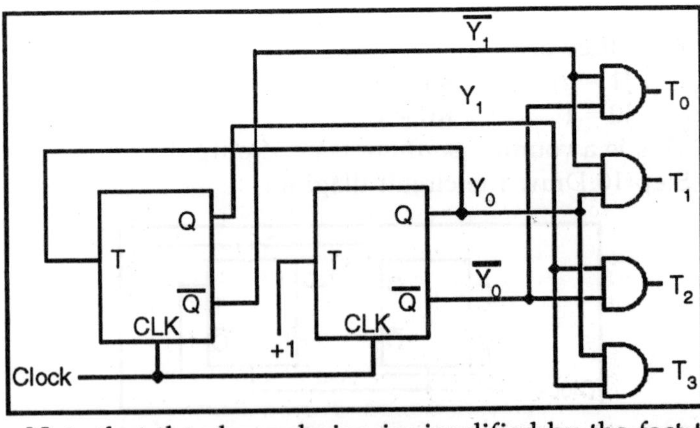

Note that the above design is simplified by the fact that the outputs Y1' and Y0' are available directly from the flip-flops and do not need to be synthesized using NOT gates.

One can achieve a simpler design at the cost of additional

flip-flops. The following design is called a one-hot design, in that it uses a shift register in which exactly one flip-flop at a time is storing a 1. This design also works as a modulo-4 counter and skips the decoder delays.

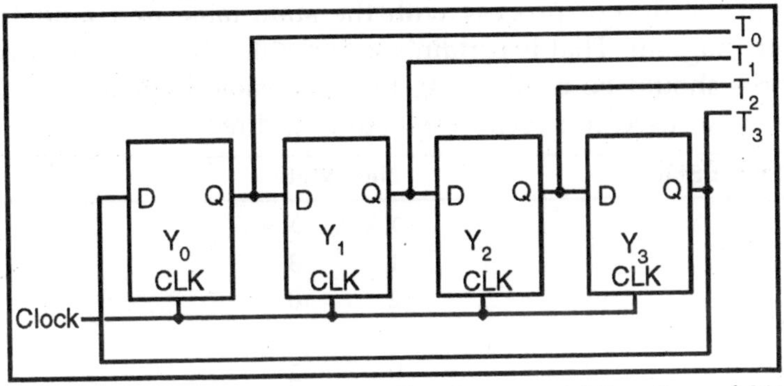

When the counter is initialized, we set Y0 = 1, and Y1 = Y2 = Y3 = 0. As the clock ticks, the single 1 is shifted by the shift register, so that the discrete signals become high in sequence.

DESIGN PROBLEM

The Modulo-4 Up-Down Counter

For the next design, we introduce a problem that uses input. This is a modulo-4 up-down counter. The input X is used to control the direction of counting.

If X = 0, the device counts up: 0, 1, 2, 3, 0, 1, 2, 3, etc.

If X = 1, the device counts down: 0, 3, 2, 1, 0, 3, 2, 1, etc.

Step 1: Derive the state diagram and state table for the circuit.

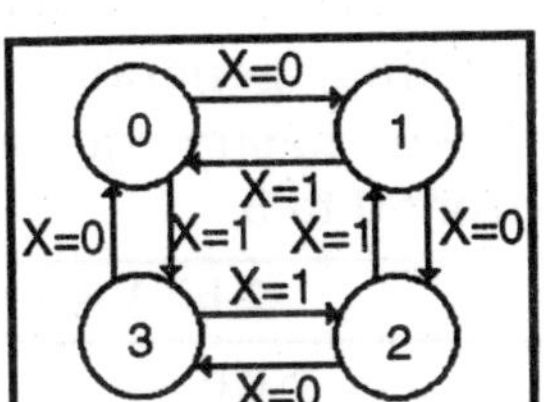

The state diagram for the modulo-4 up-down counter is shown at right. Notice that the X input is used to determine the counting direction. Again, this type of circuit does not have any output associated with the transitions; the output just reflects which of the four states the machine finds itself in at the moment. We now produce the sate table by translating the state diagram. As an aside, some students might prefer to begin the design process with the state table and omit the state diagram. That is certainly acceptable practice; whatever works should be used. Here, the state table depends on X - the input used to specify the counting direction.

Present State	**Next State**	
	X = 0	X = 1
0	1	3
1	2	0
2	3	1
3	0	2

Step 2: Count the number of states in the state diagram (call it N) and calculate the number of flip-flops needed (call it P) by solving the equation 2P-1 < N 2P.

The number of states on a modulo-N counter is simply N; these are labeled 0 through (N - 1). Specifically, a modulo-4 counter has four states: labeled 0, 1, 2, and 3.

We solve the equation 2P-1 < 4 2P by noting that 21 = 2 and 22 = 4, so we have determined that 21 < 4 22, hence P = 2. We shall see later that there are valid solutions with more than two flip-flops, but there are none with fewer.

Step 3: Assign a unique P-bit binary number (state vector) to each state. Often, the first state = 0, the next state = 1, etc.

Some sequential circuits suggest an innovative numbering system, but modulo-N counters never do. We go with the obvious labeling, generated by assigning each decimal number its two-bit binary equivalent as an unsigned integer in the range from 0 to 3.

State	**2-bit Vector**
0	0 0
1	0 1
2	1 0
3	1 1

Step 4: Derive the state transition table and the output table.

There is no output table for any modulo-N counter, as the output associated with this type of table is the output on a transition, as is seen in a sequence detector. The transition table is a direct translation of the state table, using the assignments from the previous step.

The transition table for the modulo-4 up-down counter is as follows.

Present State		**Next State**	
		X = 0	X = 1
0	00	01	11
1	01	10	00
2	10	11	01
3	11	00	10

Step 5: Separate the state transition table into P tables, one for each flip-flop.

Here we separate the state transition table into 2 tables, one for each flip-flop. Note that the flip-flops will be numbered 0 and 1, with flip-flop 0 storing the least significant bit of the state information. Thus, we shall refer to the state information as Y1Y0.

Flip-Flop 1			Flip-Flop 0		
PS	Next State		PS	Next State	
Y_1Y_0	Y_1, X = 0	Y_1, X = 1	Y_1Y_0	Y_0, X = 0	Y_0, X = 1
0 0	0	1	0 0	1	1
0 1	1	0	0 1	0	0
1 0	1	0	1 0	1	1
1 1	0	1	1 1	0	0

The student who is paying attention at this point will notice an interesting feature concerning flip-flop 0; specifically that its next state does not depend on X. This is due to the fact that in considering a modulo-N counter, one moves from odd numbers to even numbers and from even numbers to odd numbers in both counting up and counting down.

Step 6: Decide on the types of flip-flops to use. When in doubt, use all JK's.

Up to this point, we have made no assumptions about the type of flip-flop to use. In order to proceed any farther with the design, we must now commit to a specific type. In line with this author's preferences, he chooses to use two JK flip-flops.

Q(t)	Q(t+1)	J	K
0	0	0	d
0	1	1	d
1	0	d	1
1	1	d	0

The excitation table for a JK flip-flop is shown at right. Recall that the"d" stands for"Don't Care". For example, if we have Q(t) = 0 and want Q(t+1) = 0, we can use either J = 0, K = 0 or J = 0, K = 1. Similarly either J = 1 and K = 0 or J = 1 and K = 1 will take Q(t) = 0 to Q(t + 1) = 1.

Step 7: Derive the input table for each flip-flop using the excitation tables for the type.

Here is the input table for flip-flop 1. Note that the arrangement of the table has been altered to reflect the fact that we now have a binary input.

	X = 0			X = 1		
Y_1Y_0	Y_1	J_1	K_1	Y_1	J_1	K_1
0 0	0	0	d	1	1	d
0 1	1	1	d	0	0	d
1 0	1	d	0	0	d	1
1 1	0	d	1	1	d	0

Here is the input table for flip-flop 0.

	X = 0	X = 1				
Y_1Y_0	Y_0	J_0	K_0	Y_1	J_0	K_0
0 0	1	1	d	1	1	d
0 1	0	d	1	0	d	1
1 0	1	1	d	1	1	d
1 1	0	d	1	0	d	1

Step 8: Derive the input equations for each flip-flop based as functions of the input and current state of all flip-flops.

At this point, we try to derive an expression that matches each column.

Formal methods can be used, but generally are more trouble than they are worth. Here is this author's set of rules to match an expression to a given column.

- If a column does not have a 0 in it, match it to the constant value 1.
  If a column does not have a 1 in it, match it to the constant value 0.
- If the column has both 0's and 1's in it, try to match it to a single variable,
  which must be part of the present state. Only the 0's and 1's in a column must match the suggested function.
- If every 0 and 1 in the column is a mismatch, match to the complement of a function.
- If all the above fails, try for simple combinations of the present state.

The reader will note that there are two columns for each variable for which an equation is desired; one column for X = 0 and one column for X = 1.

For example, consider the table for flip-flop 0, just above. If we work on a column-by column basis, we shall arrive at four equations.One for J0 when X = 0,

one for K_0 when X = 0,

one for J_0 when X = 1, and

one for K_0 when X = 1.

However, we need a single equation for J0 and a single equation for K0.

REGISTERS AND COUNTERS

REGISTERS

Introduction

Registers are simply a set of flip-flops used to store a

number of binary bits. A set of n flip-flops can store bits. 1-bit is a simple form of register.

This register consists of a 1-bit input (I), and enable signal (enb), and a 1-bit output (Q).

When enb=1, the register loads the value of I on the rising clock edge. When enb=0, the register holds the current value. We create a module by name of Reg1.

The register consists of an interface of 4 ports, clk, I, enb, Q. // 1-bit Register

```
module Reg1(clk, I enb, Q);
endmodule
```

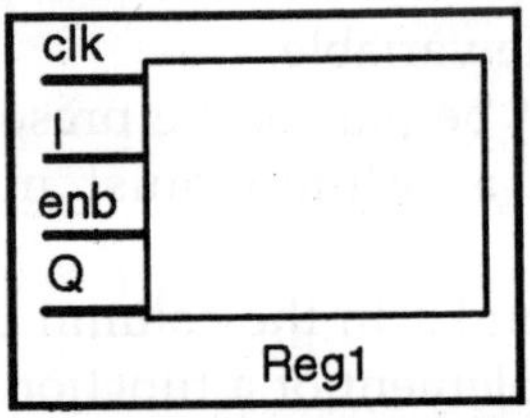

We next specify what type the ports are. In this example, clk, I, and enb are input ports. Port Q is an output port.

Notice in addition to declaring Q as an output, we must also declare Q as a register so we can assign values to Q.

```
// 1-bit Register
module Reg1(clk, I enb, Q);
input clk;
input I, enb;
output Q;
reg Q;
endmodule
```

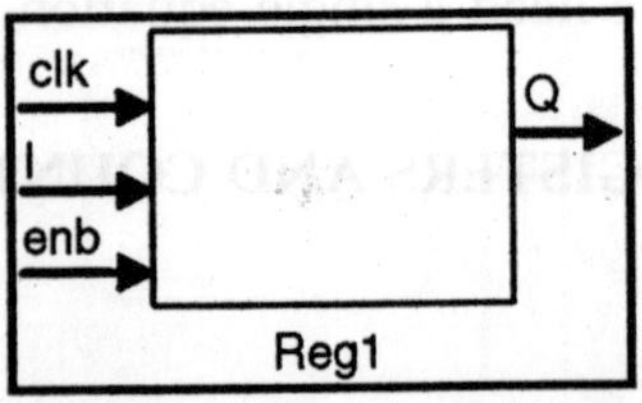

We then create a sensitivity list, which executes the code between the"begin" and"end" statements onv every rising edge of the clk.// 1-bit Register

```
module Reg1(clk, I enb, Q);
input clk;
input I, enb;
output Q;
reg Q;
always @ (posedge clk)
begin
end
endmodule
```

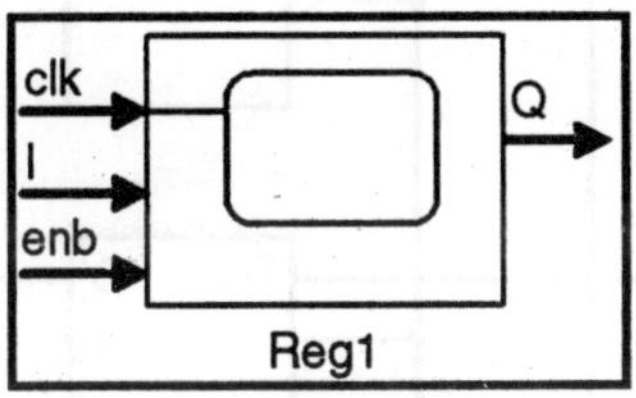

If enb=1 on the rising edge of the clk, then we store the value of input I. // 1-bit Register

```
module Reg1(clk, I enb, Q);
input clk;
input I, enb;
output Q;
reg Q;
always @ (posedge clk)
begin
if(enb == 1)
Q ⇐ I;
end
endmodule
```

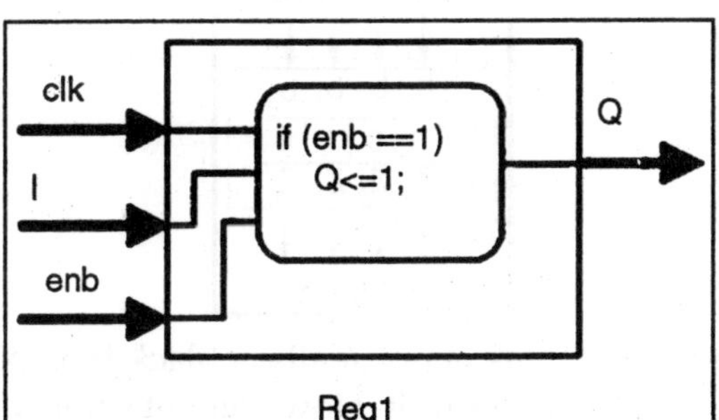

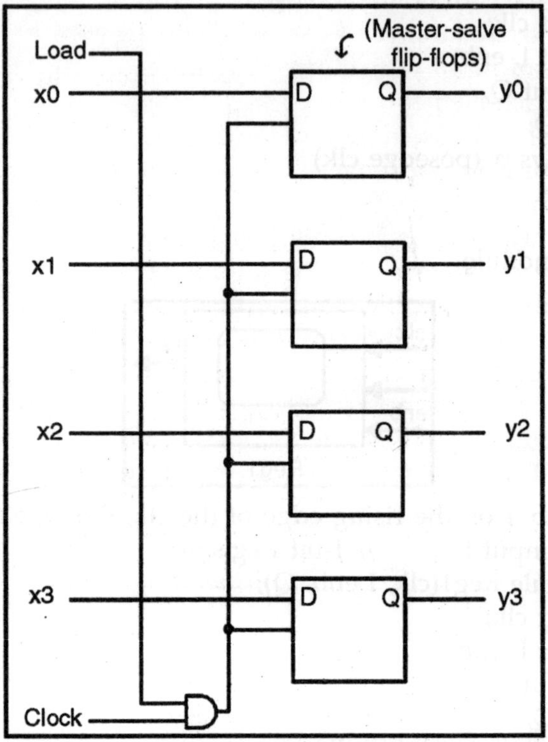

Description

A CPU contains very fast memory called registers. For example, a MIPS ISA stores 32 32-bit registers.

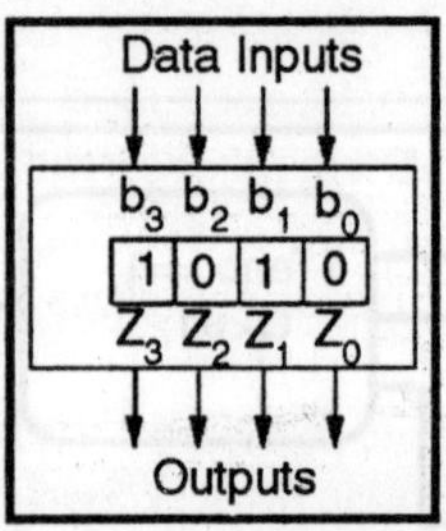

In some sense, this is not really a black box, because we have some idea of what's in it. However, let's not worry about that.

The black box shown above has four inputs. The register can do one of two things: it can parallel load the inputs, that is, it can read in all four inputs and store the four bits into the array. Each element of the array can store a single bit.

It can also choose to ignore the inputs, and the values of the arrays remain unchanged. In this case, we say the array is"holding" its values.

The array's values is continuously being sent as output. Thus, if we could measure the output of the register (say, with a voltmeter), the four bits being output would correspond to the four bits currently being stored in the array.

This output is sent to the outside world where other devices can read the values, if they want to.

A register can have more than 4 bits stored in it. In fact, modern CPUs either store 32 or 64 bits in registers.

In reality, one bit of a register is really a flip flop, which is a device that can store one bit. We will discuss flip flops at some later point.

Parallel Load Register

This register has a name. It's called a parallel load register. It supports two operations. The operation is controlled by a single control bit, called c.

c	Operation
0	Hold
1	Parallel Load

Like combinational logic circuits, the c refers to a control bit. Recall that control bits are used to determine which operation or function a device performs.

Unlike combinational logic circuits, registers use clocks. Here's an important feature of registers (and sequential logic devices in general).

A device that is edge-triggered (which this register is) can only change values when there is a clock edge. In particular, we assume a register is positive-edge triggered, so it can only change values whenever a positive edge occurs.

Specifically, when the clock reaches a positive edge, the

register detects this event. It then reads in the value of c, the control bit, and based on the value, either parallel loads (i.e., sets $z_3z_2z_1z_0 = x_3x_2x_1x_0$) or it holds. If a clock is not at a positive edge, then the value of the registers is held, and does not change.

Hold

You may wonder why we have a"hold" operation? After all, when there's no positive edge, the register seems to hold the value already.

Here's an analogy. Many years ago, milk was delivered by a milkman, much in the same way newspapers are delivered today. (I guess in those days, they were always men, though if milkmen existed today they'd probably be called"milk attendants"). Imagine that the milkman comes by your house once a day during the weekdays. You don't always want to have milk dropped off each day. When you are done with a milk bottle (usually made of glass), you leave it outside your door. The milkman sees the bottle, picks it up, and replaces it with a new bottle. However, when the milkman does not see the bottle then no new bottle is dropped off. He assumes that you have not yet completed a bottle of milk.

Similarly, a positive edge occurs on a regular basis (just like the milkman appears on a daily basis), and it's not always the case that you want to parallel load every time this happens. You want to control when a register is loaded. Sometimes you want it to parallel load, sometimes to hold its value. Thus, the need for a control signal.

Registers are Memory

Registers store information over time, which makes them devices with memory. There are other kinds of circuits (combinational logic circuits and wires) which merely process inputs and produce outputs, but do not store any values.

Clock

When we study combinational logic, we won't use a clock there. Combinational logic circuits are made from AND gates,

OR gates, etc. These circuits can be modeled using a graph. Such graphs are acyclic, i.e., there are no cycles.

However, in general, it's useful to design circuits with feedback (i.e., cycles). Circuits with feedback are easier to design if we can control how often the circuit is updated.

Thus, the need for a clock. For now, just believe that it's important for a register to have a clock.

Diagram of a 4-bit Register

Let's look at a picture of a 4-bit register.

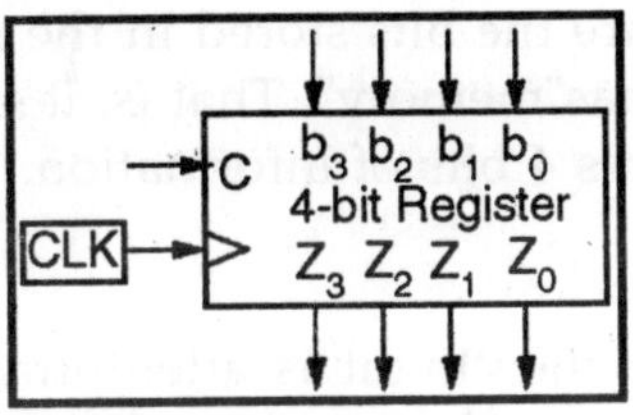

A 4-bit register has the following inputs and outputs:

- 4 bits of data input b3-0
- 1 control bit, c, which indicates whether to perform a parallel load or hold.
- A clock (which is an input), used for timing. The register will only perform the operation when there is a positive edge from the clock.

Example

Let's see an example of how a register behaves.

In particular, let's see what happens when a c = 0. I've added boxes inside the register diagram so you can see the"bits".

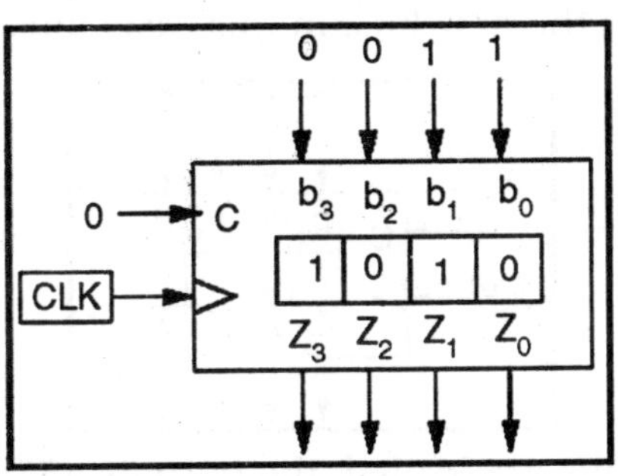

Suppose the register contains bits 1010. The inputs are 0011. When c == 0 and there is a positive clock edge, then the register maintains the value 1010. That is, itholds this value.

The bits being fed into the input, i.e. 0011, are ignored.

If the clock is not currently at a positive edge (i.e., it's at a level 1, or a level 0, or a negative edge), then the register also holds the value. That is, it ignores the inputsb3-0, and maintains the value stored in the register, in this case, 1010.

A register always outputs the bits it stores. Thus, z3-0 = 1010, since those are the bits stored in the register.

This register has"memory". That is, it stores information. In this case, it stores 4 bits of information.

Parallel Load

Now suppose the circuit is attempting a parallel load. That is, c == 1. Assume the positive edge has not yet arrived, and the register looks like:

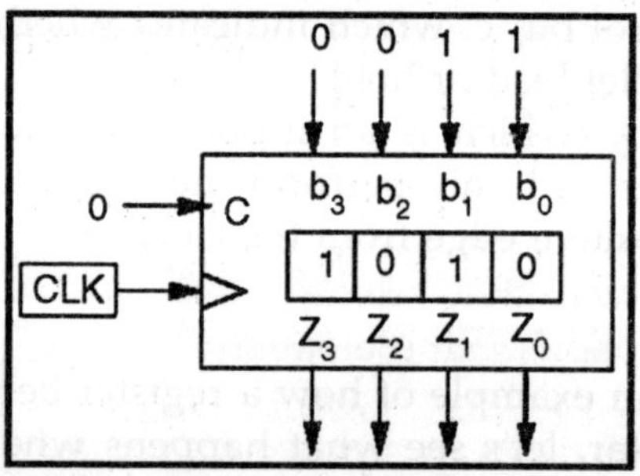

After a positive edge occurs, the 4 bits are read in from the input, in parallel. This overwrites the previous bits, and replaces it with the new bits. In this case, those bits are 0011.

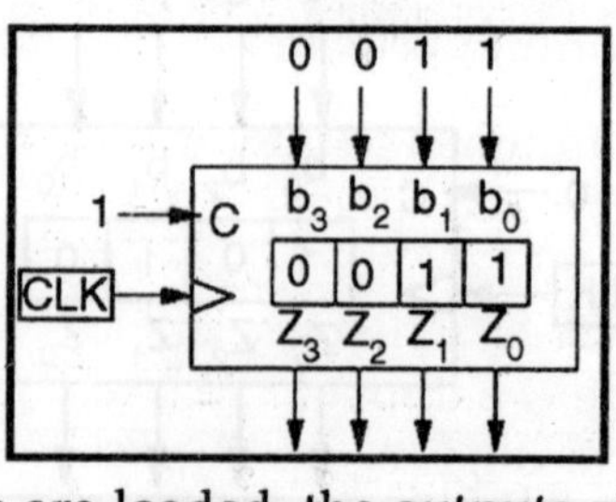

Once the bits are loaded, the outputs z3-0 is 0011.

Points to Remember

- A k-bit register contains k flip flops.
- Each flip flop can store a single bit.
- A positive edge-triggered flip flop (thus, a register) can only change the value of the bit on a positive edge.
- When a positive edge occurs, a register can either hold its value (if c == 0) or parallel load (if c == 1).
- A parallel load means the bits are read in from the input bits (b(k-1)-0) and stored in the k-bits within the register.
- A hold means the registers do not read in the bits, but maintains the current values of the bits.
- A register can only change its value at most once per positive edge.
- When the clock is not at a positive edge, the register maintains ("holds") its value.
- A k-bit register always outputs its values through z(k-1)-0.

COUNTERS

Counters can be classified into two broad categories according to the way they are clocked:

- Asynchronous (Ripple) Counters - the first flip-flop is clocked by the external clock pulse, and then each successive flip-flop is clocked by the Q or Q' output of the previous flip-flop.
- Synchronous Counters - all memory elements are simultaneously triggered by the same clock.

Asynchronous (Ripple) Counters

A two-bit asynchronous counter is shown on the left. The external clock is connected to the clock input of the first flip-flop (FF0) only. So, FF0 changes state at the falling edge of each clock pulse, but FF1 changes only when triggered by the falling edge of the Q output of FF0. Because of the inherent propagation delay through a flip-flop, the transition of the input clock pulse and a transition of the Q output of FF0 can never occur at exactly the same time. Therefore, the flip-flops cannot be triggered simultaneously, producing an asynchronous operation.

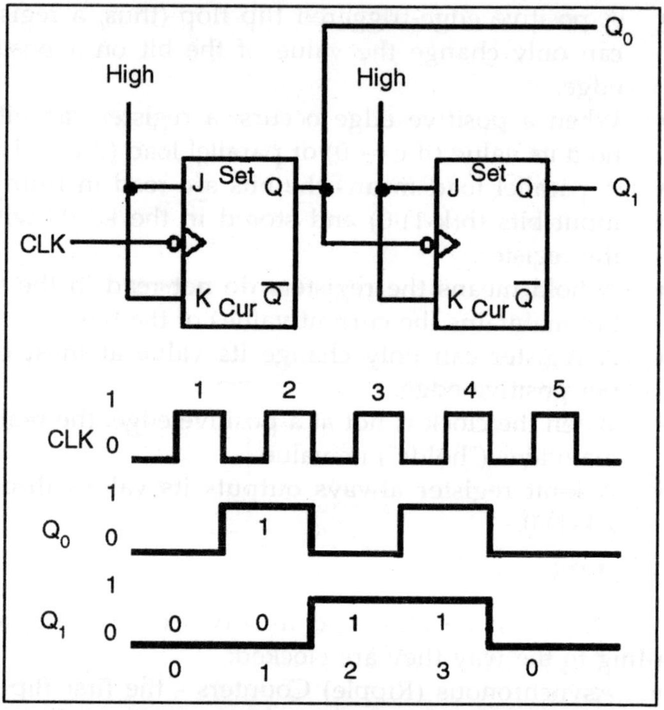

Note that for simplicity, the transitions of Q0, Q1 and CLK in the timing diagram above are shown as simultaneous even though this is an asynchronous counter. Actually, there is some small delay between the CLK, Q0 and Q1 transitions. 0

Usually, all the CLEAR inputs are connected together, so that a single pulse can clear all the flip-flops before counting starts. The clock pulse fed into FF0 is rippled through the other counters after propagation delays, like a ripple on water, hence the name Ripple Counter.

The 2-bit ripple counter circuit above has four different states, each one corresponding to a count value. Similarly, a counter with n flip-flops can have 2 to the power n states.

The number of states in a counter is known as its mod (modulo) number. Thus a 2-bit counter is amod-4 counter. A mod-n counter may also described as a divide-by-n counter. This is because the most significant flip-flop (the furthest flip-flop from the original clock pulse) produces one pulse for every n pulses at the clock input of the least significant flip-flop (the one triggers by the clock pulse). Thus, the above counter is an example of a divide-by-4 counter.

The following is a three-bit asynchronous binary counter 0 and its timing diagram for one cycle. It works exactly the same way as a two-bit asynchronous binary counter mentioned above, except it has eight states due to the third flip-flop.

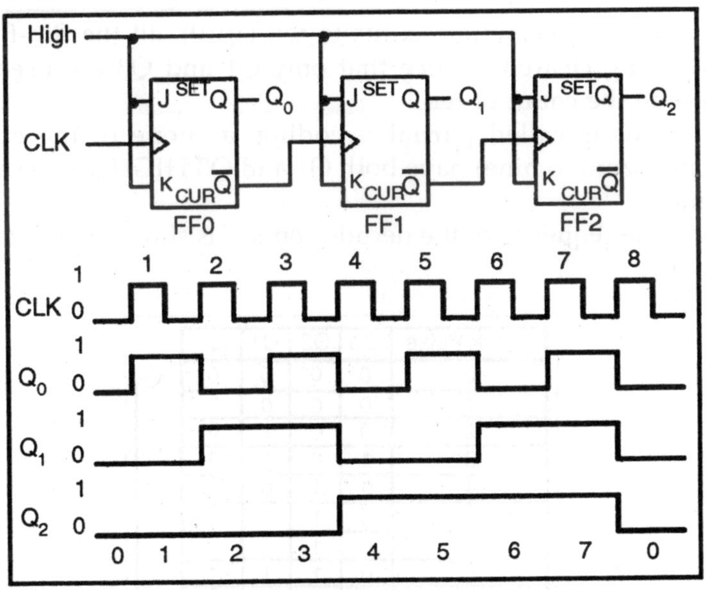

Asynchronous Decade Counters

The binary counters previously introduced have two to the power n states. But counters with states less than this number are also possible. They are designed to have the number of states in their sequences, which are called truncated sequences. These sequences are achieved by forcing the counter to recycle before going through all of its normal states. A common modulus for counters with truncated sequences is ten.

A counter with ten states in its sequence is called a decade counter. The circuit below is an implementation of a decade counter.

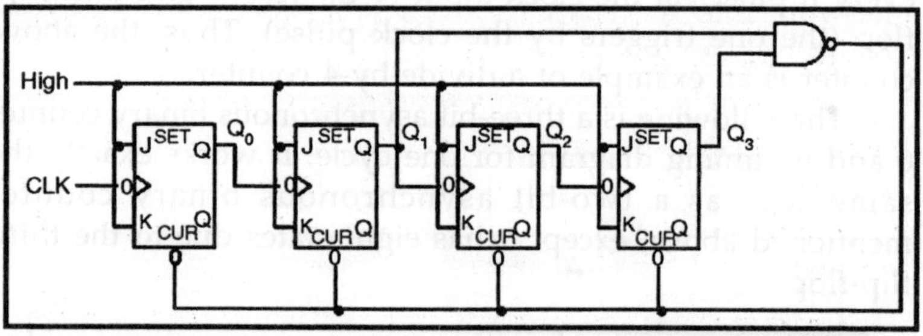

Once the counter counts to ten (1010), all the flip-flops are being cleared. Notice that only Q1 and Q3 are used to decode the count of ten.

This is called partial decoding, as none of the other states (zero to nine) have both Q1 and Q3 HIGH at the same time.

The sequence of the decade counter is shown in the table below:

Clock Pulse	Q3	Q2	Q1	Q0
0	0	0	0	0
1	0	0	0	1
2	0	0	1	0
3	0	0	1	1
4	0	1	0	0
5	0	1	0	1
6	0	1	1	0
7	0	1	1	1
8	1	0	0	0
9	1	0	0	1

Asynchronous Up-Down Counters

In certain applications a counter must be able to count both up and down. The circuit below is a 3-bit up-down counter. It counts up or down depending on the status of the control signals UP and DOWN.

When the UP input is at 1 and the DOWN input is at 0, the NAND network between FF0 and FF1 will gate the non-inverted output (Q) of FF0 into the clock input of FF1. Similarly, Q of FF1 will be gated through the other NAND network into the clock input of FF2. Thus the counter will count up.

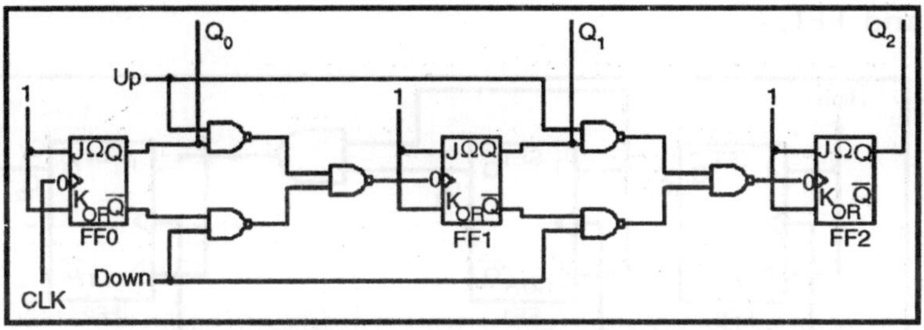

When the control input UP is at 0 and DOWN is at 1, the inverted outputs of FF0 and FF1 are gated into the clock inputs of FF1 and FF2 respectively. If the flip-flops are initially reset to 0's, then the counter will go through the following sequence as input pulses are applied.

FF2	FF1	FF0
0	0	0
1	1	1
1	1	0
1	0	1
1	0	0
0	1	1
0	1	0
0	0	1

Notice that an asynchronous up-down counter is slower than an up counter or a down counter because of the additional propagation delay introduced by the NAND networks.

Synchronous Counters

In synchronous counters, the clock inputs of all the flip-flops are connected together and are triggered by the input pulses. Thus, all the flip-flops change state simultaneously (in parallel).

The circuit below is a 3-bit synchronous counter. The J and K inputs of FF0 are connected to HIGH.

FF1 has its J and K inputs connected to the output of FF0, and the J and K inputs of FF2 are connected to the output of an AND gate that is fed by the outputs of FF0 and FF1.

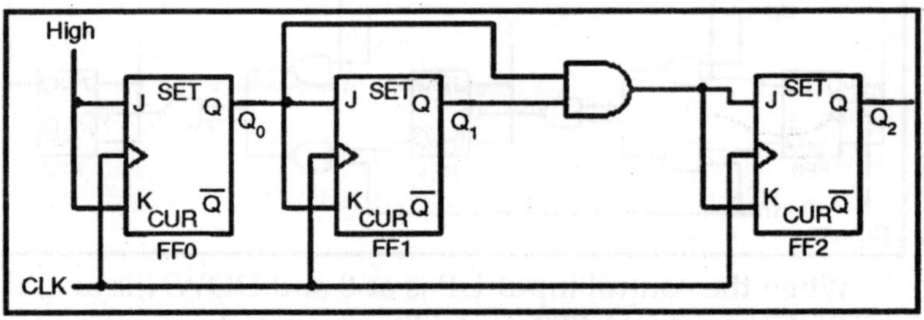

Pay attention to what happens after the 3rd clock pulse. Both outputs of FF0 and FF1 are HIGH. The positive edge of the 4th clock pulse will cause FF2 to change its state due to the AND gate.

Synchronous Decade Counters

Similar to an asynchronous decade counter, a synchronous decade counter counts from 0 to 9 and then recycles to 0 again.

This is done by forcing the 1010 state back to the 0000 state. This so called truncated sequence can be constructed by the following circuit.

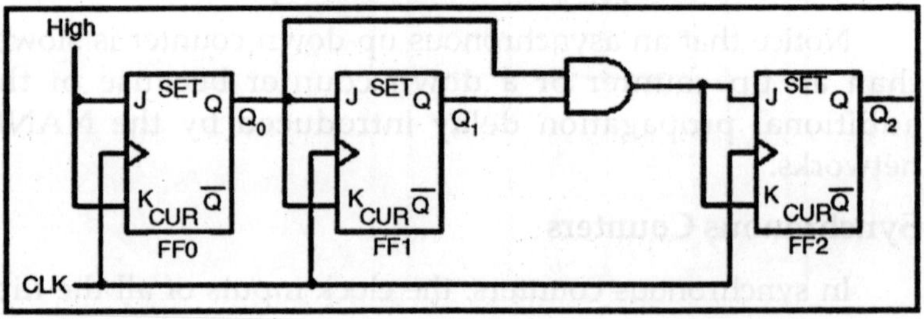

Clock Pulse	Q3	Q2	Q1	Q0
0	0	0	0	0
1	0	0	0	1
2	0	0	1	0
3	0	0	1	1
4	0	1	0	0
5	0	1	0	1
6	0	1	1	0
7	0	1	1	1
8	1	0	0	0
9	1	0	0	1

From the sequence on the left, we notice that:

- Q0 toggles on each clock pulse.
- Q1 changes on the next clock pulse each time Q0=1 and Q3=0.
- Q2 changes on the next clock pulse each time Q0=Q1=1.
- Q3 changes on the next clock pulse each time Q0=1, Q1=1 and Q2=1 (count 7), or when Q0=1 and Q3=1 (count 9).

Synchronous Up-Down Counters

A circuit of a 3-bit synchronous up-down counter and a table of its sequence are shown below.

Similar to an asynchronous up-down counter, a synchronous up-down counter also has an up-down control input. It is used to control the direction of the counter through a certain sequence.

Up ↓ Down ↑

Q2	Q1	Q0
0	0	0
0	0	1
0	1	0
0	1	1
1	0	0
1	0	1
1	1	0
1	1	1

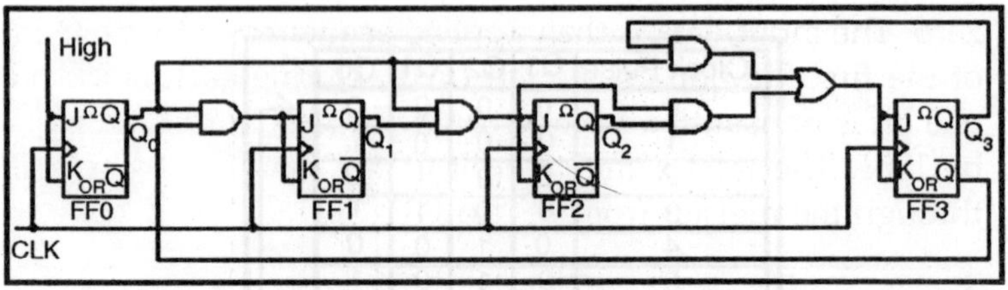

An examination of the sequence table shows:

- For both the UP and DOWN sequences, Q0 toggles on each clock pulse.
- For the UP sequence, Q1 changes state on the next clock pulse when Q0=1.
- For the DOWN sequence, Q1 changes state on the next clock pulse when Q0=0.
- For the UP sequence, Q2 changes state on the next clock pulse when Q0=Q1=1.
- For the DOWN sequence, Q2 changes state on the next clock pulse when Q0=Q1=0.

SHIFT REGISTERS

DEFINITION

Shift registers are a type of sequential logic circuit, mainly for storage of digital data. They are a group of flip-flops connected in a chain so that the output from one flip-flop becomes the input of the next flip-flop. Most of the registers possess no characteristic internal sequence of states. All the flip-flops are driven by a common clock, and all are set or reset simultaneously.

In this chapter, the basic types of shift registers are studied, such as Serial In - Serial Out, Serial In - Parallel Out, Parallel In - Serial Out, Parallel In - Parallel Out, and bidirectional shift registers. A special form of counter - the shift register counter, is also introduced.

SERIAL IN - SERIAL OUT SHIFT REGISTERS

A basic four-bit shift register can be constructed using four D flip-flops, as shown below. The operation of the circuit is as follows. The register is first cleared, forcing all four outputs to zero. The input data is then applied sequentially to the D input of the first flip-flop on the left (FF0). During each clock pulse, one bit is transmitted from left to right. Assume a data word to be 1001. The least significant bit of the data has to be shifted through the register from FF0 to FF3.

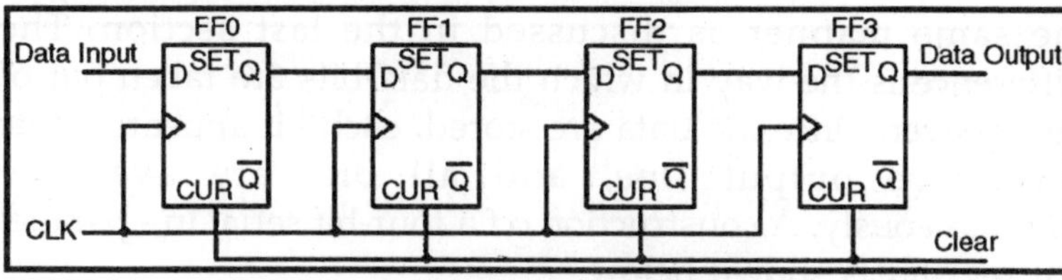

	FF0	FF1	FF2	FF3
Clear	0	0	0	0

In order to get the data out of the register, they must be shifted out serially. This can be done destructively or non-destructively. For destructive readout, the original data is lost and at the end of the read cycle, all flip-flops are reset to zero.

	FF0	FF1	FF2	FF3	
0000	1	0	0	1	0000

To avoid the loss of data, an arrangement for a non-destructive reading can be done by adding two AND gates, an OR gate and an inverter to the system. The construction of this circuit is shown below.

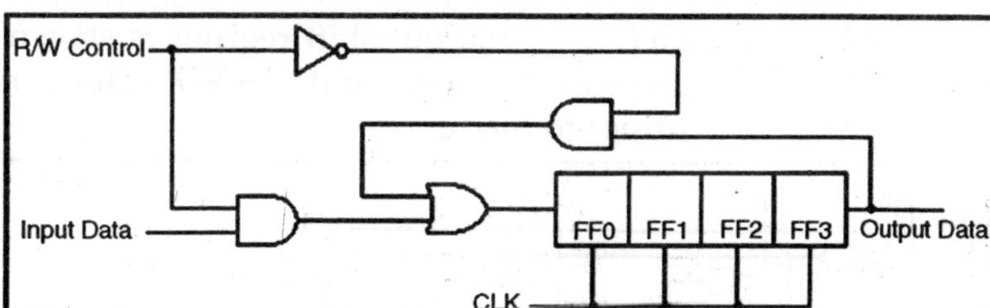

The data is loaded to the register when the control line is HIGH (ie WRITE). The data can be shifted out of the register when the control line is LOW (ie READ). This is shown in the animation below.

Write 1001	FF0	FF1	FF2	FF3
	0	0	0	0

SERIAL IN - PARALLEL OUT SHIFT REGISTERS

For this kind of register, data bits are entered serially in the same manner as discussed in the last section. The difference is the way in which the data bits are taken out of the register. Once the data are stored, each bit appears on its respective output line, and all bits are available simultaneously. A construction o f a four-bit serial in - parallel out register is shown below.

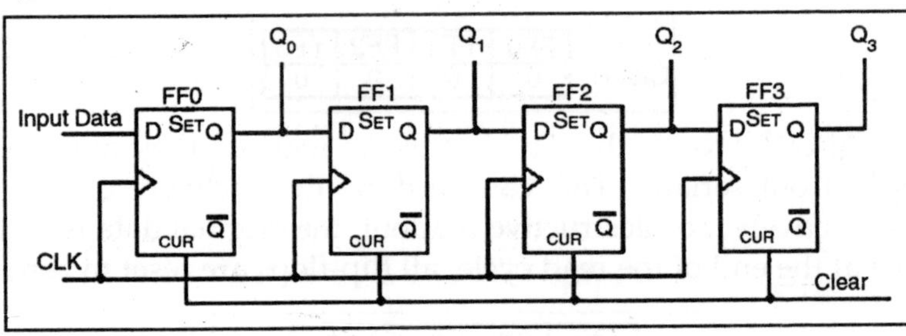

In the animation below, we can see how the four-bit binary number 1001 is shifted to the Q outputs of the register.

Clear 1001	Q0	Q1	Q2	Q3
	0	0	0	0

PARALLEL IN - SERIAL OUT SHIFT REGISTERS

A four-bit parallel in - serial out shift register is shown below. The circuit uses D flip-flops and NAND gates for entering data (ie writing) to the register.

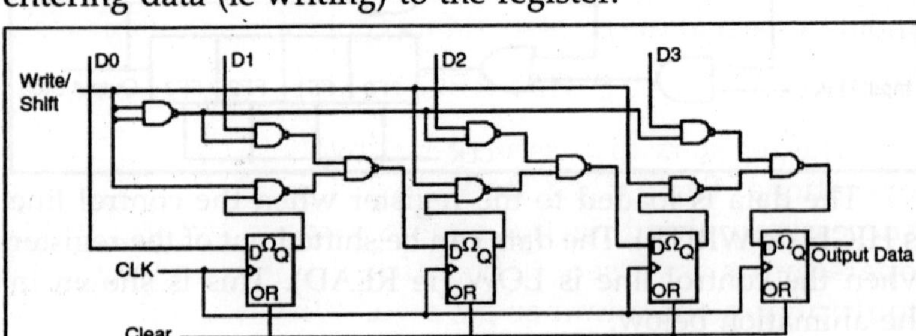

D0, D1, D2 and D3 are the parallel inputs, where D0 is the most significant bit and D3 is the least significant bit. To write data in, the mode control line is taken to LOW and the data is clocked in. The data can be shifted when the mode control line is HIGH as SHIFT is active high. The register performs right shift operation on the application of a clock pulse, as shown in the animation below.

	Q0	Q1	Q2	Q3
Clear	0	0	0	0

PARALLEL IN - PARALLEL OUT SHIFT REGISTERS

For parallel in - parallel out shift registers, all data bits appear on the parallel outputs immediately following the simultaneous entry of the data bits. The following circuit is a four-bit parallel in - parallel out shift register constructed by D flip-flops.

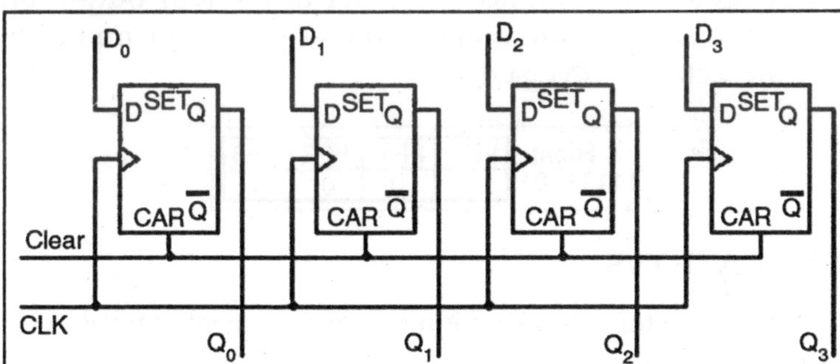

The D's are the parallel inputs and the Q's are the parallel outputs. Once the register is clocked, all the data at the D inputs appear at the corresponding Q outputs simultaneously.

BIDIRECTIONAL SHIFT REGISTERS

The registers discussed so far involved only right shift operations. Each right shift operation has the effect of successively dividing the binary number by two. If the operation is reversed (left shift), this has the effect of multiplying the number by two. With suitable gating arrangement a serial shift register can perform both operations. A bidirectional, or reversible, shift register is one in which the data can be shift either left or right. A four-bit bidirectional shift register using D flip-flops is shown below.

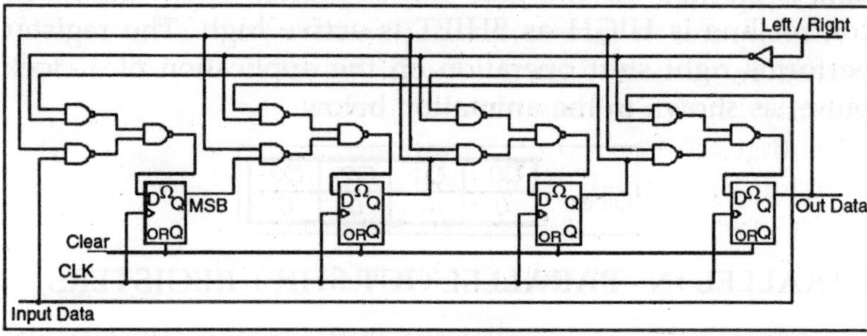

Here a set of NAND gates are configured as OR gates to select data inputs from the right or left adjacent bistables, as selected by the LEFT/RIGHT control line.

The animation below performs right shift four times, then left shift four times. Notice the order of the four output bits are not the same as the order of the original four input bits. They are actually reversed!

Right	FF0	FF1	FF2	FF3
11111001	0	0	0	0

APPLICATIONS

Shift registers can be found in many applications. Here is a list of a few.

To produce time delay

The serial in -serial out shift register can be used as a time delay device. The amount of delay can be controlled by:

- The number of stages in the register
- The clock frequency

The ring counter technique can be effectively utilized to implement synchronous sequential circuits. A major problem in the realization of sequential circuits is the assignment of binary codes to the internal states of the circuit in order to reduce the complexity of circuits required. By assigning one flip-flop to one internal state, it is possible to simplify the combinational logic required to Realise the complete sequential circuit. When the circuit is in a particular state, the flip-flop corresponding to that state is set to HIGH and all other flip-flops remain LOW.

A computer or microprocessor-based system commonly requires incoming data to be in parallel format. But frequently, these systems must communicate with external devices that send or receive serial data. So, serial-to-parallel conversion is required. As shown in the previous sections, a serial in - parallel out register can achieve this.

RIPPLE COUNTER

DEFINITION

An n-stage counter that is formed from n cascaded flip-flops. The clock input to each of the individual flip-flops, with the exception of the first, is taken from the output of the preceding one. The count thus ripples along the counter's length due to the propagation delay associated with each stage of counting. A ripple counter contains a chain of flip-flops with the output of each one feeding the input of the next. A flip-flop output changes state every time the input changes from high to low (on the falling-edge). This simple arrangement works well, but there is a slight delay as the effect of the clock'ripples' through the chain of flip-flops.

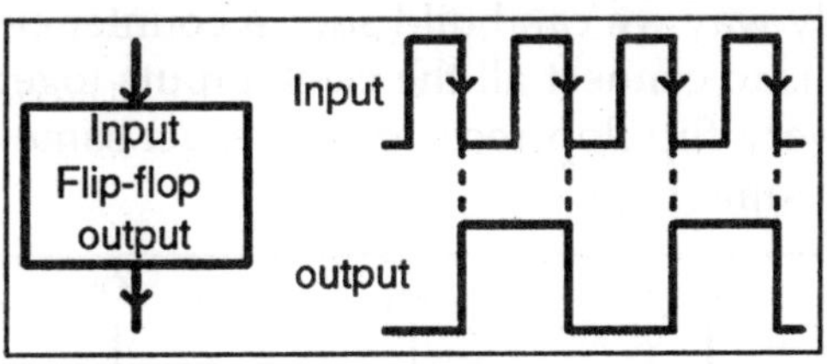

In most circuits the ripple delay is not a problem because it is far too short to be seen on a display. However, a logic system connected to ripple counter outputs will briefly see false counts which may produce'glitches' in the logic system and may disrupt its operation. For example a ripple counter changing from 0111 (7) to 1000 (8) will very briefly show 0110, 0100 and 0000 before 1000!

LINKING RIPPLE COUNTERS

The diagram below shows how to link standard ripple counters. Notice how the highest output QD of.each counter drives the clock (CK) input of the next counter. This works because ripple counters have clock inputs that are'active-low' which means that the count advances as the clock input becomes low, on the falling-edge.

Remember that with all ripple counters there will be a slight delay before the later outputs respond to the clock signal, especially with a long counter chain. This is not a problem in simple circuits driving displays, but it may cause glitches in logic systems connected to the counter outputs.

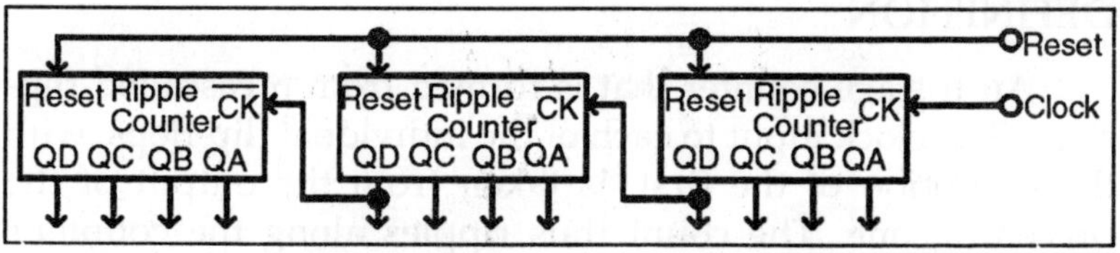

SYNCHRONOUS COUNTER

DESCRIPTION

A synchronous counter, in contrast to an asynchronous counter, is one whose output bits change state simultaneously, with no ripple.

The only way we can build such a counter circuit from J-K flip-flops is to connect all the clock inputs together, so that each and every flip-flop receives the exact same clock pulse at the exact same time:

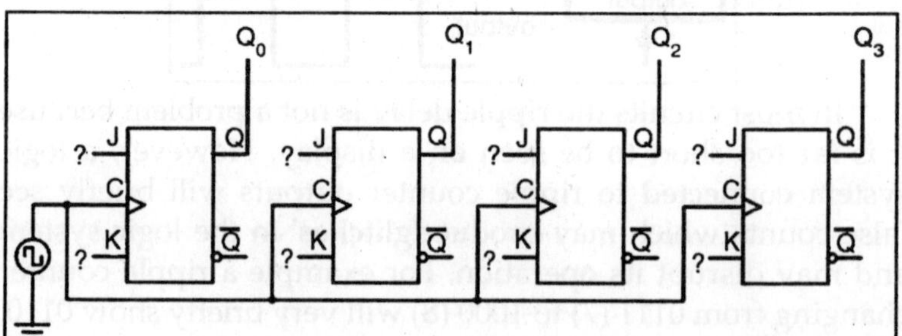

OPERATION

Now, the question is, what do we do with the J and K inputs? We know that we still have to maintain the same divide-by-two frequency pattern in order to count in a binary sequence, and that this pattern is best achieved utilizing the"toggle" mode of the flip-flop, so the fact that the J and K inputs must both be (at times)"high" is clear.

However, if we simply connect all the J and K inputs to the positive rail of the power supply as we did in the asynchronous circuit, this would clearly not work because all the flip-flops would toggle at the same time: with each and every clock pulse!

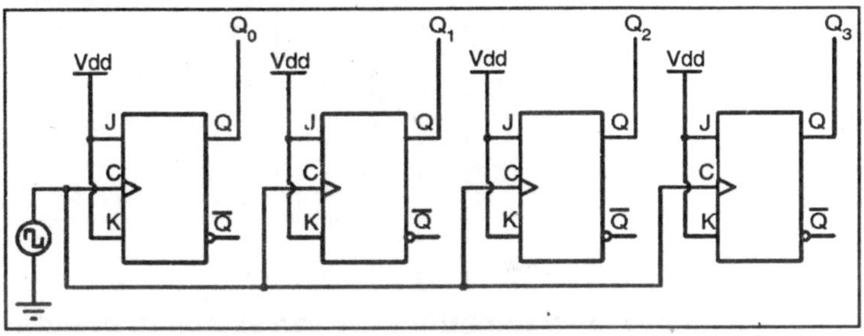

Fig. This Circuit will not Function as a counter!

EXAMPLE

Let's examine the four-bit binary counting sequence again, and see if there are any other patterns that predict the toggling of a bit.

Asynchronous counter circuit design is based on the fact that each bit toggle happens at the same time that the preceding bit toggles from a"high" to a"low" (from 1 to 0). Since we cannot clock the toggling of a bit based on the toggling of a previous bit in a synchronous counter circuit (to do so would create a ripple effect) we must find some other pattern in the counting sequence that can be used to trigger a bit toggle:

Examining the four-bit binary count sequence, another predictive pattern can be seen. Notice that just before a bit toggles, all preceding bits are"high:"

0	0	0	0
0	0	0	1
0	0	1	0
0	0	1	1
0	1	0	0
0	1	0	1
0	1	1	0
0	1	1	1
1	0	0	0
1	0	0	1
1	0	1	0
1	0	1	1
1	1	0	0
1	1	0	1
1	1	1	0
1	1	1	1

This pattern is also something we can exploit in designing a counter circuit. If we enable each J-K flip-flop to toggle based on whether or not all preceding flip-flop outputs (Q) are"high," we can obtain the same counting sequence as the asynchronous circuit without the ripple effect, since each flip-flop in this circuit will be clocked at exactly the same time:

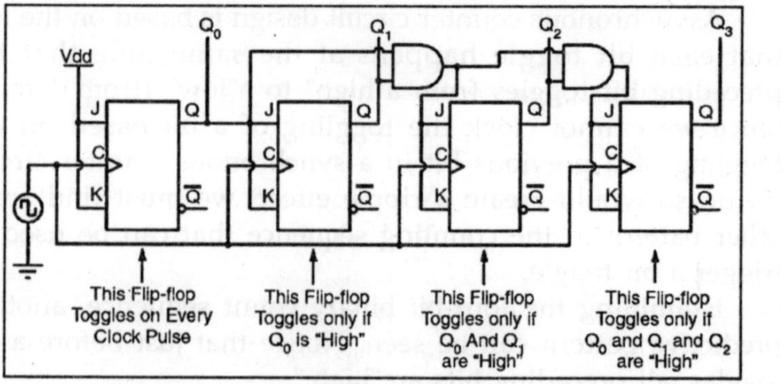

Fig. A Four-bit Synchronous "up" Counter

The result is a four-bit synchronous"up" counter. Each of the higher-order flip-flops are made ready to toggle (both J and K inputs"high") if the Q outputs of all previous flip-flops are"high." Otherwise, the J and K inputs for that flip-flop will both be"low," placing it into the"latch" mode where it will maintain its present output state at the next clock pulse. Since the first (LSB) flip-flop needs to toggle at every clock pulse, its J and K inputs are connected to Vcc or Vdd, where they will be"high" all the time. The next flip-flop need only"recognize" that the first flip-flop's Q output is high to be made ready to toggle, so no AND gate is needed. However, the remaining flip-flops should be made ready to toggle only when all lower-order output bits are"high," thus the need for AND gates. To make a synchronous"down" counter, we need to build the circuit to recognize the appropriate bit patterns predicting each toggle state while counting down. Not surprisingly, when we examine the four-bit binary count sequence, we see that all preceding bits are"low" prior to a toggle (following the sequence from bottom to top):

0 0 0 0
0 0 0 1
0 0 1 0
0 0 1 1
0 1 0 0
0 1 0 1
0 1 1 0
0 1 1 1
1 0 0 0
1 0 0 1
1 0 1 0
1 0 1 1
1 1 0 0
1 1 0 1
1 1 1 0
1 1 1 1

Since each J-K flip-flop comes equipped with a Q' output as well as a Q output, we can use the Q' outputs to enable the toggle mode on each succeeding flip-flop, being that each Q' will be"high" every time that the respective Q is"low:"

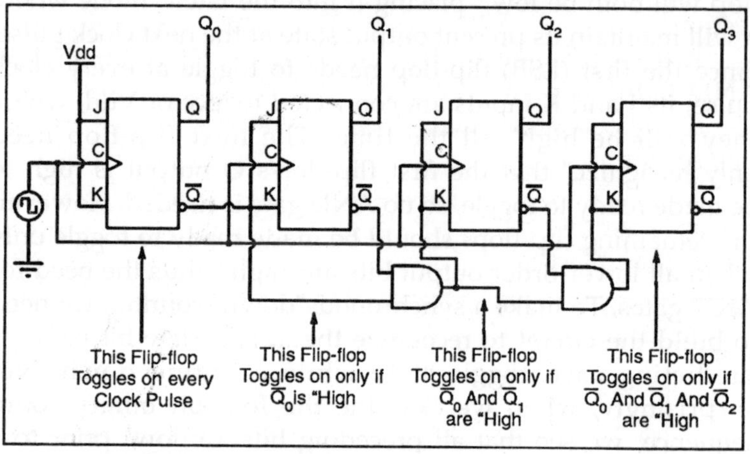

Fig. A Four-bit Synchronous "Down" Counter

Taking this idea one step further, we can build a counter circuit with selectable between"up" and"down" count modes by having dual lines of AND gates detecting the appropriate bit conditions for an"up" and a"down" counting sequence, respectively, then use OR gates to combine the AND gate outputs to the J and K inputs of each succeeding flip-flop:

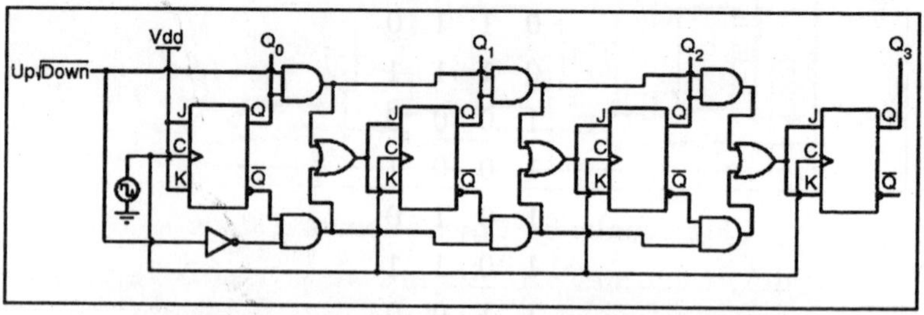

Fig. A Fout-bit Synchronous "up/down" Counter

This circuit isn't as complex as it might first appear. The Up/Down control input line simply enables either the upper string or lower string of AND gates to pass the Q/Q' outputs to the succeeding stages of flip-flops.

If the Up/Down control line is"high," the top AND gates become enabled, and the circuit functions exactly the same as the first ("up") synchronous counter circuit shown in this section.

If the Up/Down control line is made"low," the bottom AND gates become enabled, and the circuit functions identically to the second ("down" counter) circuit shown in this section.

To illustrate, here is a diagram showing the circuit in the"up"-counting mode (all disabled circuitry shown in grey rather than black):

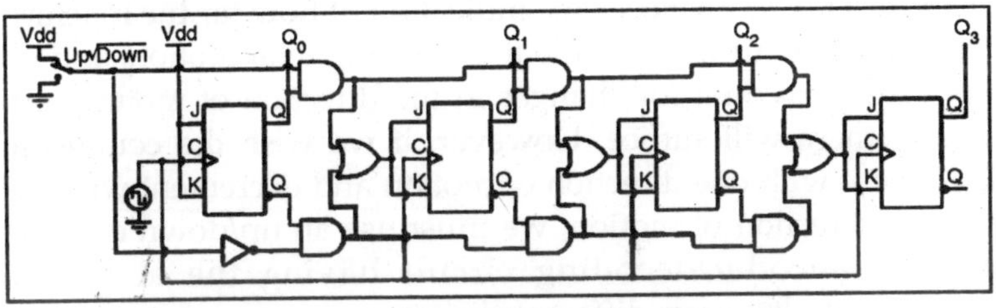

Fig. Counter in "up" Counting Mode

Here, shown in the"down" counting mode, with the same grey colouring representing disabled circuitry:

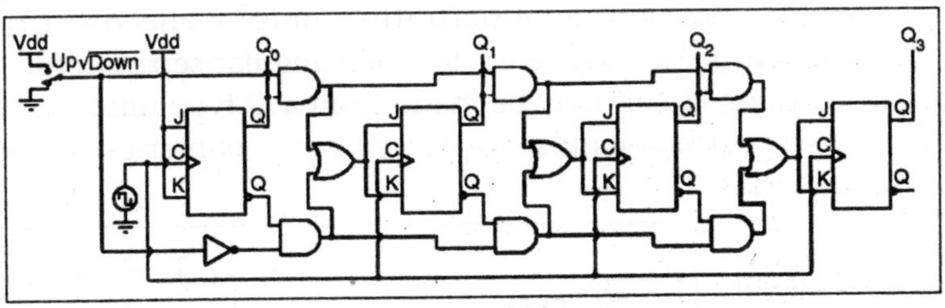

Fig. Counter in "Down" Counting Mode

Up/down counter circuits are very useful devices. A common application is in machine motion control, where devices called rotary shaft encoders convert mechanical rotation into a series of electrical pulses, these pulses"clocking" a counter circuit to track total motion:

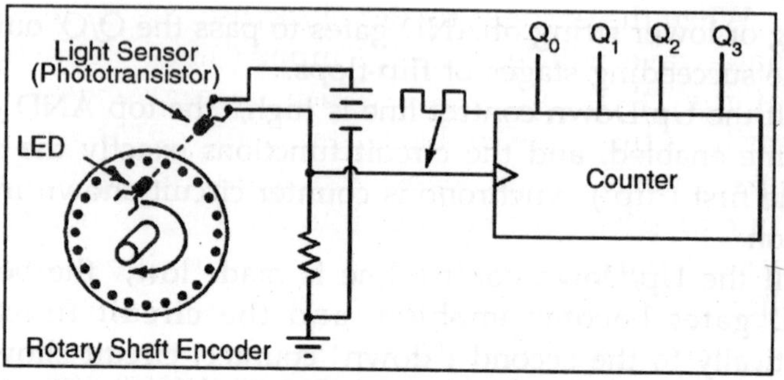

As the machine moves, it turns the encoder shaft, making and breaking the light beam between LED and phototransistor, thereby generating clock pulses to increment the counter circuit. Thus, the counter integrates, or accumulates, total motion of the shaft, serving as an electronic indication of how far the machine has moved. If all we care about is tracking total motion, and do not care to account for changes in the direction of motion, this arrangement will suffice. However, if we wish the counter to increment with one direction of motion and decrement with the reverse direction of motion, we must use an up/down counter, and an encoder/decoding circuit having the ability to discriminate between different directions.

If we re-design the encoder to have two sets of LED/ phototransistor pairs, those pairs aligned such that their square-wave output signals are 90o out of phase with each other, we have what is known as aquadrature output encoder (the word"quadrature" simply refers to a 90o angular separation). A phase detection circuit may be made from a D-type flip-flop, to distinguish a clockwise pulse sequence from a counter-clockwise pulse sequence:

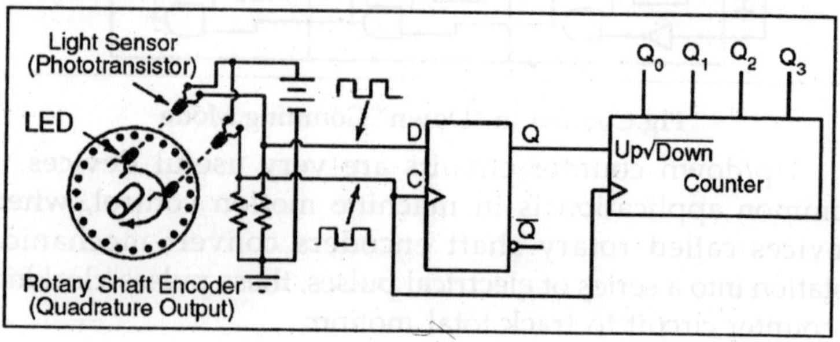

When the encoder rotates clockwise, the"D" input signal square-wave will lead the"C" input square-wave, meaning that the"D" input will already be"high" when the"C" transitions from"low" to"high," thus settingthe D-type flip-flop (making the Q output"high") with every clock pulse. A"high" Q output places the counter into the"Up" count mode, and any clock pulses received by the clock from the encoder (from either LED) will increment it.

Conversely, when the encoder reverses rotation, the"D" input will lag behind the"C" input waveform, meaning that it will be"low" when the"C" waveform transitions from"low" to"high," forcing the D-type flip-flop into the reset state (making the Q output"low") with every clock pulse. This"low" signal commands the counter circuit to decrement with every clock pulse from the encoder.

This circuit, or something very much like it, is at the heart of every position-measuring circuit based on a pulse encoder sensor. Such applications are very common in robotics, CNC machine tool control, and other applications involving the measurement of reversible, mechanical motion.

Chapter 5

Memory and Programmable Logic

INTRODUCTION

Memory inside a computer is organised in a matrix of rows and collums. Each word of memory (or location as it is often caleld) is uniquely identified by the combined row and column values - known as the address. This arrangement resembles a set of pigeon holes used to sort post. Each item of post has an assigned address, which indicates the pigeon hole into which it is to be placed:

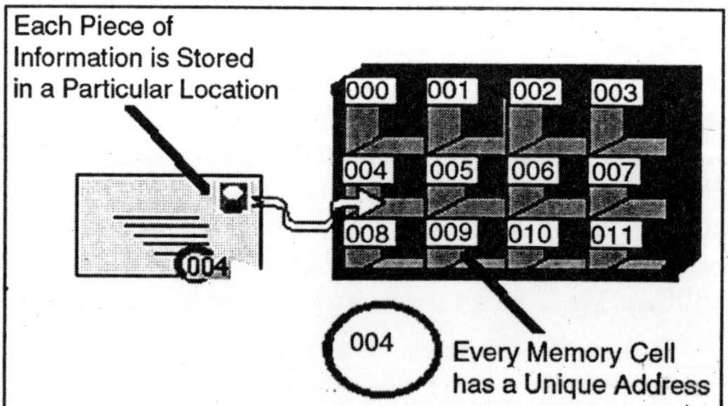

For instance to read the value stored at a memory location 4, the following steps of actions are performed:

- Set the memory address value to 4 to indicate that we are going to deal with the 4th memory location
- Set the Figure below shows a segment of a sequential PAL. memory control logic to READ (enables the memory)

- The data register returns the value at the location specified by the memory address (e.g. 23 in this example)
- Disable the memory control logic

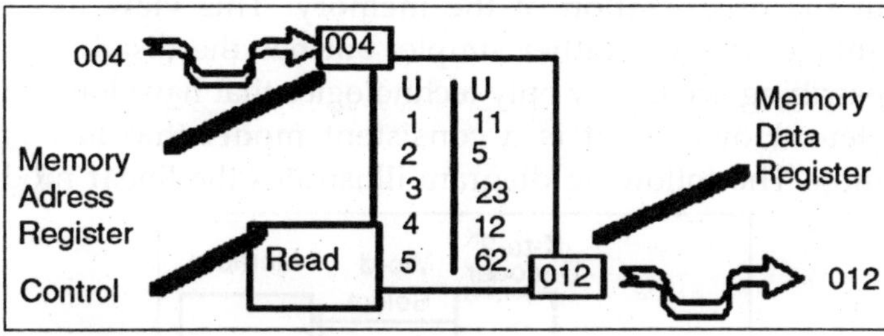

MEMORY HIERARCHY

As often is the case, we utilize a number of logical models of our memory system, depending on the point we want to make. The simplest view of memory is that of a monolithic linear memory; specifically a memory fabricated as a single unit (monolithic) that is organized as a singly dimensioned array (linear). This is satisfactory as a logical model, but it ignores very many issues of considerable importance.

Consider a memory in which an M-bit word is the smallest addressable unit. For simplicity, we assume that the memory contains N = 2K words and that the address space is also N = 2K. The memory can be viewed as a one-dimensional array, declared something like

Memory: Array [0.. (N - 1)] of M-bit word.

The monolithic view of the memory is shown in the following figure.

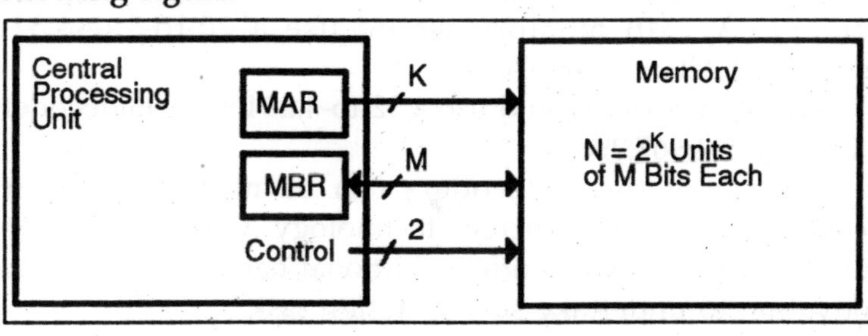

Fig. Monolithic View of Computer Memory

In this monolithic view, the CPU provides K address bits to access N = 2K memory entries, each of which has M bits, and at least two control signals to manage memory.

The linear view of memory is a way to think logically about the organization of the memory. This view has the advantage of being rather simple, but has the disadvantage of describing accurately only technologies that have long been obsolete. However, it is a consistent model that is worth mention. The following diagram illustrates the linear model.

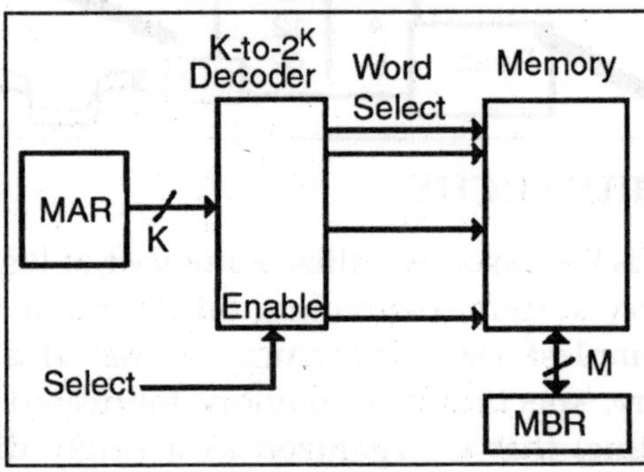

There are two problems with the above model, a minor nuisance and a"show-stopper".

The minor problem is the speed of the memory; its access time will be exactly that of plain variety DRAM (dynamic random access memory), which is about 50 nanoseconds. We must have better performance than that, so we go to other memory organizations.

The"show-stopper" problem is the design of the memory decoder. Consider two examples for common memory sizes: 1MB (220 bytes) and 4GB (232 bytes) in a byte-oriented memory. A 1MB memory would use a 20-to-1,048,576 decoder, as 220 = 1,048,576.

A 4GB memory would use a 32-to-4,294,967,296 decoder, as 232 = 4,294,967,296.

Neither of these decoders can be manufactured at acceptable cost using current technology. One should note that since other designs offer additional benefits, there is no motivation to undertake such a design task.

We now examine two design choices that produce easy-to-manufacture solutions that offer acceptable performance at reasonable price. The first is the memory hierarchy, using various levels of cache memory, offering faster access to main memory. Before discussing the ideas behind cache memory, we must first speak of two technologies for fabricating memory.

RAM

Random Access Memory (RAM) is used for storing most programs and data in a computer. Most computers also use some Read Only Memory (ROM) or Erasable-Programmable Read Only Memory (EPROM).

This stores programs (or libraries of procedures) which do not need to be changed. (This usually includes the programme that is executed when the computer is first turned on, and the procedures required to access permanently connected peripherals - such as the keyboard, display, disk drive,...).

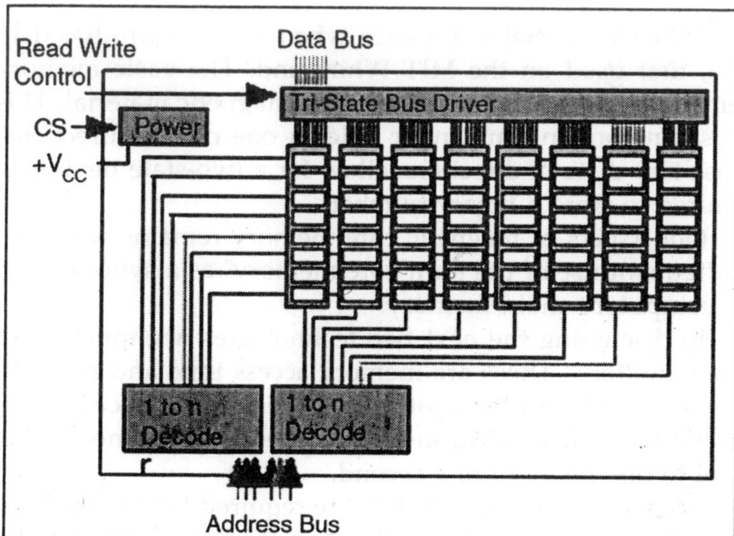

SRAM (STATIC RAM) AND DRAM (DYNAMIC RAM)

We now discuss technologies used to store binary

information. The first topic is to make a list of requirements for devices used to implement binary memory.

- Two well defined and distinct states.
- The device must be able to switch states reliably.
- The probability of a spontaneous state transition must be extremely low.
- State switching must be as fast as possible.
- The device must be small and cheap so that large capacity memories are practical.

There are a number of memory technologies that were developed in the last half of the twentieth century. Most of these are now obsolete. There are three that are worth mention:

- Core Memory (now obsolete, but new designs may be introduced soon)
- Static RAM
- Dynamic RAM

Core Memory

This was a major advance when it was introduced in 1952, first used on the MIT Whirlwind. The basic memory element is a torus (tiny doughnut) of magnetic material. This torus can contain a magnetic field in one of two directions. These two distinct directions allow for a two-state device, as required to store a binary number.

One aspect of magnetic core memory remains with us - the frequent use of the term"core memory" as a synonym for the computer's main memory.

In discussing the next two technologies, we must make two definitions. These are memory access time and memory cycle time. The measure of real interest is the access time. The unit for measuring memory times is the nanosecond, equal to one billionth of a second.

Memory access time is the time required for the memory to access the data; specifically, it is the time between the instant that the memory address is stable in the MAR and the data are available in the MBR.

Memory cycle time is the minimum time between two

independent memory accesses. It should be clear that the cycle time is at least as great as the access time, because the memory cannot process an independent access while it is in the process of placing data in the MBR.

STATIC RAM

Static RAM (SRAM) is a memory technology based on flip-flops. SRAM has an access time of 2 - 10 nanoseconds. From a logical view, all of main memory can be viewed as fabricated from SRAM, although such a memory would be unrealistically expensive.

DYNAMIC RAM

Dynamic RAM (DRAM) is a memory technology based on capacitors - circuit elements that store electronic charge. Dynamic RAM is cheaper than static RAM and can be packed more densely on a computer chip, thus allowing larger capacity memories. DRAM has an access time in the order of 60 - 100 nanoseconds, slower than SRAM.

Our goal in designing a memory would be to create a memory unit with the performance of SRAM, but the cost and packaging density of DRAM. Fortunately this is possible by use of a design strategy called"cache memory", in which a fast SRAM memory fronts for a larger and slower DRAM memory.

This design has been found to be useful due to a property of computer programme execution called"programme locality". It is a fact that if a programme accesses a memory location, it is likely both to access that location again and to access locations with similar addresses. It is programme locality that allows cache memory to work.

Static RAM is composed of D-Type Flip-Flops, and is extremely fast, however it is also expensive. It is therefore usually reserved for applications requiring a high speed (such as graphics display memory or cache memory. The main computer memory is usually formed from Dynamic RAM (DRAM), which uses an array of capacitor storage elements. Although slower than SRAM it is also much cheaper.

ROM

There is a type of memory that stores data without electrical current; it is the ROM (Read Only Memory) or is sometimes called non-volatile memory as it is not erased when the system is switched off. This type of memory lets you stored the data needed to start up the computer. Indeed, this information cannot be stored on the hard disk since the disk parameters (vital for its initialisation) are part of these data which are essential for booting.

Different ROM-type memories contain these essential start-up data, i.e.:

- The BIOS is a programme for controlling the system's main input-output interfaces, hence the nameBIOS ROM which is sometimes given to the read-only memory chip of the mother board which hosts it.
- *The bootstrap loader*: a programme for loading (random access) memory into the operating system and launching it. This generally seeks the operating system on the floppy drive then on the hard disk, which allows the operating system to be launched from a system floppy disk in the event of malfunction of the system installed on the hard disk.
- The CMOS Setup is the screen displayed when the computer starts up and which is used to amend the system parameters (often wrongly referred to as BIOS).
- The Power-On Self Test (POST), a programme that runs automatically when the system is booted, thus allowing the system to be tested (this is why the system"counts" the RAM at start-up).

Given that ROM are much slower than RAM memories (access time for a ROM is around 150 ns whereas for SDRAM it is around 10 ns), the instructions given in the ROM are sometimes copied to the RAM at start-up; this is known as shadowing, though is usually referred to as shadow memory).

TYPES OF ROM

ROM memories have gradually evolved from fixed read-only memories to memories than can be programmed and then re-programmed.

ROM

The first ROMs were made using a procedure that directly writes the binary data in a silicon plate using a mask. This procedure is now obsolete. There is a type of memory that stores data without electrical current; it is the ***ROM*** (*Read Only Memory*) or is sometimes called *non-volatile memory* as it is not erased when the system is switched off.

This type of memory lets you stored the data needed to start up the computer. Indeed, this information cannot be stored on the hard disk since the disk parameters are part of these data which are essential for booting.

Different *ROM*-type memories contain these essential start-up data, i.e.:

- The BIOS is a programme for controlling the system's main input-output interfaces, hence the name *BIOS ROM* which is sometimes given to the read-only memory chip of the mother board which hosts it.
- The bootstrap loader: a programme for loading (random access) memory into the operating system and launching it. This generally seeks the operating system on the floppy drive then on the hard disk, which allows the operating system to be launched from a system floppy disk in the event of malfunction of the system installed on the hard disk.
- The CMOS Setup is the screen displayed when the computer starts up and which is used to amend the system parameters (often wrongly referred to as *BIOS*).
- The Power-On Self Test (*POST*), a programme that runs automatically when the system is booted, thus allowing the system to be tested (this is why the system "counts" the RAM at start-up).

Given that ROM are much slower than RAM memories (access time for a ROM is around 150 ns whereas for SDRAM it is around 10 ns), the instructions given in the ROM are sometimes copied to the RAM at start-up; this is known as *shadowing*, though is usually referred to as *shadow memory*).

Read-only memory (ROM) is similar in design to static or dynamic RAM circuits, except that the "latching" mechanism is made for one-time (or limited) operation. The simplest type of ROM is that which uses tiny "fuses" which can be selectively blown or left alone to represent the two binary states.

Obviously, once one of the little fuses is blown, it cannot be made whole again, so the writing of such ROM circuits is one-time only. Because it can be written (programmed) once, these circuits are sometimes referred to as PROMs (Programmable Read-Only Memory).

However, not all writing methods are as permanent as blown fuses. If a transistor latch can be made which is resettable only with significant effort, a memory device that's something of a cross between a RAM and a ROM can be built. Such a device is given a rather oxymoronic name: the EPROM (Erasable Programmable Read-Only Memory).

Eproms come in two basic varieties: Electrically-erasable (EEPROM) and Ultraviolet-erasable (UV/EPROM). Both types of Eproms use capacitive charge Mosfet devices to latch on or off.

UV/EPROMs are "cleared" by long-term exposure to ultraviolet light. They are easy to identify: they have a transparent glass window which exposes the silicon chip material to light. Once programmed, you must cover that glass window with tape to prevent ambient light from degrading the data over time.

EPROMs are often programmed using higher signal voltages than what is used during "read-only" mode. The earliest forms of digital data storage involving moving parts was that of the punched paper card.

Joseph Marie Jacquard invented a weaving loom in 1780 which automatically followed weaving instructions set by carefully placed holes in paper cards.

This same technology was adapted to electronic computers in the 1950's, with the cards being read mechanically (metal-to-metal contact through the holes), pneumatically (air blown through the holes, the presence of a hole sensed by air nozzle backpressure), or optically (light shining through the holes).

An improvement over paper cards is the paper tape, still used in some industrial environments (notably the CNC machine tool industry), where data storage and speed demands are low and ruggedness is highly valued. Instead of wood-fibre paper, mylar material is often used, with optical reading of the tape being the most popular method.

Magnetic tape (very similar to audio or video cassette tape) was the next logical improvement in storage media. It is still widely used today, as a means to store "backup" data for archiving and emergency restoration for other, faster methods of data storage.

Like paper tape, magnetic tape is sequential access, rather than random access. In early home computer systems, regular audio cassette tape was used to store data in modulated form, the binary 1's and 0's represented by different frequencies (similar to FSK data communication). Access speed was terribly slow (if you were reading ASCII text from the tape, you could almost keep up with the pace of the letters appearing on the computer's screen!), but it was cheap and fairly reliable.

Tape suffered the disadvantage of being sequential access. To address this weak point, magnetic storage "drives" with disk- or drum-shaped media were built. An electric motor provided constant-speed motion.

A movable read/write coil (also known as a "head") was provided which could be positioned via servo-motors to various locations on the height of the drum or the radius of the disk, giving access that is almost random (you might still have to wait for the drum or disk to rotate to the proper position once the read/write coil has reached the right location).

The disk shape lent itself best to portable media, and thus the *floppy disk* was born. Floppy disks (so-called because the magnetic media is thin and flexible) were originally made in

8-inch diameter formats. Later, the 5-1/4 inch variety was introduced, which was made practical by advances in media particle density.

All things being equal, a larger disk has more space upon which to write data. However, storage density can be improved by making the little grains of iron-oxide material on the disk substrate smaller.

Today, the 3-1/2 inch floppy disk is the preeminent format, with a capacity of 1.44 Mbytes (2.88 Mbytes on SCSI drives). Other portable drive formats are becoming popular, with IoMega's 100 Mbyte "ZIP" and 1 Gbyte "JAZ" disks appearing as original equipment on some personal computers.

Still, floppy drives have the disadvantage of being exposed to harsh environments, being constantly removed from the drive mechanism which reads, writes, and spins the media. The first disks were enclosed units, sealed from all dust and other particulate matter, and were definitely *not* portable. Keeping the media in an enclosed environment allowed engineers to avoid dust altogether, as well as spurious magnetic fields. This, in turn, allowed for much closer spacing between the head and the magnetic material, resulting in a much tighter-focused magnetic field to write data to the magnetic material.

PROM

PROM (Programmable Read Only Memory) memories were developed at the end of the 70s by a company called Texas Instruments. These memories are chips comprising thousands of fuses (or diodes) that can be"burnt" using a device called a" ROM programmer", applying high voltage (12V) to the memory boxes to be marked. The fuses thus burnt correspond to 0 and the others to 1.

EPROM

EPROM (Erasable Programmable Read Only Memory) memories are PROMs that can be deleted. These chips have a glass panel that lets ultra-violet rays through. When the chip is subjected to ultra-violet rays with a certain wavelength, the fuses are reconstituted, meaning that all the memory bits return to 1. This is why this type of PROM is called erasable.

EEPROM

EEPROM (Electrically Erasable Read Only Memory memories are also erasable PROMs, but unlike EPROMs, they can be erased by a simple electric current, meaning that they can be erased even when they are in position in the computer.

There is a variant of these memories known as flash memories (also Flash ROM or Flash EPROM). Unlike the classic EEPROMs that use 2 to 3 transistors for each bit to be memorised, the EPROM Flash uses only one transistor. Moreover, the EEPROM may be written and read word by word, while the Flash can be erased only in pages (the size of the pages decreases constantly).

PLA

INTRODUCTION

One way to design a combinational logic circuit it to get gates and connect them with wires. One disadvantage with this way of designing circuits is its lack of portability. You can now get chips called PLA (programmable logic arrays) and"programme" them to implement Boolean functions. I'll explain what it means to programme a PLA. Fortunately, a PLA is quite simple to learn, and produces nice neat circuits too.

The ROM implementation of a function may become quite expensive for functions with a large number of variables, because all potential minterms of the function are implemented, whether or not they are needed.

A programmable logic array (PLA) requires that only the minterms required for a function be implemented, and allows the implementation of several functions simultaneously. Moreover, the functions can be implemented directly from their minterm forms (although it is often possible to eliminate some of the minterms, further decreasing the cost of the PLA).

The PLA can be considered as a direct POS (or SOP)

implementation of a set of switching functions, with a set of AND functions followed by a set of OR functions. A PLA is often said to have an "AND" plane followed by an "OR" plane. In practice, either NAND or NOR gates are normally used, with the resulting PLA said to be a NAND/NAND or a NOR/NOR device.

Special logic for Data Acquisition or Trigger applications in physics experiments is developed either in ASICs or in Programmable Logic chips. The design methologies are similar: Device-independent high-level design and simulation languages like VHDL Verilog, SystemC are used to design and simulate the electrical behaviour prior to a synthesis & routing process which is specific for the chip.

Programmable Logic has less on chip gate resources and is inferior ins speed compared to an ASIC however up to 5 Million user gates may be at disposition to be configured into complex logic systems and certain devices reach up to 300 MHz system clock.

Programmable logic may also contain embedded ASIC subsystems like processors, network interfaces or bus interfaces or use commercial or free IP software cores to integrate these as subsystems. The programmable logic is usually favoured for fast turn-around, low volume (compared to ASIC), online reconfiguration and logic upgrading. It is also the basis for building general purpose electronic cards which can be configured for a variety of different applications (Our example: PCI-FLIC and its FPGA design environment: Visual HDL/ Synfinity/ Foundry)

FPGA (Field Programmable Gate Arrays) are the most common programmable chips to implement complex logic systems: The binary congfiguration code which contains the routed application is programmed either into an external Prom or an internal Flash (Antifuse see below) which load these default configurations at power-up. Usually configuration updates can also be loaded dynamically via instrumentation buses like JTAG, I2C, and sometimes via the PCI..bus. The bit code of the internal logic configuration is stored in either SRAM, Flash or an Antifuse layer inside the

FPGA chip. Some companies (AMI, Altera, Xilinx) provide services for FPGA to ASIC conversion. FPGAs with Anti-fuses (Actel, Quicklogic) are considered more radiation tolerant due to their radiation hardened latches and do not require verification of configuration as in SRAM based FPGAs, hence they are interesting for FPGA logic in exposed logic of physics experiments. The antifuses configuration technique is a non-volatile, non-backreadable storage requiring no external Prom nor power-up delay and operates at low power consumption. However the programming procedure per chip may take 1/2 hour and the aging properties should be considered.

STARTING OUT

The first part of a PLA looks like:

Each variable is hooked to a wire, and to a wire with a NOT gate. So the top wire is x2 and the one just below is its negation, \x2.

Then there's x1 and just below it, its negation, \x1.

The next part is to draw a vertical wire with an AND gate. I've drawn 3 of them.

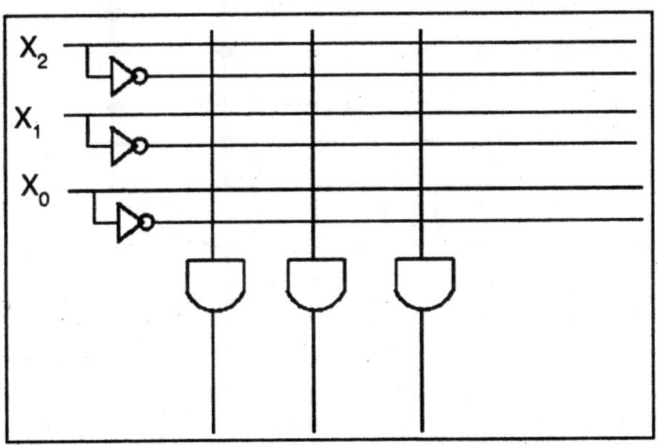

Let's try to implement a truth table with a PLA.

x_2	x_1	x_0	z_1	z_0
0	0	0	0	0
0	0	1	1	0
0	1	0	0	0
0	1	1	1	0
1	0	0	1	1
1	0	1	0	0
1	1	0	0	0
1	1	1	0	1

Each of the vertical lines with an AND gate corresponds to a minterm. For example, the first AND gate (on the left) is the minterm: $\backslash x_2 \backslash x_1 x_0$.

The second AND gate (from the left) is the minterm: $\backslash x_2 x_1 x_0$.

The third AND gate (from the left) is the minterm: $x_2 \backslash x_1 \backslash x_0$.

I've added a fourth AND gate which is the minterm: $x_2 x_1 x_0$.

The first three minterms are used to implement z_1. The third and fourth minterm are used to implement z0.

This is how the PLA looks after we have all four minterms.

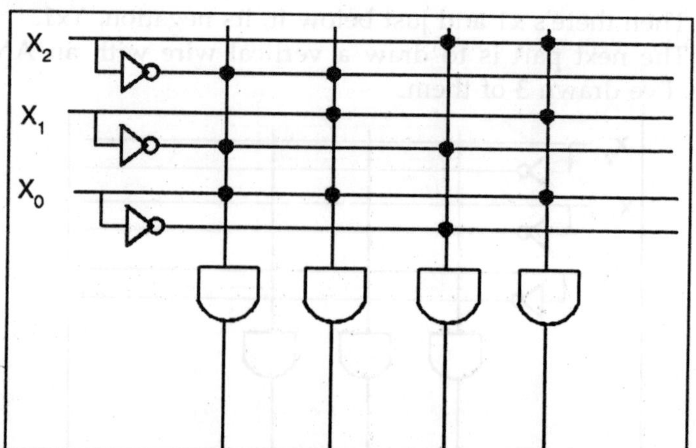

Now you might complain. How is it possible to have a

one input AND gate? How can three inputs be hooked to the same wire to an AND gate? Isn't that invalid for combinational logic circuits?

That's true, it is invalid. However, the diagram is merely a simplification. I've drawn the each of AND gate with three input wires, which is what it is in reality (there is as many input wires as variables). For each connection (shown with a black dot), there's really a separate wire. We draw one wire just to make it look neat.

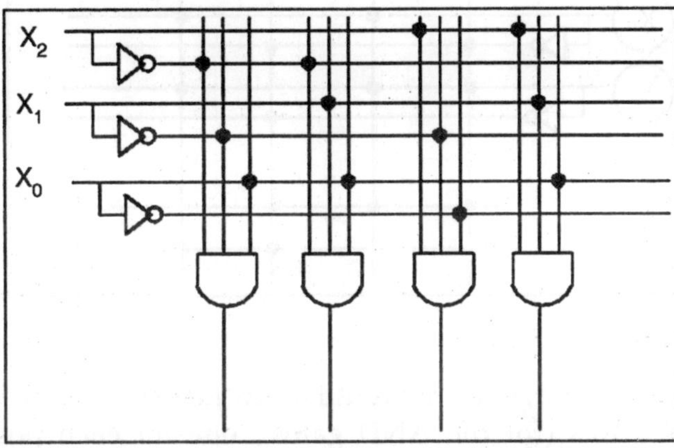

The vertical wires are called the AND plane. We often leave out the AND gates to make it even easier to draw.

We then add OR gates using horizontal wires, to connect the minterms together.

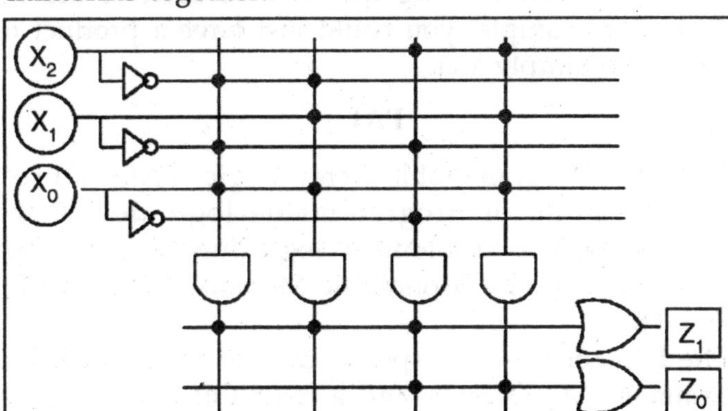

Again, a single wire into the OR gate is really 4 wires.

We use the same simplification to make it easier to read. The horizontal wires make up the OR plane. This is how the PLA looks when we leave out the AND gates and the OR gates. It's not that the AND gates and OR gates aren't there---they are, but they've been left out to make the PLA even easier to draw.

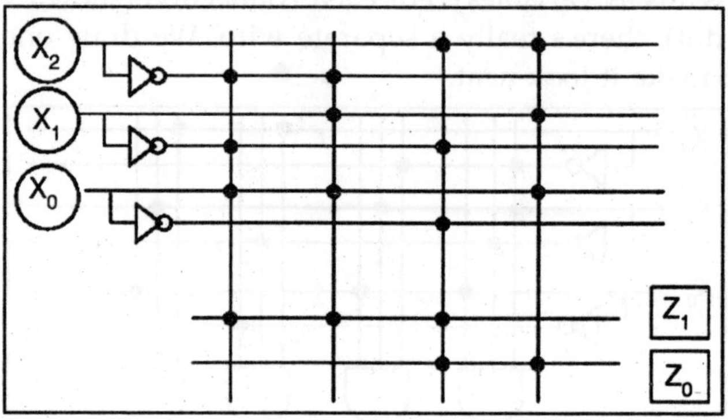

MINTERMS

Given n variables, it would seem necessary to have 2n vertical wires (for the AND gates), one for each possible minterm.

However, 2n grows VERY quickly. So, sometimes there aren't 2n vertical wires. You can generally get around the problem by not connecting the wire to each of the three variables. For example, you could just have a product term x2\x0 or even simply \x1.

PAL

The term Programmable Array Logic (PAL) is used to describe a family of programmable logic device semi-conductors used to implement logic functions in digital circuits introduced by Monolithic Memories, Inc. (MMI) in March 1978.

The PAL device is a special case of PLA which has a programmable AND array and a fixed OR array. The basic structure of Rom is same as PLA.

It is cheap compared to PLA as only the AND array is

programmable. It is also easy to programme a PAL compared to PLA as only AND must be programmed. PAL devices consisted of a small PROM (programmable read-only memory) core and additional output logic used to implement particular desired logic functions with few components.

Using specialized machines, PAL devices were"field-programmable". Each PAL device was"one-time programmable" (OTP), meaning that it could not be updated and reused after its initial programming. (MMI also offered a similar family called HAL, or"hard array logic", which were like PAL devices except that they were mask-programmed at the factory.)

The figure below shows a segment of an unprogrammed PAL. The input buffer with non inverted and inverted outputs is used, since each PAL must drive many AND Gates inputs. When the PAL is programmed, the fusible links (F1, F2, F3...F8) are selectively blown to leave the desired connections to the AND Gate inputs. Connections to the AND Gate inputs in a PAL are represented by Xs, as shown here:

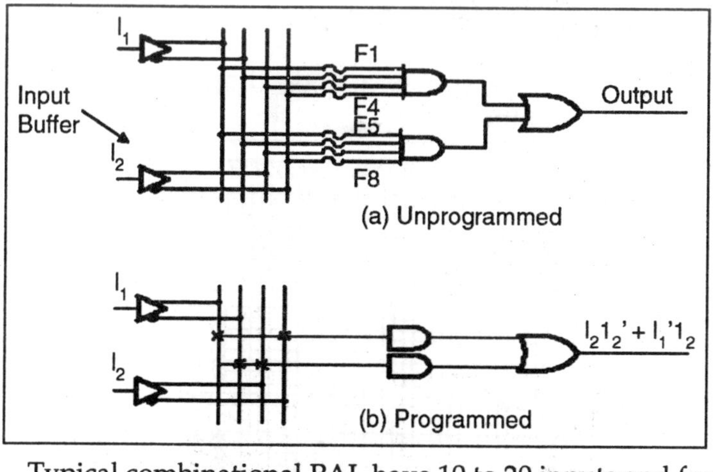

Typical combinational PAL have 10 to 20 inputs and from 2 to 10 outputs with 2 to 8 AND gates driving each OR gate. PALs are also available which contain D flip-flops with inputs driven from the programming array logic. Such PAL provides a convenient way of realizing sequential networks.

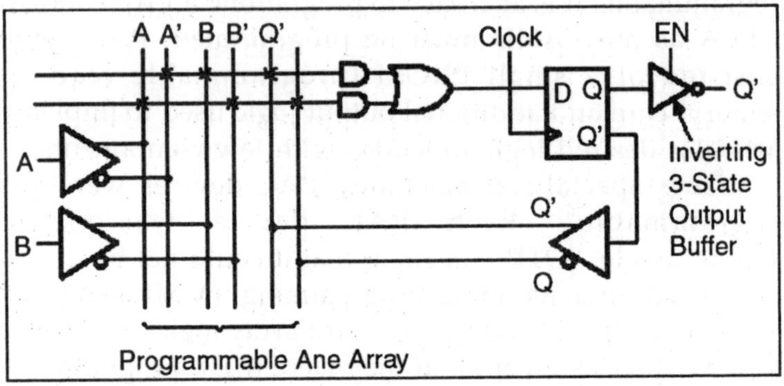

Fig. Below Shows a Segment of a Sequential PAL.

The D flip-flop is driven from the OR gate, which is fed by two AND gates. The flip-flop output is fed back to the programmable AND array through a buffer. Thus the AND gate inputs can be connected to A, A', B, B', Q, or Q'. The Xs on the diagram show the realization of the next-state equation.

Q+ = D = A'BQ' + AB'Q

The flip-flop output is connected to an inverting tristate buffer, which is enabled when

EN = 1

Figure below shows a logic diagram for a typical sequential PAL, the 16R4

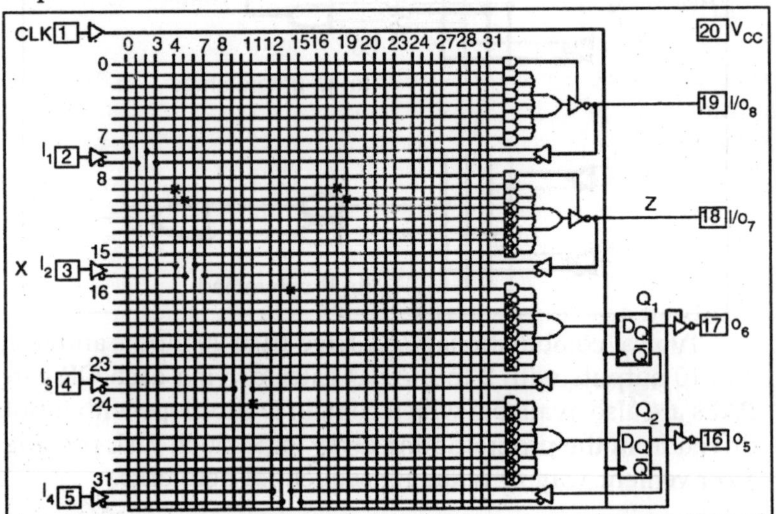

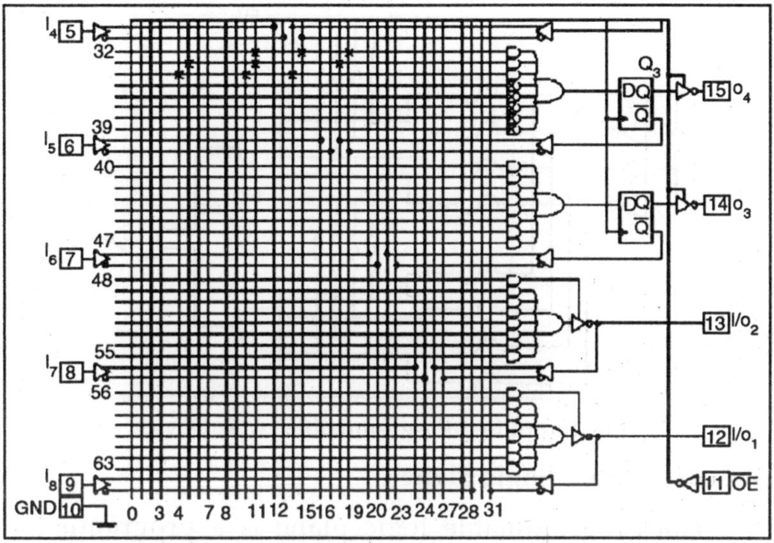

This PAL has an AND gate array with 16 input variables, and it has 4 D flip-flops. Each flip-flop output goes through a tristate-inverting buffer (output pins 14-17). One input (pin 11) is used to enable these buffers. The rising edge of a common clock (pin 1) causes the flip-flops to change the state. Each D flip-flop input is driven from an OR gate, and each OR gate is fed from 8 AND gates.

The AND gate inputs can come from the external PAL inputs (pins2-9) or from the flip-flop outputs, which are fed back internally. In addition there are four input/output (i/o) terminals (pins 12,13,18 and 19), which can be used as either network outputs or as inputs to the AND gates. Thus each AND gate can have a maximum of 16 inputs (8 external inputs, 4 inputs fed back from the flip-flop outputs, and 4 inputs from the i/o terminals). When used as an output, each I/O terminal is driven from an inverting tristate buffer. Each of these buffers is fed from an OR gate and each OR gate is fed from 7 AND gates. An eighth AND gate is used to enable the buffer.

PAL ARCHITECTURE

The PAL architecture consists of two main components: a logic plane and output logic macrocells.

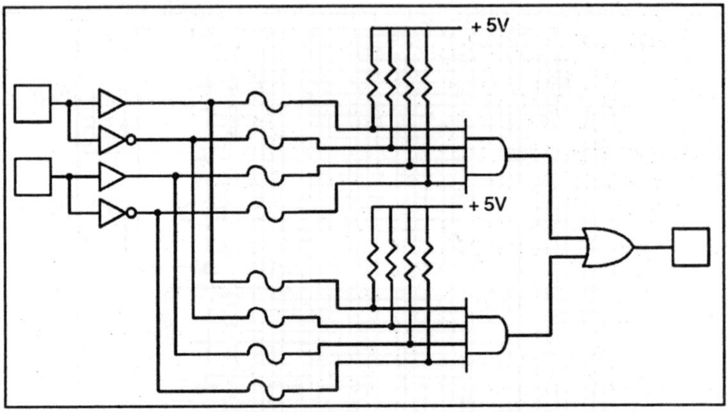

Fig. Simplified Programmable Logic Device

Programmable Logic Plane

The programmable logic plane is a programmable (PROM) array that allows the signals present on the devices pins (or the logical complements of those signals) to be routed to an output logic macrocell.

PAL devices have arrays of transistor cells arranged in a"fixed-OR, programmable-AND" plane used to implement"sum-of-products" binary logic equations for each of the outputs in terms of the inputs and either synchronous or asynchronous feedback from the outputs.

Output Logic

The early 20-pin PALs had 10 inputs and 8 outputs. The outputs were active low and could be registered or combinational. Members of the PAL family were available with various output structures called"output logic macrocells" or OLMCs.

Prior to the introduction of the"V" (for"variable") series, the types of OLMCs available in each PAL were fixed at the time of manufacture. (The PAL16L8 had 8 combinational outputs and the PAL16R8 had 8 registered outputs.

The PAL16R6 had 6 registered and 2 combinational while the PAL16R4 had 4 of each.) Each output could have up to 8 product terms (effectively AND gates), however the combinational outputs used one of the terms to control a bidirectional output buffer. There were other combinations that had fewer outputs with more product term per output and were available with active high outputs.

The 16X8 family or registered devices had an XOR gate before the register. There were also similar 24-pin versions of these PALs.

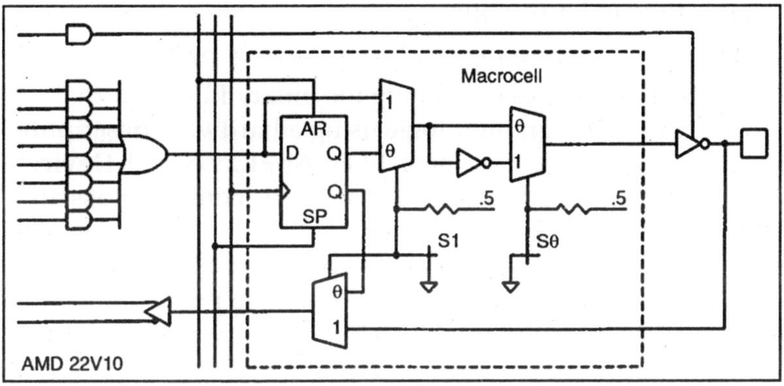

This fixed output structure often frustrated designers attempting to optimize the utility of PAL devices because output structures of different types were often required by their applications. (For example, one could not get 5 registered outputs with 3 active high combinational outputs.) So, in June 1983 AMD introduced the 22V10, a 24 pin device with 10 output logic macrocells. Each macrocell could be configured by the user to be combinational or registered, active high or active low. The number of product term allocated to an output varied from 8 to 16. This one device could replace all of the 24 pin fixed function PAL devices. Members of the PAL"V" ("variable") series included the PAL16V8, PAL20V8 and PAL22V10.

PROGRAMMING PALS

PALs were programmed electrically using binary patterns and a special electronic programming system available from either the manufacturer or a third-party, such as DATA/IO. In addition to single-unit device programmers, device feeders and gang programmers were often used when more than just a few PALs needed to be programmed. (For large volumes, electrical programming costs could be eliminated by having the manufacturer fabricate a custom metal mask used to programme the customers' patterns at the time of manufacture; MMI used the term"hard array logic" (HAL) to refer to devices programmed in this way.)

Programming Languages

Though some engineers programmed PAL devices by manually editing files containing the binary fuse pattern data, most opted to design their logic using a hardware description language(HDL) such as Data I/O's ABEL, Logical Devices' CUPL, or MMI's PALASM. These were computer-assisted design (CAD) (now referred to as"design automation") programs which translated (or"compiled") the designers' logic equations into binary fuse map files used to programme (and often test) each device.

Chapter 6

Sequential Logic

ANALYSIS PROCEDURE

An asynchronous sequential circuit is a sequential circuit whose behaviour depends only on the order in which its input signals change and can be affected at any instant of time. In addition to the FFs, a register may have combinational gates that control when and how new information is transferred into the register.

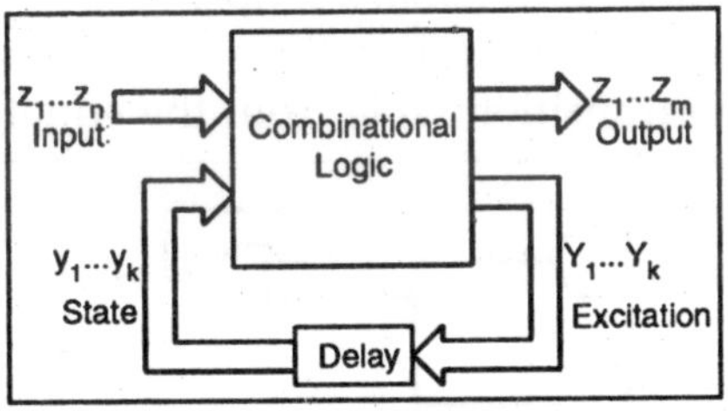

Fig. Asynchronus Sequential Circuit Model

$x = (x_1, x_2,...x_n)$: n input Variables

$z = (z_1, z_2,...z_m)$: m Output Variables

$y = (y_1, y_2,...y_k)$: k State Variables (Present State)

$Y = (Y_1, Y_2,...Y_k)$: k Excitation Variables (next Stae)

In the above circuit, the state transition occurs when there is an input change (no clock pulses). Memory (delay) elements are either latches (unclocked) or time-delay elements (instead of clocked FFs as in a synchronous sequential circuit). An asynchronous sequential circuit quite often resembles a combinational circuit with feedback. Faster and often cheaper than synchronous ones, but more difficult to design, verify, or test (due to possible timing problems involved in the feedback path).

- *Steady-state condition*: To ensure proper operation, simultaneous changes of 2 or more input variables are usually prohibited.
- *Fundamental-mode operation*: only one input variable can change at any time, and the time between 2 input changes must be longer than the time it takes the circuit to reach a stable state.

ANALYSIS PROCEDURE

The analysis consists of obtaining a table or a diagram that describes the sequence

of internal states and outputs as a function of changes in the input variables.

- Determine all feedback loops.
- Designate each feedback-loop output with Yi and its corresponding input with yi for i = 1;:::; k, where k is the number of feedback loops.
- Derive the boolean functions for all Y's.
- Plot the transition table from the equations.

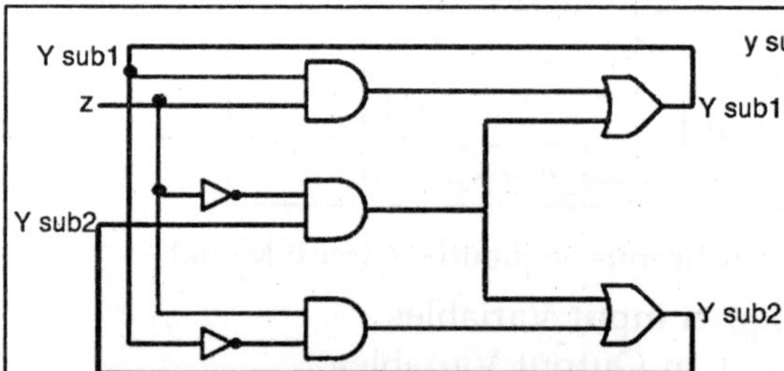

y sub 1 ysub2	0	1
00	(00)	01
01	11	(01)
11	(11)	10
10	00	(10)

Transition Table

Excitation Variables: Y_1 and Y_2

Secondary Variables: y_1 and y_2

$$y_1 = xy_1 + x'y_2$$

$$y_2 = xy_1 + x'y_2$$

The delay associated with each feedback loop is obtained from the propagation delay between each y input and its corresponding Y output.

In an asynchronous sequential circuit, the internal state can change immediately after a change in the input.

- *Total state*: internal state + input value.
- *Flow table*: a transition table in which states are named by letter symbols instead of specific binary values.

The flow table also includes the output values of the circuit for each

stable state.

- *Primitive flow table*: one that has only one stable state in each row. To obtain the circuit described by a flow table, it is necessary to assign to each state a distinct binary value, which converts the flow table into a transition table.
- *Race condition*: when 2 or more binary state variables change value in response to a change in an input variable.

May cause the state variables to change in an unpredictable manner.

- *Noncritical race*: final stable state does not depend on the order in which the state variables change.
- *Critical race:* final stable state depends on the order in which the state variables change.

For proper operation, critical races must be avoided.

Races may be avoided by making a proper state assignment. Races can be avoided by directing the circuit through intermediate unstable states with a unique state-variable change.

DESIGN PROCEDURE

- Obtain a primitive flow table.
- Reduce the flow table.
- Assign binary state variables to obtain the transition table.
- Assign output values to the dashes to obtain the output maps.
- Simplify the excitation and output functions.
- Draw the logic diagram.

We will design a gated latch circuit with 2 inputs, G (gate) and D (data), and one output, Q. The binary value at the D input is transferred to the Q output when and only when G =

1. When G falls to 0, the latch retains the value at the Q output, which does not change even if D changes.

The table of total states and the corresponding primitive flow table is shown below. Note that both inputs are not allowed to change simultaneously.

State	Inputs D	Inputs G	Output Q	Comments
a	0	1	0	D = Q
b	1	1	1	D = Q
c	0	0	0	After a or d
d	1	0	0	After c
e	1	0	1	After b or f
f	0	0	1	After e

Table of Total States

	DG = 00	01	11	10
a	c,–	(a)0	b,–	–,–
b	–,–	a,–	(b)1	e,–
c	(c)0	a,–	–,–	d,–
d	c,–	–,–	b,–	(d)0
e	f,–	–,–	b,–	(d)1
f	(f)1	a,–	–,–	e,–

Primitive Flow Table   States to be Merged

The next step is to reduce the primitive flow table, which is shown below. Then,

	DG = 00	01	11	10
a,b,c	(c)0	(a)0	b,–	(a)0
b,e,f	(f)1	a,–	(b) 1	(e) 1

→

	DG = 00	01	11	10
a	(a) 0	(a) 0	b,–	(a) 0
b	(b) 0	a,–	(b) 0	(b) 0

following state assignment, we convert the flow table into a transition table (by assigning a = 0 and b = 1). From the table, the simplified O/P function (Q) and the excitation function (Y) with respect to D, G, and y can be derived using the K-map method. Note that the don't-cares are assigned such that Q = Y

$Y = DG + G'y$: $Q = Y$.

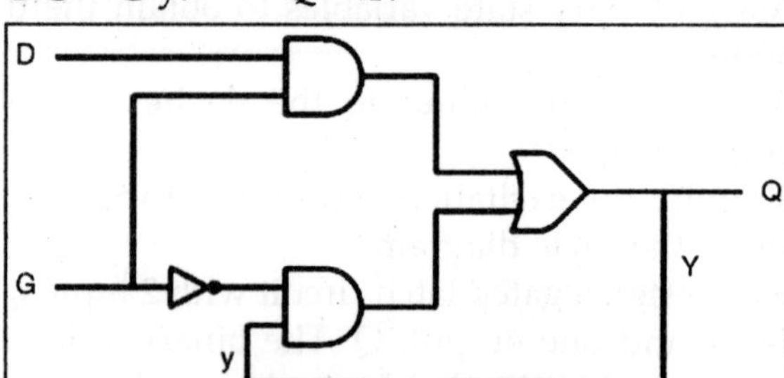

REDUCTION OF STATE

The procedure for reducing the number of internal states in an asynchronous sequential circuit resembles the procedure that is used for synchronous circuits.

IMPLICATION TABLE

The state-reduction procedure for completely specified state tables is based on the algorithm that two states in a state table can be combined into one if they can be shown to be equivalent. There are occasions when a pair of states do not have the same next states, but, nonetheless, go to equivalent next states. Consider the following state table:

Present State	Next State		output	
	x = 0	x = 1	x = 0	x = 1
a	c	b	0	1
b	d	a	0	1
c	a	d	1	0
d	b	d	1	0

(a, b) imply (c, d) and (c, d) imply (a, b). Both pairs of states are equivalent; i.e., a and b are equivalent as well as c and d. The checking of each pair of states for possible equivalence in a table with a large number of states can be done systematically by means of an implication table. This a chart that consists of squares, one for every possible pair of states, that provide spaces for listing any possible implied states.

Consider the following state table:

Present State	Next State		output	
	x = 0	x = 1	x = 0	x = 1
a	d	6	0	0
b	e	a	0	0
c	g	f	0	1
d	a	d	1	0
e	a	d	1	0
f	c	b	0	0
g	a	e	1	0

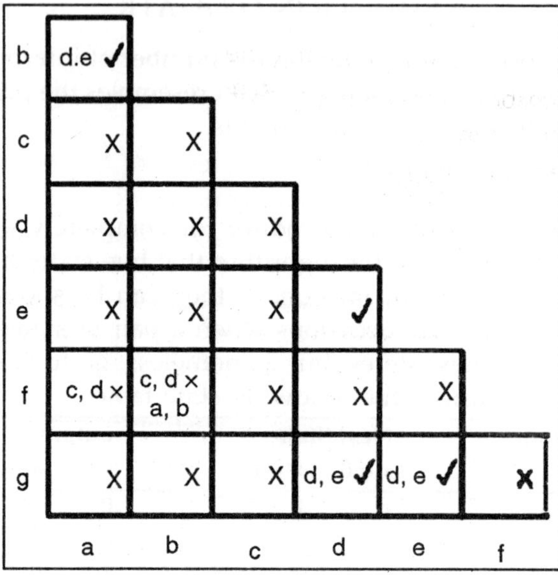

On the left side along the vertical are listed all the states defined in the state table except the last, and across the bottom horizontally are listed all the states except the last. The states that are not equivalent are marked with a'x' in the corresponding square, whereas their equivalence is recorded with a'?'. Some of the squares have entries of implied states that must be further investigated to determine whether they are equivalent or not. The step-by-step procedure of filling in the squares is as follows:

- Place a cross in any square corresponding to a pair of states whose outputs are not equal for every input.
- Enter in the remaining squares the pairs of states that are implied by the pair of states representing the squares. We do that by starting from the top square in the left column and going down and then proceeding with the next column to the right.
- Make successive passes through the table to determine whether any additional squares should be marked with a'x'. A square in the table is crossed out if it contains at least one implied pair that is not equivalent.

- Finally, all the squares that have no crosses are recorded with check marks. The equivalent states are: (a, b), (d, e), (d, g), (e, g).

We now combine pairs of states into larger groups of equivalent states. The last three pairs can be combined into a set of three equivalent states (d, e, g) because each one of the states in the group is equivalent to the other two. The final partition of these states consists of the equivalent states found from the implication table, together with all the remaining states in the state table that are not equivalent to any other state:

(a, b) (c) (d, e, g) (f)

The reduced state table is:

Present State	Next State		output	
	x = 0	x = 1	x = 0	x = 1
a	d	a	0	0
c	d	f	0	1
d	a	d	1	0
f	a	c	0	0

FLOW TABLE

There are occasions when the state table for a sequential circuit is incompletely specified.

Incompletely specified states can be combined to reduce the number of states in the flow table. Such states cannot be called equivalent, but, instead they are said to be compatible.

The process that must be applied in order to find a suitable group of compatibles for the purpose of merging a flow table is divided into three steps:

- Determine all compatible pairs by using the implication table.
- Find the maximal compatibles using a merger diagram.
- Find a minimal collection of compatibles that covers all the states and is closed.

We will now proceed to show and explain the three procedural steps using the following primitive flow table:

	DG 00	01	11	10
a	C, –	(a) 0	b, –	–, –
b	–, –	a, –	(b) 1	e, –
c	(c) 0	a, –	–, –	d, –
d	c, –	–, –	b, –	(d) 0
e	f, –	–, –	b, –	(e) 0
f	(f), 0	a, –	–, –	e, –

COMPATIBLE PAIRS

Two states are compatible if in every column of the corresponding rows in the flow table, they are identical or compatible states and if there is no conflict in the output values. The compatible pairs (√) are:

(a, b) (a, c) (a, d) (b, e) (b, f) (c, d) (e, f)

	a	b	c	d	e
b	✓				
c	✓	d, e ×			
d	✓	d, e ×	✓		
e	C, f ×	✓	d, e × c, f ×	×	
f	C, f ×	✓	×	d, e × C, f ×	✓

MAXIMAL COMPATIBLES

The maximal compatible is a group of compatibles that contains all the possible combinations of compatible states. The maximal compatible can be obtained from a merger diagram:

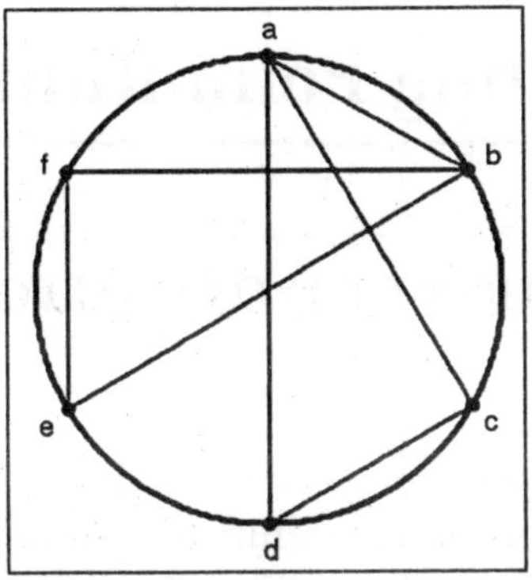

The above merger diagram is obtained from the list of compatible pairs derived from the previous implication table. A line represents a compatible pair. A triangle constitutes a compatible with three states.

The maximal compatibles are:

(a, b) (a, c, d) (b, e, f)

In the case where a state is not compatible to any other state, an isolated dot represents this state.

Chapter 7

Floating Point Rithmetic

REPRESENTATION OF FLOATING POINT NUMBERS

DEFINITION

A floating point number is one in which the position of the point is determined within the number itself. Working with floating point values, the position of the point in each number must be determined at processing time. This means that these calculations are much slower than fixed point. The reason for using floating point representation is that the range of possible values is much greater.

Floating point representation is similar to scientific notation and details of how values are represented vary from one machine to another. One of the standard floating point representations is the IEEE standard and it is useful to understand how this works.

The number uses a 32-bit string. This string has 3 distinct parts:

The sign bit	1 bit. With the value 1 for negative and 0
for positive.	
The mantissa	23 bits
The exponent	8 bits

Using binary, the value of the number is:
Sign (+/ –) 1.mantissa*$2^{exponent}$

REPRESENTATION

The IEEE Standard for Binary Floating-Point Arithmetic

defines binary formats for single and double precision numbers. Each number is composed of three parts: asign bit (s), an exponent (E) and a fraction (f). The numerical value of the combination (s,E,f) is given by the following formula,

```
(-1)^s (1.fffff...) 2^E
```

The sign bit is either zero or one. The exponent ranges from a minimum value E_min to a maximum value E_max depending on the precision.

The exponent is converted to an unsigned number e, known as the biased exponent, for storage by adding a bias parameter, e = E + bias. The sequence fffff... represents the digits of the binary fraction f. The binary digits are stored in normalized form, by adjusting the exponent to give a leading digit of 1. Since the leading digit is always 1 for normalized numbers it is assumed implicitly and does not have to be stored. Numbers smaller than 2^(E_min) are be stored in denormalized form with a leading zero,

```
(-1)^s (0.fffff...) 2^(E_min)
```

This allows gradual underflow down to 2^(E_min - p) for p bits of precision. A zero is encoded with the special exponent of 2^(E_min - 1) and infinities with the exponent of 2^(E_max + 1).

The format for single precision numbers uses 32 bits divided in the following way,

```
seeeeeeeefffffffffffffffffffffff
s = sign bit, 1 bit
e = exponent, 8 bits (E_min=-126, E_max=127,
bias=127)
f = fraction, 23 bits
```

The format for double precision numbers uses 64 bits divided in the following way,

```
seeeeeeeeeeeffffffffffffffffffffffffffffffffffffffffffffffffffff
s = sign bit, 1 bit
e = exponent, 11 bits (E_min=-1022,
E_max=1023, bias=1023)
f = fraction, 52 bits
```

It is often useful to be able to investigate the behaviour of a calculation at the bit-level and the library provides functions for printing the IEEE representations in a human-readable form.

- Function: void gsl_ieee_fprintf_float (FILE * stream, const float * x)
- Function: void gsl_ieee_fprintf_double (FILE * stream, const double * x)

These functions output a formatted version of the IEEE floating-point number pointed to by x to the stream stream. A pointer is used to pass the number indirectly, to avoid any undesired promotion from float to double. The output takes one of the following forms,

`NaN`
the Not-a-Number symbol
`Inf, -Inf`
positive or negative infinity
`1.fffff...*2^E, -1.fffff...*2^E`
a normalized floating point number
`0.fffff...*2^E, -0.fffff...*2^E`
a denormalized floating point number
`0, -0`
positive or negative zero

The output can be used directly in GNU Emacs Calc mode by preceding it with 2# to indicate binary.

- Function: void gsl_ieee_printf_float (const float * x)
- Function: void gsl_ieee_printf_double (const double * x)

These functions output a formatted version of the IEEE floating-point number pointed to by x to the stream stdout.

The following programme demonstrates the use of the functions by printing the single and double precision representations of the fraction 1/3. For comparison the representation of the value promoted from single to double precision is also printed.

```
#include <stdio.h>
#include <gsl/gsl_ieee_utils.h>
int
main (void)
{
```

```
float f = 1.0/3.0;
double d = 1.0/3.0;
double fd = f;/* promote from float to double
*/
printf (" f="); gsl_ieee_printf_float(&f);
printf ("\n");
printf ("fd="); gsl_ieee_printf_double(&fd);
printf ("\n");
printf (" d="); gsl_ieee_printf_double(&d);
printf ("\n");
return 0;
}
```

The binary representation of 1/3 is 0.01010101.... The output below shows that the IEEE format normalizes this fraction to give a leading digit of 1,

```
f= 1.01010101010101010101011*2^-2
fd = 1.0101010101010101010101100000000000000000000000
0000000*2^-2
d = 1.0101010101010101010101010101010101010101010
10101010101*2^-2
```

The output also shows that a single-precision number is promoted to double-precision by adding zeros in the binary representation.

Example 1

Sign bit 1 negative.

Sign	Exponent	Mantissa
1	10000111	10110011010000000000000

Exponent. The exponent is shown with excess 127. This means that the machine exponent is the actual exponent with 127 added. This has the effect of giving a range of 0 to 255 for the machine representation while the range of actual values is –128 to +127. If the excess was not used there would have to be a mechanism for showing a negative exponent.

In the example the actual exponent is 1000 (decimal 8).

The machine representation is:

0000 1000 (8) + 0111 1111 (127) = 1000 0111 (decimal 135)

Mantissa. The mantissa is the number being encoded.

Before the number is encoded the point is moved(or floated) left or right until the value of the number is in the range:

$$1 < n < 2$$

This is known as normalisation. Since the first digit is now always going to be 1 there is no need to encode this digit. The mantissa only includes the digits after the point and the leading 1 is assumed.

The number shown above is -1.1011 0011 01*28

In un-normalised form this is -110110011.01

Example 2

To encode the binary number 101.1110 01:

Step 1	The sign bit is 0 for positive.
*Step*2:	normalise Move the point 2 places to the left: 1.01111 001 the digits after the point are the mantissa. All trailing bits are 0.
Step 3	The point was moved 2 places to the left. The exponent is now used to multiply the mantissa by 22 This effectively returns the mantissa to its original size. However, remember that excess 127 is used so the exponent will be 2 + 127 = 129.

Sign	Exponent	Mantissa
0	10000001	01111001000000000000000

Using this representation the 32-bit number has 23 bits giving the detail of the value and 8 bits in the exponent which means that the number can be increased or decreased by 2127.

A 32-bit integer can show 32 bits of detail but has lower magnitude. This is the trade-off between floating point and fixed point numbers.

FLOATING POINT MULTIPLICATION

Multiplying two floating point values isn't so difficult, at least, if you're mostly interested in understanding how it works, rather than developing hardware to do the multiplication.

Multiplying floating point requires you to add the exponents of two values, then multiply the mantissas, then renormalize that result, adjusting the exponent if necessary.

Finally, you deal with the sign bit by XORing the sign bit. Multiplying in real hardware involves rounding, dealing with overflow and underflow. Our goal is to be able to do the multiplication on paper, just to get an idea of what's going on. In the second multiplication study, we have developed a scheme based upon a redundant 3-bit Booth encoding of the multiplier.

This redundant encoding reduces the number of partial products to be summed by one-third over a full (53 bit) tree partial product summation, but it avoids the requirement of forming plus or minus three multiples of the multiplicand. Coupled to the multiplier encoding, we have developed techniques that allow us to handle irregular counter implementations of the partial product tree.

State-of-the-art implementations of partial product trees have focused on 4-2 and similar approaches that provide a regularity in wiring of the partial product tree. We have shown with this work that it is possible to use irregular implementations based upon 3-2 counters with the assistance of CAD tools, which automatically optimize the routing and path length through the partial product tree.

Using the combined techniques of the redundant multiplier encoding, and the CAD-assisted layout of the partial product tree, we have implemented a full IEEE floating-point multiplier. This is being implemented now in ECL with the sponsorship of SUN Microsystems. The full multiplier is expected to have an overall delay of five nanoseconds.

1 - input (t = 0) 3-final Prcduce (t = 3.2ns)

2- Output of tree (t = 4.3ns) 4 - multiples ready (3x, 1x) t = 0.6ns

Suppose you want to multiply two floating-point numbers, X and Y.

Here's how to multiply floating-point numbers.

- First, convert the two representations to scientific notation. Thus, we explicitly represent the hidden 1.
- Let x be the exponent of X. Let y be the exponent of Y. The resulting exponent (call it z) is the sum of the

two exponents. z may need to be adjusted after the next step.

- Multiply the mantissa of X to the mantissa of Y. Call this result m.
- If m is does not have a single 1 left of the radix point, then adjust the radix point so it does, and adjust the exponent z to compensate.
- Add the sign bits, mod 2, to get the sign of the resulting multiplication.
- Convert back to the one byte floating point representation, truncating bits if needed.

EXAMPLE

Let's multiply the following two numbers:

Variable	sign	exponent	fraction
X	0	1001	010
Y	0	0111	110

Here are the steps again:

- First, convert the two representations to scientific notation. Thus, we explicitly represent the hidden 1. In this case, X is 1.01 X 22 and Y is 1.11 X 20.
- Let x be the exponent of X. Let y be the exponent of Y. The resulting exponent (call it z) is the sum of the two exponents. z may need to be adjusted after the next step.

  For now, the resulting exponent is 2 + 0 = 2
- Multiply the mantissa of X to the mantissa of Y. Call this result m.

  Multiplying 1.01 by 1.11 results in 10.0011
- If m is does not have a single 1 left of the radix point, then adjust the radix point so it does, and adjust the exponent z to compensate.

  Now, we have to renormalize 10.0011 to 1.00011 and increase the exponent by 1 to 3
- Add the sign bits, mod 2, to get the sign of the resulting multiplication.

The sign bit is 0 + 0 = 0.

- Convert back to the one byte floating point representation, truncating bits if needed.

We need to truncate 1.00011 x 23 to 1.000 x 23 and convert.

Product	sign	exponent	fraction
X * Y	0	1010	000

Negative Values

Unlike floating point addition, negative values are simple to take care of in floating point multiplication. Treat the sign bit as 1 bit UB, and add modulo 2. This is the same as XORing the sign bit.

Bias

Does the bias representation help us in floating point multiplication? In multiplication, it's more of a pain to use bias representation because we need to sum the exponents. Adding exponents represented in bias notation requires special hardware for biased representation. You're better off converting to two's complement, and adding. Thus, the bias makes it more challenging to add exponents.

FLOATING POINT OPERATIONS

The operation of floating point includes addition, subtraction, multiplication, or division of two floating-point operands to produce a floating-point result.

ADDITION

Here's how to add floating point numbers:

- First, convert the two representations to scientific notation. Thus, we explicitly represent the hidden 1.
- In order to add, we need the exponents of the two numbers to be the same. We do this by rewriting Y. This will result in Y being not normalized, but value is equivalent to the normalized Y.

  Add x - y to Y's exponent. Shift the radix point of the mantissa (signficand) Y left by x - y to compensate for the change in exponent.

- Add the two mantissas of X and the adjusted Y together.
- If the sum in the previous step does not have a single bit of value 1, left of the radix point, then adjust the radix point and exponent until it does.
- Convert back to the one byte floating point representation.

Example 1

Let's add the following two numbers:

Variable	Sign	Exponent	Fraction
X	0	1001	110
Y	0	0111	000

Here are the steps again:

- First, convert the two representations to scientific notation. Thus, we explicitly represent the hidden 1. In normalized scientific notation, X is 1.110 x 22, and Y is 1.000 x 20.
- In order to add, we need the exponents of the two numbers to be the same. We do this by rewriting Y. This will result in Y being not normalized, but value is equivalent to the normalized Y.

Add x - y to Y's exponent. Shift the radix point of the mantissa (signficand) Y left by x - y to compensate for the change in exponent.

The difference of the exponent is 2. So, add 2 to Y's exponent, and shift the radix point left by 2. This results in 0.0100 x 22. This is still equivalent to the old value of Y. Call this readjusted value, Y'

- Add the two mantissas of X and the adjusted Y' together.

  We add 1.110two to 0.01two. The sum is: 10.0two. The exponent is still the exponent of X, which is 2.
- If the sum in the previous step does not have a single bit of value 1, left of the radix point, then adjust the radix point and exponent until it does.

  In this case, the sum, 10.0two, has two bits left of the radix point. We need to move the radix point left by 1, and increase the exponent by 1 to compensate.

This results in: 1.000 x 23.

- Convert back to the one byte floating point representation.

Sum	Sign	Exponent	Fraction
X + Y	0	1010	000

Example 2: Let's add the following two numbers:

Variable	Sign	Exponent	Fraction
X	0	1001	110
Y	0	0110	110

Here are the steps again:

- First, convert the two representations to scientific notation. Thus, we explicitly represent the hidden 1. In normalized scientific notation, X is 1.110 x 22, and Y is 1.110 x 2-1.
- In order to add, we need the exponents of the two numbers to be the same. We do this by rewriting Y. This will result in Y being not normalized, but value is equivalent to the normalized Y.

Add x - y to Y's exponent. Shift the radix point of the mantissa (signficand) Y left by x - y to compensate for the change in exponent.

The difference of the exponent is 3. So, add 3 to Y's exponent, and shift the radix point of Y left by 3. This results in 0.00111 x 22. This is still equivalent to the old value of Y. Call this readjusted value, Y'

- Add the two mantissas of X and the adjusted Y' together.

  We add 1.110two to 0.00111two. The sum is: 1.11111two. The exponent is still the exponent of X, which is 2.
- If the sum in the previous step does not have a single bit of value 1, left of the radix point, then adjust the radix point and exponent until it does.

  In this case, the sum, 1.11111two, has a single 1 left of the radix point. So, the sum is normalized. We do not need to adjust anything yet.

  So the result is the same as before: 1.11111 x 23.

- Convert back to the one byte floating point representation.

We only have 3 bits to represent the fraction. However, there were 5 bits in our answer. Obviously, it looks like we should round, and real floating point hardware would do rounding.

However, for simplicity, we're going to truncate the additional two bits. After truncating, we get 1.111 x 22. We convert this back to floating point.

Sum	Sign	Exponent	Fraction
X + Y	0	1010	111

This example illustrates what happens if the exponents are separated by too much. In fact, if the exponent differs by 4 or more, then effectively, you are adding 0 to the larger of the two numbers.

PROGRAMMABLE GATE ARRAYS

INTRODUCTION

A field programmable gate array (FPGA) is an integrated circuit (IC) that includes a two-dimensional array of general-purpose logic circuits, called cells or logic blocks, whose functions are programmable.

An FPGA is a programmable integrated circuit which provides a customised logic array and functionality to a particular customer.

Programmable logic devices are widely used in the electronics industry. Contemporary programmable logic devices typically comprise a homogeneous, general-purpose logic array.

Such programmable logic devices use typically requires various programmable logic devices to serve multiple purposes. Instead of designing specific gate arrays for each purpose, multiple homogeneous programmable gate arrays are programmed to serve each required purpose.

Field programmable gate arrays (FPGAs) are typically used for these purposes. Digital logic can be implemented using any of several available integrated circuit architectures, including hardwired application-specific integrated circuits (ASIC), mask or fuse-programmed custom gate arrays (CGA), programmable array logic (PAL), programmable logic arrays (PLA) and other programmable logic devices (PLD) that typically employ nonvolatile EPROM or EEPROM memory cell technology for configuration by the user, and field programmable gate arrays (FPGA) which generally use SRAM configuration bits that are set during each power-up of the chip.

Application specific integrated circuits (ASICs) offer the electronics designer the ability to customise standard integrated circuits to provide a unique set of performance characteristics by integrating complex functionality and input/output (I/O) on a single integrated circuit. The significant benefits regarding the use of ASICs are customization, the ability to create unique functionality, and economies of scale for devices destined to be mass-produced.

Alternative devices, such as field programmable gate arrays permit the digital logic designer access to standard digital logic functions and capabilities, and additionally allow certain functions and I/O to be programmed rather than fixed during production.

Programmability offers the advantages of greater design flexibility and faster product implementation during subsequent system development efforts. FPGAs offer the advantages of low non-recurring engineering costs, fast turnaround, and low risk since designs can be easily amended late on in the product design cycle.

For purposes of low volume applications and the creation of prototype units, FPGAs typically exhibit lower unit costs than do ASICs. Field programmable gate arrays have been widely used in telecommunication applications, Internet applications, switching applications, routing applications, and a variety of other end user applications.

Field programmable gate arrays have become the solution of choice for logic design implementation in applications where time to market is a critical product development factor.

WORKING

The FPGA is made up of look-up tables (LUT), routing blocks, dedicated RAM and some common logical blocks such as multipliers or adders.

The LUT is a one-bit storage block and acts as a programmable gate. The input refers to the address lines of the storage element and the output is the stored value at that address. A flip-flop is placed between the gate and the output for clocked logic.

One or more routing blocks with wires connect inputs and outputs to various LUTs to each other. Routing blocks are designed so that only certain paths through the block are allowed. The LUTs and routing blocks are placed in an array in the FPGA. Hardware description language like VHDL and Verilog are used to programme the instructions.

SELECTION

- *Configurable logic blocks (CLB)*: contain RAM LUTs and flip-flops. CLBs can be programmed to store data (e.g. 62,208 nos).
- *IOBs*: control data flow between I/O pins and the logic elements of the device.
- *Block RAM*: for data storage (e.g. 432/ 576/ 1728 K).
- Multiplier Blocks: use 18-bit binary numbers as input (e.g. 24, 32, 96).
- *DCM*: digital clock manager for internal calibration between elements (e.g. 4).

DEVICES USED IN FPGAS

- *PROMs (programmable read only memory)*: Data can be written only once.
- *EPROM (erasable programmable read-only memory)*: Exposing the chip to ultraviolet rays can erase data and a new programme can be written.
- *PLAs (programmable logic array)*: This has a programmable AND plane and a fixed OR plane.
- *PAL/GALs (programmable array logic/generic array logic)*: These use a combination of different types of arrays.

APPLICATIONS

Some of the manufacturers of FPGAs are Xilinx, Altera, Lattice Semiconductor, Actel, Cypress, Atmel, QuickLogic and ST Microelectronics.

FPGAs are used in digital signal processing, software-defined radio, aerospace and Defence systems, ASIC prototyping, medical imaging and many other emerging markets like computer vision, speech recognition, cryptography, bioinformatics, etc.

PROGRAMMABLE LOGIC DEVICES

As the technology surrounding programmable devices improved, new devices were developed which combined several PLDs together on a single integrated circuit to form complex programmable logic devices, CPLDs. CPLD was introduced in late of 1970 with extension of SPLD devices. The concept is to have a few PLD blocks or macrocells on a single device with a general-purpose interconnect in-between.

Basically, a CPLD consists of several blocks, each of which is a PLD, which are connected together. I/Os of each of the PLD blocks are connected by a global interconnect array.

Each logic block contains 4 to 16 macrocells depending on the vendor and the architecture. A macrocell on most modern CPLDs contains a sum-of-products combinatorial logic function and an optional flip-flop. The combinatorial logic function typically supports four to 16 product terms with wide fan-in. In other words, a macrocell function can have many inputs, but the complexity of the logic function is limited.

CPLDs are generally best for control- oriented designs due in part to their fast pin-to-pin performance. The wide fan-in of their macrocells makes them well-suited to complex, high-performance state machines.

CPLD has less flexible internal architecture and the delay through a CPLD (measured in nanoseconds) is more predictable and usually shorter. In addition to programming the individual SPLD blocks, the connections between the blocks can be programmed by means of the programmable interconnection matrix, which give greater flexibility to user and become more popular among designers. The devices are programmed using programmable elements that, depending on the technology of the manufacturer, can be EPROM cells, E2PROM cells, or Flash EPROM cells. The Figure below shows general architecture of CPLD devices.

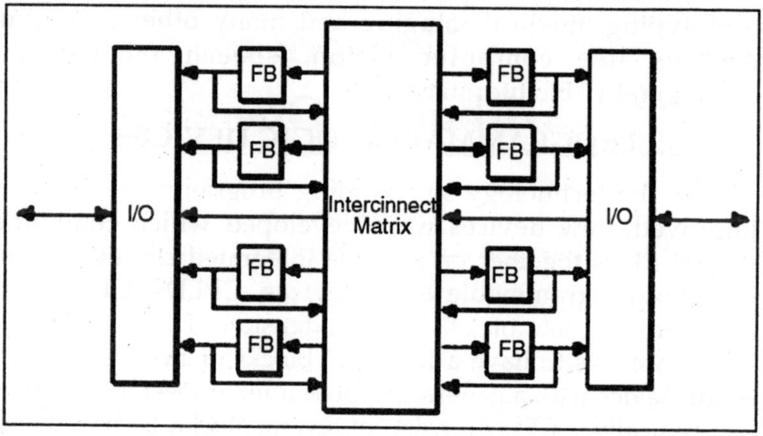

Chapter 8

Network for Arithmatic Operations

SERIAL ADDER WITH ACCUMULATOR

A control circuit for a digital system is a sequential network that outputs a sequence of control signals. These signals cause operations such a addition and shifting to take place at appropriate times. Figure shows the block diagram for serial adder with accumulator. Two shift registers are used to hold the 4-bit numbers to be added, X and Y. The box at the left end of each shift register shows the inputs: Sh (shift), SI(serial input), and clock. When Sh=1 and the clock is pulsed, SI is entered into x3(or y3) as the contents of register are shifted right one position.

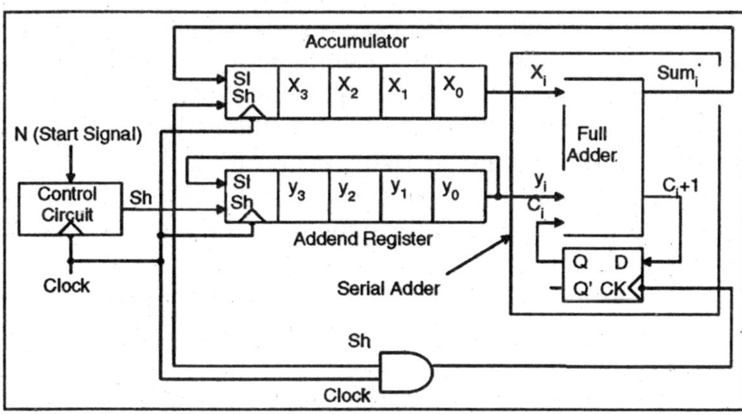

Fig: Serial Adder with Accumulator

The X-register serves as the accumulator, and after four shifts, the number X is replaced with the sum of X and Y. The addend register is connected as a cyclic shift register, so after four shifts it is back to its original state and the number Y is not lost.

The serial adder consists of a full adder and a carry flip - flop. At each clock time, one pair of bits is added.

When Sh=1, the falling edge of the clock shifts the sum bit into the accumulator, stores the carry bit in the flip-flop, and causes the addend register to rotate left. Additional connections needed for initially loading the X and Y registers and clearing the carry flip-flop are not shown in the block diagram.

Table below illustrates the operation of the serial adder Initially, at time t0 the accumulator contains X, the addend register contains Y, and the carry flip-flop is clear.

	x	y	c_1	Sum_i	C_{i+1}
t_0	0101	0111	0	0	1
t_1	0010	1011	1	0	1
t_2	0001	1101	1	1	1
t_3	1000	1110	1	1	0
t_4	1100	0111	0	(1)	(0)

Since the full adder is a combinational network, x0 = 1, y0 = 1, and c0 = 0 are added after a short propagation delay to give 10, so sum0 = 0 and carry c1 = 1. when the first clock occurs, sum is shifted into the accumulator, and the remaining accumulator digits are shifted right one position.

The same shift pulse stores c1 in the carry flip-flop and cycles the addend register right one position.

The next pair of bits, x1=0 and y1 = 1, are now at the full adder input, and the adder generates the sum and carry, sum1=0 and c2 = 1.

The second clock pulse shifts sum into the accumulator, stores c2 in the carry flip-flop and cycles the addend register right.

Bits x2 and y2 are now at the adder input, and the process continues until all bit pairs have been added. After four clocks (time t4), the sum of X and Y is in the accumulator, and the addend register is back to its original state.

The control circuit for the adder must now be designed so that after receiving a start signal, the control circuit will output Sh=1 for four clocks and then stop. Figure below shows the state graph and table for the control circuit. The network remains in S0 until a start signal (N) is received, at which time the network outputs Sh = 1 and goes to S1. then Sh=1 for three more clock times, and the network returns to S0. It will be assumed that the start signal is terminated before the network returns to state S0, so no further action occurs until another start signal is received. Dashes (don't cares) on the graph indicate the once S1 is reached, the network operation continues regardless of the value of N.

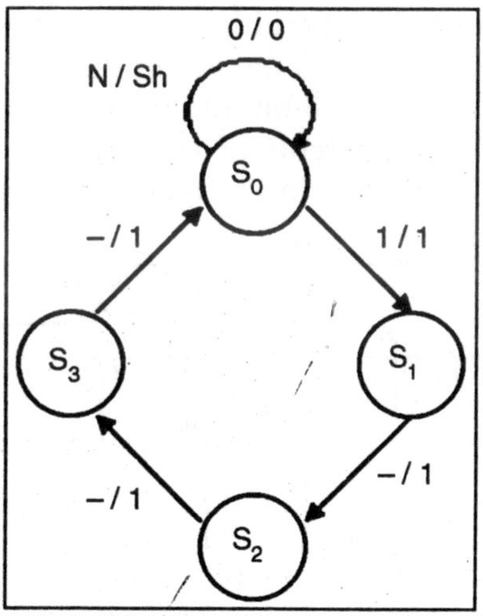

Present Stat state	Next State N=0	Next State N=1	Present Output (Sh) N=0	Present Output (Sh) N=1
S_0	S_0	S_1	0	1
S_1	S_2	S_2	1	1
S2				

STATE GRAPH

Binary multiplication requires only shifting and adding. For example, multiplication 13_{10} by 05_{10} in binary:

```
        Multiplicand   → 1 1 0 1   (13)
        Multiplier     → 0 1 0 1   (05)
Partial Product        →   1 1 0 1
                         0 0 0 0
                         0 1 1 0 1
                       1 1 0 1
                       1 0 0 0 0 0 1
                     0 0 0 0
                     0 1 0 0 0 0 0 1   (65)
```

Note that each partial product is either the multiplicand (1101) shifted over by the appropriate number of places or zero. Multiplication of two 4-bit numbers requires a 4-bit multiplicand register, a 4-bit multiplier register, a 4-bit full adder, and an 8-bit register for the product. The product register serves as an accumulator to accumulate the sum of the partial products. If the multiplicand were shifted left each time before it was added to the accumulator, as was done in the previous example, an 8-bit adder would be needed. So it is better to shift the contents of the product register to the right each time, as shown in the block diagram as shown in figure below:

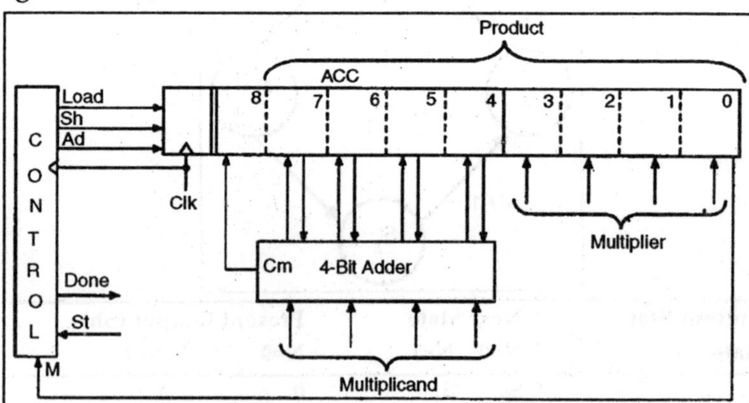

Fig. Block Diagram for Binary Multiplier

This type of multiplier is sometimes referred to as a serial - parallel multiplier, since the multiplier bits are processed serially, but the addition takes place in parallel. As indicated by the arrows on the diagram, 4 bits from the accumulator

(ACC) and 4 bits from the multiplicand register are connected to the adder inputs; the 4 sum bits and the carry output from the adder are connected back to the accumulator. When an add signal (Ad) occurs, the adder outputs are transferred to the accumulator by the next clock pulse, thus causing the multiplicand to be added to the accumulator. An extra bit at the left end of the product register temporarily stores any carry that is generated when the multiplicand is added to the accumulator. When a shift signal (Sh) occurs, all 9 bits of ACC are shifted right by the next clock pulse.

Since the lower 4 bits of the product register are initially unused, we will store the multiplier in this location instead of in a separate register. As each multiplier bit is used, it is shifted out the right end of the register to make room for additional product bits.

Multiplication Steps:		
Initial Contents of product Register	0 0 0 0 0 0 1 0 1	← M (5)
(Add Multiplicand Since M=1)	1 1 0 1	
After Addition	0 1 1 0 1 0 1 0 1	
After Shift	0 0 1 1 0 1 0 1 0	←M
(Skip Addition Since M=0)	0 0 0 0	
After Addition	0 0 1 1 0 1 0	
After Shift	0 0 0 1 1 0 1 0 1	← M
(Add Multiplicand Since M=1)	1 1 0 1	
After Addition	1 0 0 0 0 0 1 0 1	
After Shift	0 1 0 0 0 0 0 1 0	
(Skip Addition Since M=0)		
After Shift (Final Answer)	0 0 1 0 0 0 0 0 1	

A shift signal (Sh) causes the contents of the product register (including the multiplier) to be shifted right one place when the next clock pulse occurs. The control circuit puts out the proper sequence of add and shift signals after a start signal

(St=1) has been received. If the current multiplier bit (M) is 1, the multiplicand is added to the accumulator followed by a right shift; if the multiplier bit is 0, the addition is skipped, and only the right shift occurs. The multiplication example (13X05) is reworked below showing the location of the bits in the registers at each clock time.

The control circuit must be designed to output the proper sequence of add and shift signals. Figure below shows a state graph for the control circuit.

In this Figure, S0 is the reset state, and the network stays in S0 until a start signal (St=1) is received. This generates a load signal, which causes the multiplier to be loaded into the lower 4 bits of the Accumulator (ACC) and the upper 5 bits of the accumulator to be cleared.

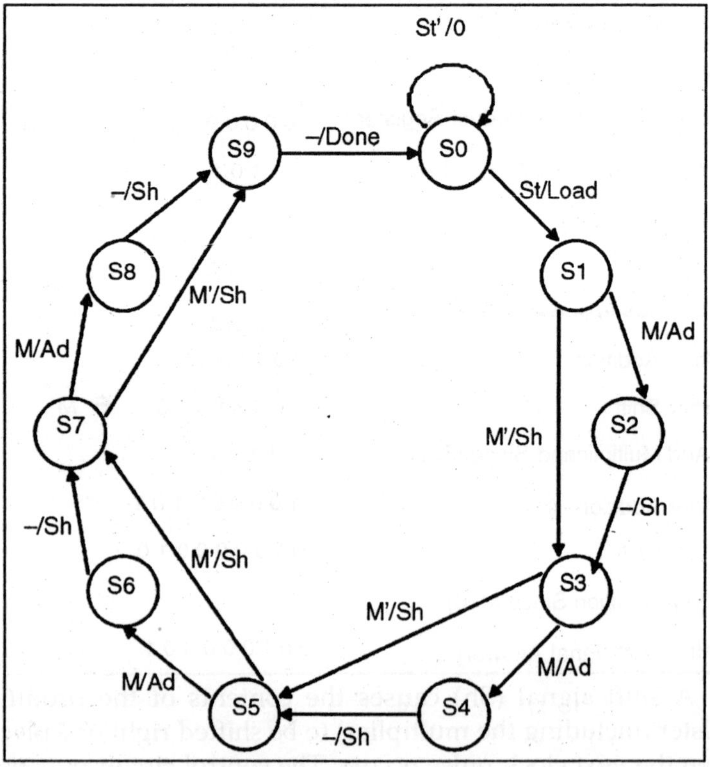

In state S1, the low-order bit of the multiplier (M) is

tested. If M=1, an add signal is generated, and if M=0, a shift signal is generated. Similarly, in states S3, S5 and S7, the current multiplier bit (M) is teted to determine whether to generate an add or shift signal. A shift signal is always generated at the next clock time following an add signal (states S2, S4, S6, and S8). After four shifts have been generated, the control network goes to S9, and a done signal is generated before returning to S0.

The behavioural VHDL model (Figure below) corresponds directly to the state graph. Since there are 10 states, we have declared an integer range 0 to 9 for the state signal. The signal ACC represents the 9-bit accumulator output.

The statement alias M: bit is ACC(0); allows us to use the name M in place of ACC(0) The done signal needs to be turned on only in state 9. If we had used the statement when 9 ⇒ State ⇐ 0; Done ⇐'1', Done would be turned on at the same time the State changed to 0. This is too late, since we want Done to turn on when the state becomes 9.

Therefore, we used a separate concurrent assignment statement. This statement is placed outside the process so that Done will be updated whenever State changes.

```
    Figure Behavioural model for 4 × 4 Binary
Multiplier
    - This is behavioural model of a multiplier
    for unsigned
    - Binary numbers. It multiplies a 4-bit
    multiplicand
    - By a 4-bit multiplier to give an 8-bit
    product.
    - The maxiumum number of clock cycles needed
    for a
    - Multiply is 10.
    - Library bitlib:
    use BITLIB. bit_pack. all;
    entity mult4 × 4 is
        Port (Clk, st: in bit;)
             Mplier, Mcand: in bit_ voctor (3
```

```
        downto 0);
        Done: out bit);
end mult 4 × 4;
architecture behavel of mult 4×4 is
   signal State: integer range 0 to 9
   Singnal Acc: bit_ vector (8 downto 0); -
   accumulatir
   alias M: bit is acc (0); - M is bit 0 of
   Acc
begin
   Process
   begin
        wait util CLK = '1' -executes on
        rising edge of clock
   case state is
        when 0 = ⇒-initial state
             if st=1' then
                  Acc (8 downto 4)⇐
                  "0000";-Begin cycle
                  Acc (3 downto 0)⇐
                  mplier; -load the
                  multiplier
        State ⇐ 1;
   end if;
when 1|3|5|7 ⇒ - "add/shift" state
   if M = '1' then - add multiplicand
   Acc (8 downto 4) ⇐   add 4 (7 downto
   4), Mcand, '0');
   state ⇐ state + 1;
else
   Acc ⇐ '0' & Acc (8 downto 1); -shift
   accumulator right state ⇐ state + 2;
   end if;
when 2|4|6|8 ⇒-"shift" State
   Acc ⇐'0' & Acc (8 downto 1); -Right
   Shift
   State ⇐ State +1;
```

```
when 9 ⇒ -End of cycle
    state ⇐ 0;
end Case;
    Done ⇐ '1' when state = 9 else '0';
end behavel;
If K = '1' then Nextstate ⇐ 3; -K
else Nextstate ⇐ 1;
end if;
When 3 ⇒ Done ⇐ '1'; -(stat3)
        Next state ⇐ 0;
end case;
end process;
process (CLK)
begin
if CLK = '1' then
State ⇐ Nextstate; -update State on rising
edge
end if;
end process;
end SMbehave;
```

As the state graph for the multiplier indicates, the control performs two functions generating add or shift signals as needed and counting the number of shifts. If the number of bits is large, it is convenient to divide the control network into a counter and an add-shift control, as shown in Figure below.

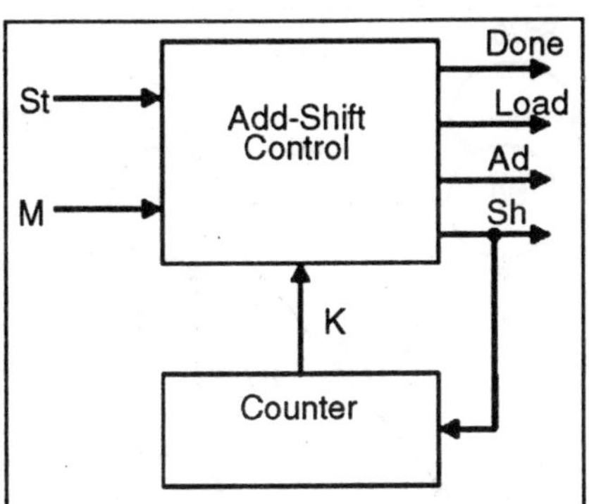

(a) Multiplier Control

First, we will derive a state graph for the add-shift control that tests St and M and outputs the proper sequence of add and shift signals below.

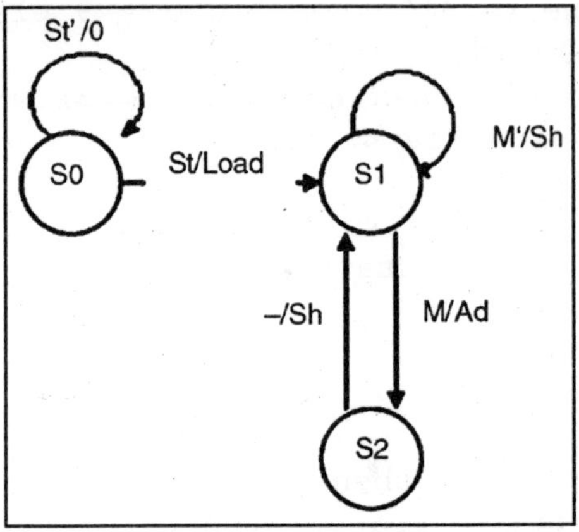

Then we will add a completion signal (K) from the counter that stops the multiplier after the proper number of shifts have been completed. Starting in S0 in Figure above, when a start signal St=1 is received, a load signal is generated and the network goes to state S_2; if M=0, a shift signal is generated and the network stays in S_1.

In S_2, a shift signal is generated since a shift always follows an add. The graph of Figure shown above will generate the proper sequence of add and shift signals, but it has no provision for stopping the multiplier.

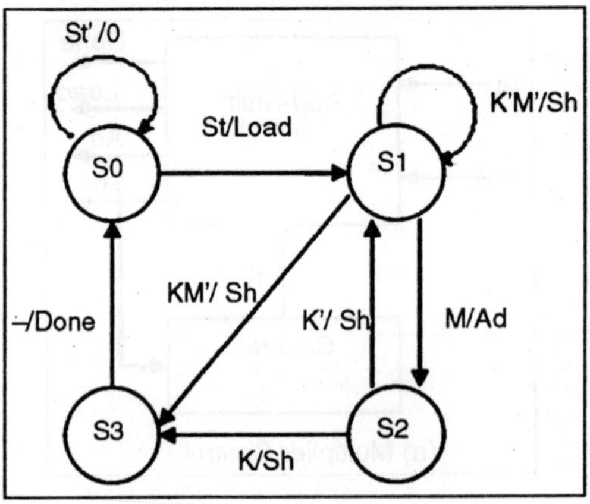

In order to determine when the multiplication is completed, the counter is incremented each time a shift signal is generated. If the multiplier is n bits, n shifts are required. We will design the counter so that a completion signal (K) is generated after n-1 shifts have occurred. When K=1, the network should perform one more addition id necessary and then do the final shift.

The control operation in above Figure (c) is the same as Figure 6(b) as long as K=0. In state S1, if K=1, we test M as usual. If M =0, we output the final shift signal and go to the done state (S3); however if M=1, we add before shifting and go to state S2. In state S2, if K=1, we output one more shift signal and then go to S3. The last shift signal will increment the counter to 0 at the same time the add-shift control goes to the done state. As an example, consider the multiplier of figure, but replace the control network with

Figure (a). Since n=4, a 2-bit counter is needed to count the 4 shifts, and K=1 when the counter is in state 3(112). Table below shows the operation of the multiplier when 1101 is multiplied by 1011. S0, S1, S2, and S3 represent states of the control circuit (Figure (c)).

Time	State	Counter	Product Register	St	M	K	Load	Ad	sh	Down
t_0	SO	00	000000000	0	0	0	0	0	0	0
t_1	SO	00	000000000	1	0	0	1	0	0	0
t_2	S1	00	000001011	0	1	0	0	1	0	0
t_3	S2	00	011011011	0	1	0	0	0	1	0
t_4	S1	01	001101101	0	1	0	0	0	1	0
t_5	S2	01	100111101	0	1	0	0	0	1	0
t_6	S1	10	010011110	0	0	0	0	0	1	0
t_7	S1	11	001001111	0	1	1	0	1	0	0
t_8	S2	11	100011111	0	1	1	0	0	1	0
t_9	S3	00	010001111	0	1	0	0	0	0	1

STATE MACHINE CHARTS

A state machine is a computational model based on automata theory. The state machine model is widely used to describe discrete systems, where the current behaviour is a function of previously occurring events.

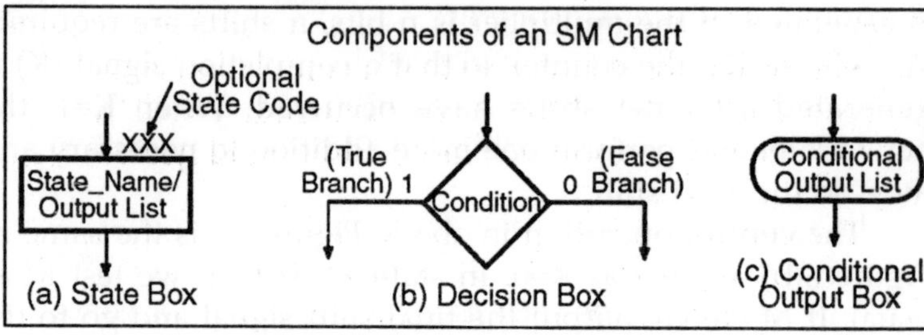

At a given point in time the system is in one of several possible states.

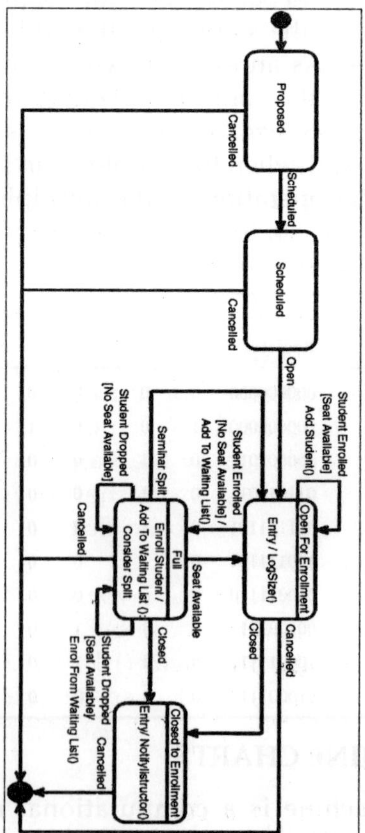

The system can change its state depending on input from the environment. As a state change occurs, actions can be performed on the environment.

The arrows in Figure represent transitions, progressions from one state to another. For example, when a seminar is in the Scheduled state, it can either be opened for enrollment or cancelled.

he notation for the labels on transitions is in the format event [guard][/method list]. It is mandatory to indicate the event which causes the transition, such as open or cancelled. Guard, conditions that must be true for the transition to be triggered, are optionally indicated.

The [not seat available] guard is shown on the student enrolled transition from the Open For Enrollment to the Closed To Enrollment state. Guards can be described in any manner, including both free form text or formal language - when I'm white boarding I'll use free form text to ensure that it's readable by everyone but with a sophisticated CASE tool I would consider using either a programming language such as Java or a modeling language such as Object Constraint Language (OCL) if the tool has the ability to actually process that information into something useful (such as executable code).

The invocation of methods, such as addToWaitingList() can optionally be indicated on transitions. The order in the listing implying the order in which they are invoked.

States are represented by the values of the attributes of an object. For example, a seminar is in the Open For Enrollment state when it has been flagged as open and seats are available to be filled.

It is possible to indicate the invocation of methods within a state, for example, upon entry into the Closed To Enrollment state the methodnotify Instructor() is invoked. The notation used within the same as that used on transitions, the only difference being that the method list is mandatory and the event is optional.

For example in the Full state the operations add to waiting list() and consider Split() are invoked whenever a student is enrolled. Had there been no event indicated those methods would be invoked continuously (in a loop) whenever the object is in that state.

I indicate the methods to run during the state when I want to indicate a method is to be run continuously, perhaps a method that polls other objects for information or a method that implements the logic of an important business process. Methods to be invoked when the object enters the state are indicated by the keyword entry, as you see with both the Open For Enrollment and Closed To Enrollment states in Figure.

Methods to be invoked as the object exits the state are indicated by the keyword exit. The capability to indicate method invocations when you enter and exit a state is useful because it enables you to avoid documenting the same method several times on each of the transitions that enter or exit the state, respectively.

Transitions are the result of the invocation of a method that causes an important change in state. Understanding that not all method invocations will result in transitions is important.

For example, the invocation of a getter method likely wouldn't cause a transition because it isn't changing the state of the object (unless lazy initialization is being applied). Furthermore, Figure indicates an attempt to enroll a student in a full seminar may not result in the object changing state, unless it is determined that the seminar should be split, even though the state of the object changes (another student is added to the waiting list).

You can see that transitions are a reflection of your business rules. For example, you see that you can attempt to enroll a student in a course only when it is open for enrollment or full, and that a seminar may be split (presumably into two seminars) when the waiting list is long enough to justify the split. You can have recursive transitions, also called self transitions, that start and end in the same state. An example of which is the student dropped transition when the seminar is full.

For the sake of convention, we say an object is always in

one and only one state, implying transitions are instantaneous. Although we know this is not completely true (every method is going to take some time to run), this makes life a lot easier for us to assume transitions take no time to complete.

Because the lifecycle of a seminar is so complex Figure 1 only depicts part of it. Figure 2 depicts the entire lifecycle, with Figure 1 shown as a substate of theEnrollment state. I could have included all of the details in Figure shown below but chose not to in order to keep the diagram simple. In fact, instead of creating a diagram such as Figure below

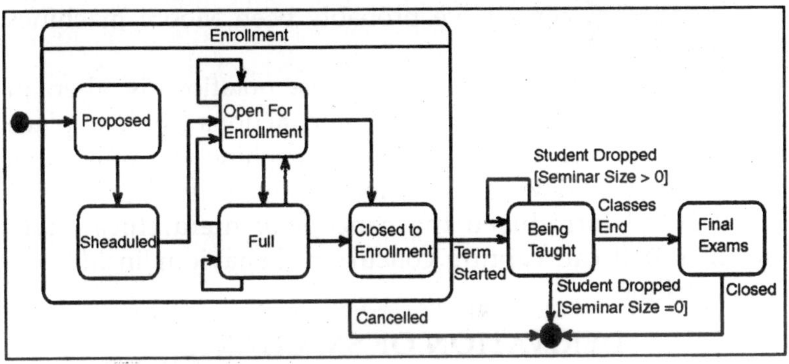

typically prefer something more along the lines of the high-level view of Figure as seen below.

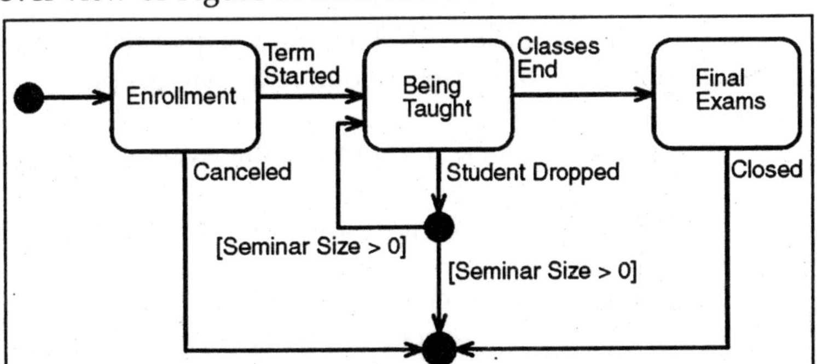

This approach keeps the diagrams small and easy to understand.

A state machine is generally defined by a set of:

States: A state embodies information about the current situation in the system.

- *Events*: An event is an input message to the state machine.
- *Transitions*: A transition is a change from one state to another, usually triggered by an event.
- *Actions*: An action is an activity to be performed by the state machine at a given point in time.
- A set of primitives to express guard conditions on transitions.

There are a number of different notations and semantics for state machines; the ones most widely used in the design of embedded systems have probably been Moore machines and Mealy machines.

The main difference between these notations is when an action can occur. In a Moore machine, actions can take place upon the entry of a state. A Mealy machine can only have actions associated with transitions between states. In 1987 David Harel introduced the concept of hierarchical state machines that can capture concurrent behaviour inside one state machine.

DERIVATION OF SM CHARTS

CONSTRUCTION OF SM CHARTS

The construction of an SM chart for a sequential control network is similar to that used to derive a state graph.

Steps are:

- First draw a block diagram of the system that we are controlling.
- Define the required input and output signals to the control network.
- Then construct the chart that tests the input signals and generates the proper sequence of output signals.

REALISATION OF SM CHARTS

The realization consists of a combinational sub network, together with Flip-flop storing the state of the network. As an example SM chart for binary multiplier is taken up. This SM chart is given in Fig shown below.

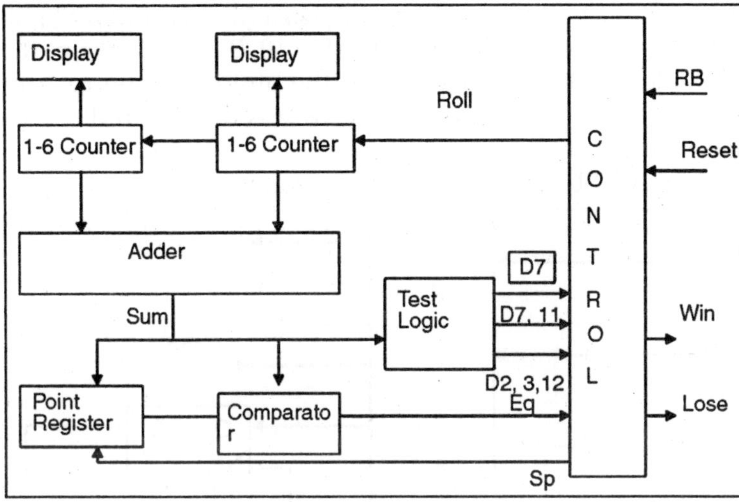

The controller for the multiplier can be realized using a PLA and D flip-flops. The controller chart has 4 states and you need 2 (2 = 4) D flip-flops. The PLA table is given as shown

	A	B	St	M	K	A+	B+	Load	Sh	Ad	Done
So	0	0	0	-	-	0	0	0	0	0	0
	0	0	1	-	-	0	1	1	0	0	0
	0	1	-	0	1	1	1	0	1	0	0
S1	0	1	-	0	1	1	1	0	1	0	0
	0	1	-	1	-	1	0	0	0	1	0
	1	0	-	-	0	0	1	0	1	0	0
S2	1	0	-	-	0	0	1	0	1	0	0
S3	1	1	-	-	-	0	0	0	0	0	1

In this the PLA has 5 inputs and 6 outputs. Each row in the table corresponds to one of the link paths in the SM chart. Since So has two exit paths the table has two rows for present state So. The first row corresponds to the St = 0 exit path. So the next state and output are 0. In the second row, St = 1, so the next state is a don't care in the corresponding rows. The outputs for each row can be filled in by tracing the corresponding link paths on the SM chart. For example, the link path from S1 to S2 passes through conditional output

Ad, so Ad = 1 in this row. Since S2 has a Moore output Sh, Sh = 1 in both of the rows for which AB = 10. By inspection of the PLA table, the logic equations for the multiplier control are:

A+ = A'BM'K + A'BM + AB'K; B+ = A'B'St + A'BM' + AB'; Load = A'B'St

Sh = A'B'St = AB'; Ad = A'BM'; Done = AB

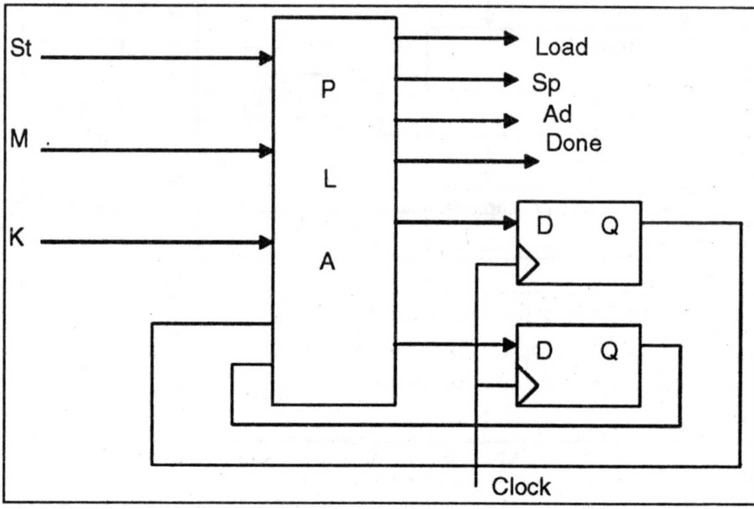

Fig. PLA Realization of Multiplier Control

IMPLEMENTATION OF DICE GAME

This is a game based on a dice, which will have 6 faces with numbers 1,2,3,4,5,6. In this game two dices will be thrown, and depending on the sum of the numbers seen on the faces of the dices, the result is decided. One can come out with many conditions to decide whether a player has won or not. The purpose of this example is to design a circuit that will simulate the above said idea.

Figure below shows the block diagram for the dice game and below shows the SM Chart of game. Two counters are used to simulate the ROLL of DICE. Each counter counts in the sequence 1,2,3,4,5,6,1,...Thus after the ROLL of the DICE the SUM of the values in the two counters will be in the range 2 through 12.

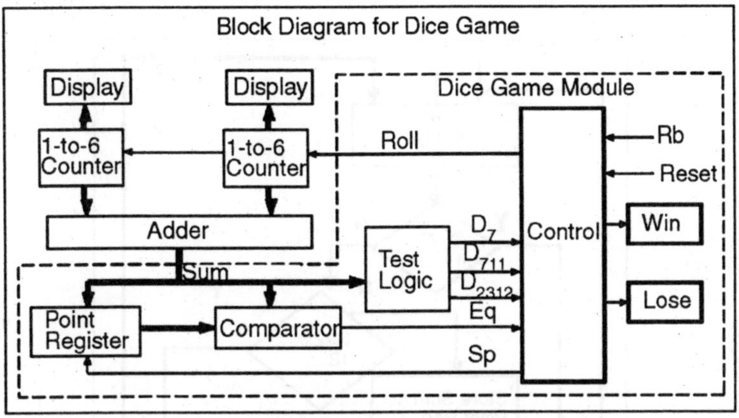
Block Diagram for Dice Game
Display
Display
Dice Game Module
1-to-6 Counter
1-to-6 Counter
Roll
Rb
Reset
Adder
Control
Win
Sum
Test Logic
D_7
D_{711}
D_{2312}
Eq
Lose
Point Register
Comparator
Sp

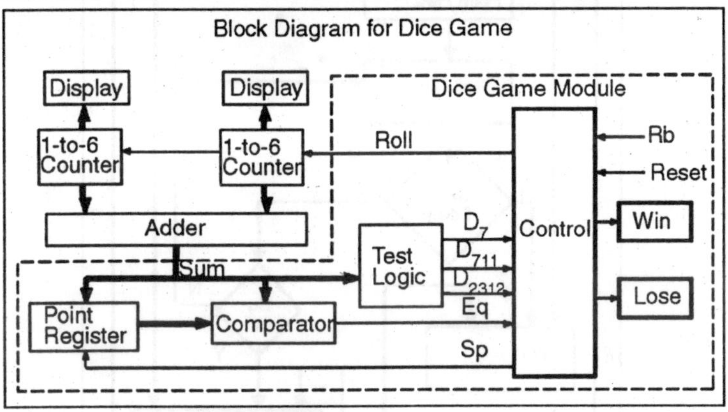
Block Diagram for Dice Game
Display
Display
Dice Game Module
1-to-6 Counter
1-to-6 Counter
Roll
Rb
Reset
Adder
Control
Win
Sum
Test Logic
D_7
D_{711}
D_{2312}
Eq
Lose
Point Register
Comparator
Sp

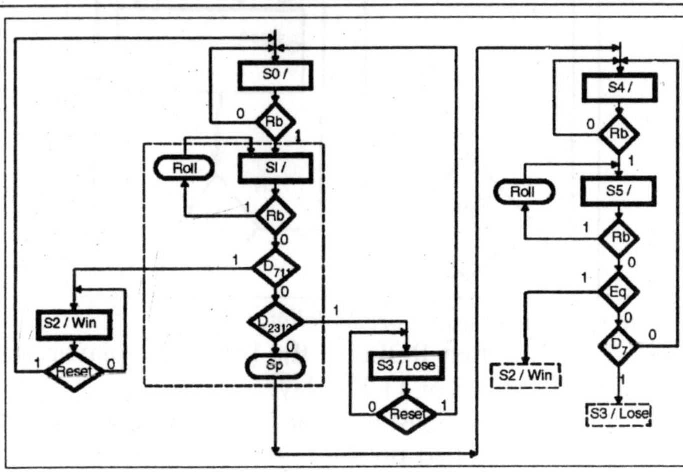
S0 /
Rb
Roll
SI /
Rb
D_{711}
D_{2312}
S2 / Win
Reset
Sp
S3 / Lose
Reset
S4 /
Rb
Roll
S5 /
Rb
Eq
D_7
S2 / Win
S3 / Lose

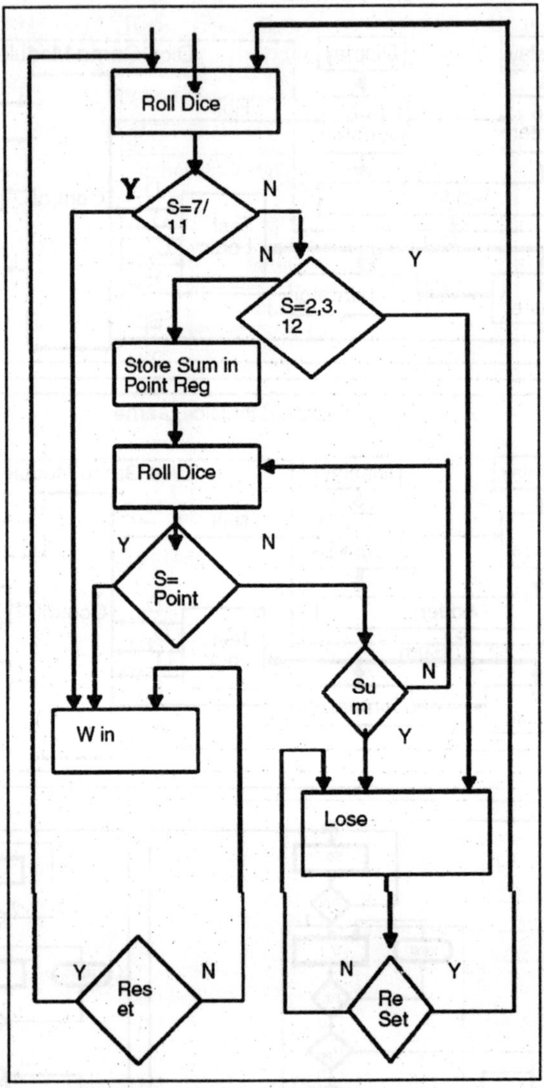

The rules of the game are as follows:

- After the first ROLL of the DICE, the player wins if the SUM is 7 or 11.Th player LOSES if the SUM is 2,3 or 12. Otherwise the SUM the player obtained on the first ROLL is referred to as a POINT, and the player must ROLL the DICE again.

- On the second or subsequent ROLL of the DICE, the player WINS if the SUM is 7.

Otherwise, the player must ROLL again until he or she finally WINS or LOSES or RESETS (starts a new game).

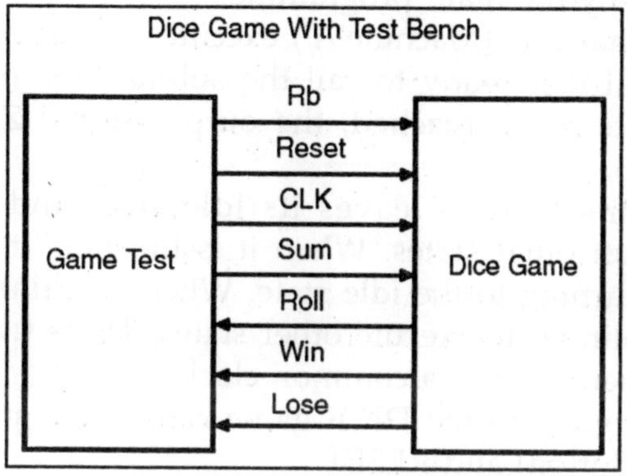

LINKED STATE MACHINE

When a sequential machine becomes large and complex, it is desirable to divide the machine up into several smaller machines that are linked together.

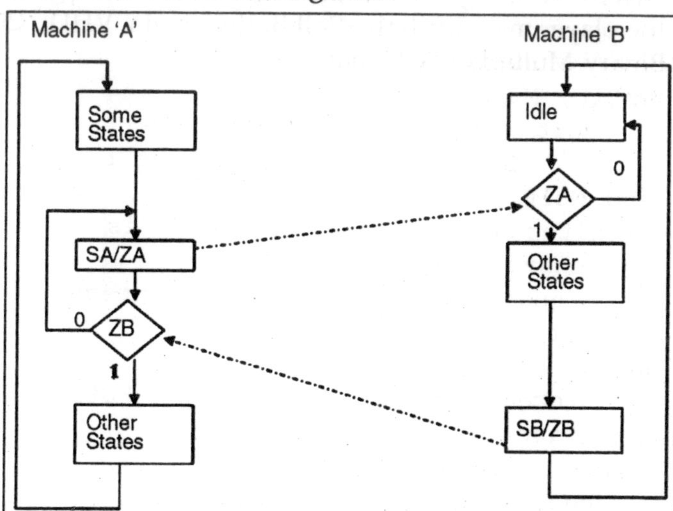

Fig. Above shows the SM Charts for two Serially Linked State machines.

Each of the smaller machines is easier to design and implement. Also, one of the submachines may be'called' in several different places by the main machine. This is analogous to dividing a large software programme into procedures that are called by the main programme.

The machine (Machine'A') executes a sequence of some states until it is ready to call the submachine (machine'B'). When state SA is reached, the output signal ZA activates machine B.

Machine B then leaves its idle state and executes a sequence of other states. When it is finished, it outputs ZB before returning to the idle state. When machine A receives ZB, it continues to execute other states. These two machines are assumed to have a common clock.

The inputs to the DICE game come from push buttons RB (Roll Button) and RESET.

RESET is used to initiate a new game. When the ROLL button is pushed, the DICE counters count at high speed. So the values cannot be read on the display. When the Roll

Button is released the values in the two counters are displayed and the game can proceed. If the WIN light is not on, the player must push the Roll Button again. VHDL CODE for Binary Multiplier SM Chart:

```
entity Multi is
   Port (CLK, St, K, M: in bit;)
        Load, sh. Ad, Done: out bit);
end Mult;
architecture SM behave of Mult is
SM behave of Mult is
   Signal state, Next State: integer range
   0 to 3;
begin
   process (St, K, M, State)   -Start if
   state or
inputs change
   begin
        Load ⇒ '0'; Sh ⇐ '0'; Ad ⇐ '0';
case State is
```

```
    when 0 ⇒ if St = '1' then -St (state 0)
  Load ⇐ '1';
  Nextstate ⇐ '1' then -M (state 1)
  Ad ⇐ '1'
  Next State ⇐ 2;
  else
  Sh ⇐ '1'
  if K = '1' then Nextstate ⇐ 3; -K
  else Next state ⇐ 1
  end if;
  end if;
  When 2 ⇒ Sh ⇐ '1' (-state 2)
```

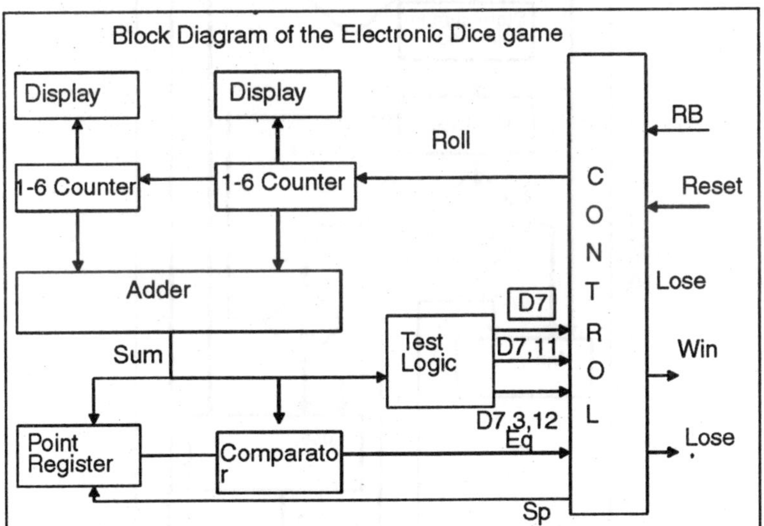

FLOW CHART FOR DICE GAME

It is given in fig. that after rolling the dice, the sum is tested If it is 7 or 11, the player wins, if it is 2,3 or 12 the player loses. Otherwise the sum is saved in the point register, and the player wins. If it is 7, he or she loses. Otherwise the player rolls again. After winning or giving it up the player must push reset button again to begin a new game.

The components of the dice game are: Adder-ads the output of two counters.

Register-stores the POINT Test Logic- determines the condition for a WIN or LOSE Control Network- Controls the dice game

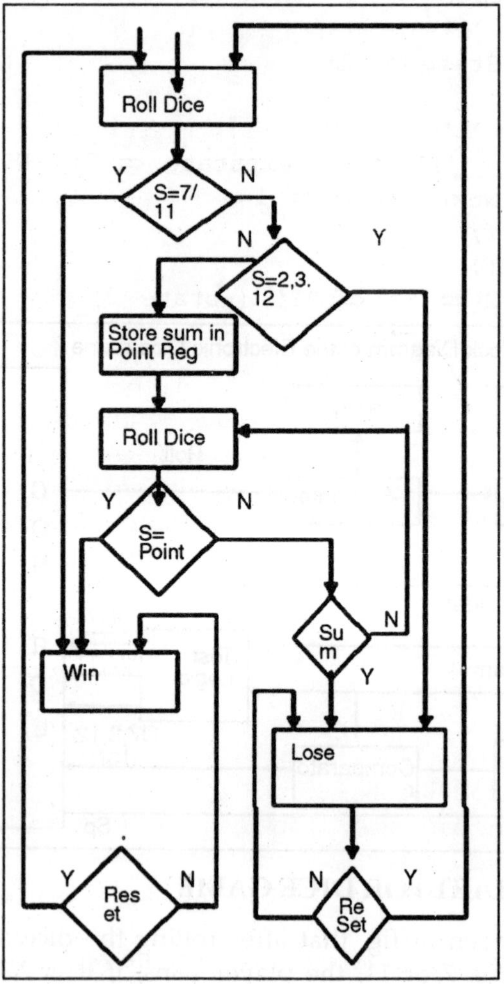

Chapter 9

Memory Models and Design

STATIC RAM

INTRODUCTION

Static RAM is a type of RAM that holds its data without external refresh, for as long as power is supplied to the circuit. This is contrasted to dynamic RAM (DRAM), which must be refreshed many times per second in order to hold its data contents. SRAMs are used for specific applications within the PC, where their strengths outweigh their weaknesses compared to DRAM:

- *Simplicity*: Srams don't require external refresh circuitry or other work in order for them to keep their data intact.
- *Speed*: SRAM is faster than DRAM.

In contrast, SRAMs have the following weaknesses, compared to DRAMs:

In contrast, SRAMs have the following weaknesses, compared to DRAMs:

- *Cost*: Sram is, byte for byte, several times more expensive than DRAM.
- *Size*: Srams take up much more space than DRAMs (which is part of why the cost is higher).

These advantages and disadvantages taken together obviously show that performance-wise, SRAM is superior to DRAM, and we would use it exclusively if only we could do so economically.

Unfortunately, 32 MB of SRAM would be prohibitively

large and costly, which is why DRAM is used for system memory. SRAMs are used instead for level 1 cache and level 2 cache memory, for which it is perfectly suited; cache memory needs to be very fast, and not very large.

SRAM is manufactured in a way rather similar to how processors are: highly-integrated transistor patterns photo-etched into silicon.

Each SRAM bit is comprised of between four and six transistors, which is why SRAM takes up much more space compared to DRAM, which uses only one (plus a capacitor). Because an SRAM chip is comprised of thousands or millions of identical cells, it is much easier to make than a CPU, which is a large die with a non-repetitive structure. This is one reason why RAM chips cost much less than processors do.

DESIGN

Each bit in an SRAM is stored on four transistors that form two cross-coupled inverters. This storage cell has two stable states which are used to denote 0 and 1. Two additional access transistors serve to control the access to a storage cell during read and write operations.

A typical SRAM uses six MOSFETs to store each memory bit. In addition to such 6T SRAM, other kinds of SRAM chips use 8T, 10T, or more transistors per bit.

This is sometimes used to implement more than one (read and/or write) port, which may be useful in certain types of video memory and register files implemented with multi ported SRAM circuitry.

Generally, the fewer transistors needed per cell, the smaller each cell can be. Since the cost of processing a silicon wafer is relatively fixed, using smaller cells and so packing more bits on one wafer reduces the cost per bit of memory. Memory cells that use fewer than 6 transistors are possible - but such 3T or 1T cells are DRAM, not SRAM (even the so-called 1T-SRAM).

Access to the cell is enabled by the word line (WL in figure) which controls the two access transistors M5 and M6 which, in turn, control whether the cell should be connected to the bit lines: BL and BL. They are used to transfer data for both read and write operations. Although it is not strictly necessary to have two bit lines, both the signal and its inverse are typically provided in order to improve noise margins.

During read accesses, the bit lines are actively driven high and low by the inverters in the SRAM cell. This improves SRAM bandwidth compared to DRAMs-in a DRAM, the bit line is connected to storage capacitors and charge sharing causes the bitline to swing upwards or downwards. The symmetric structure of SRAMs also allows for differential signalling, which makes small voltage swings more easily detectable.

Another difference with DRAM that contributes to making SRAM faster is that commercial chips accept all address bits at a time. By comparison, commodity DRAMs have the address multiplexed in two halves, i.e. higher bits followed by lower bits, over the same package pins in order to keep their size and cost down.

OPERATION

An SRAM cell has three different states it can be in: *standby* where the circuit is idle, *reading* when the data has been requested and *writing* when updating the contents. The three different states work as follows:

Standby

If the word line is not asserted, the *access* transistors M_5 and M_6 disconnect the cell from the bit lines. The two cross coupled inverters formed by M_1 – M_4 will continue to reinforce each other as long as they are connected to the supply.

Reading

Assume that the content of the memory is a 1, stored at Q. The read cycle is started by precharging both the bit lines to a logical 1, then asserting the word line WL, enabling both the *access* transistors. The second step occurs when the values stored in Q and Q are transferred to the bit lines by leaving

BL at its precharged value and discharging BL through M_1 and M_5 to a logical 0. On the BL side, the transistors M_4 and M_6 pull the bit line toward V_{DD}, a logical 1. If the content of the memory were a 0, the opposite would happen and BL would be pulled toward 1 and BL toward 0.

Writing

The start of a write cycle begins by applying the value to be written to the bit lines. If we wish to write a 0, we would apply a 0 to the bit lines, i.e. setting BL to 1 and BL to 0. This is similar to applying a reset pulse to a SR-latch, which causes the flip flop to change state.

A 1 is written by inverting the values of the bit lines. WL is then asserted and the value that is to be stored is latched in. Note that the reason this works is that the bit line input-drivers are designed to be much stronger than the relatively weak transistors in the cell itself, so that they can easily override the previous state of the cross-coupled inverters. Careful sizing of the transistors in an SRAM cell is needed to ensure proper operation.

Bus Behaviour

A RAM memory with an access time of 70 ns will output valid data within 70 ns from the time that the address lines are valid.

But the data will remain for a hold time as well (5-10 ns). Rise and fall times also influence valid timeslots with approximately ~5 ns. By reading the lower part of an address range bits in sequence (page cycle) one can read with significantly shorter access time (30 ns).

CLOCK RATE AND POWER

The power consumption of SRAM varies widely depending on how frequently it is accessed; it can be as power-hungry as dynamic RAM, when used at high frequencies, and some ICs can consume many watts at full bandwidth.

On the other hand, static RAM used at a somewhat

slower pace, such as in applications with moderately clocked microprocessors, draw very little power and can have a nearly negligible power consumption when sitting idle — in the region of a few micro-watts.

Static RAM exists primarily as:

- General purpose products
  - With *asynchronous* interface, such as the 28 pin 32Kx8 chips (usually named XXC256), and similar products up to 16 Mbit per chip
  - With *synchronous* interface, usually used for caches and other applications requiring burst transfers, up to 18 Mbit (256Kx72) per chip
- Integrated on chip
  - As RAM or cache memory in micro-controllers (usually from around 32 bytes up to 128 kilobytes)
  - As the primary caches in powerful microprocessors, such as the x86 family, and many others (from 8 kB, up to several megabytes)
  - To store the registers and parts of the state-machines used in some microprocessors
  - On application specific ICs, or ASICs (usually In the order of kilobytes)
  - In FPGAs and CPLDs (usually in the order of a few kilobytes or less)

Embedded Use

Many categories of industrial and scientific subsystems, automotive electronics, and similar, contains static RAM. Some amounts (kilobytes or less) is also embedded in practically all modern appliances, toys, etc that implements an electronic user interface. Several megabytes may be used in complex products such as digital cameras, cell phones, synthesizers, etc.

In Computers

SRAM is also used in personal computers, workstations, routers and peripheral equipment: internal CPU caches and external burst mode SRAM caches, hard disk buffers, router buffers, etc. LCD screens and printers also normally employ static RAM to hold the image displayed (or to be printed). Small SRAM buffers are also found in CDROM and CDRW drives; usually 256 kB or more are used to buffer track data, which is transferred in blocks instead of as single values. The same applies to cable modems and similar equipment connected to computers.

Hobbyists

Hobbyists often prefer SRAM due to the ease of interfacing. It is much easier to work with than DRAM as there are no refresh cycles and the address and data buses are directly accessible rather than multiplexed. In addition to buses and power connections, SRAM usually require only three controls: Chip Enable (CE), Write Enable (WE) and Output Enable (OE). In synchronous SRAM, Clock (CLK) is also included.

SRAM Memory Interface to Microcontroller

Introduction

Static random access memory (SRAM) is a type of volatile semiconductor memory to store binary logic '1' and '0' bits. SRAM uses bistable latching circuitry made of Transistors/ MOSFETS to store each bit. Compared to Dynamic RAM (DRAM), SRAM does't have a capacitor to store the data, hence SRAM works without refreshing. In SRAM the data is lost when the memory is not electrically powered.

SRAM is faster and more reliable than the more common DRAM . While DRAM supports access times (access time is the time required to read or write data to/from memory) of about 60 nanoseconds, SRAM can give access times as low as 10 nanoseconds. In addition, its cycle time is much shorter than that of DRAM because it does not need to pause between accesses. Unfortunately, it is also much more expensive to produce than DRAM. Due to its high cost, SRAM is often used only as a memory cache.

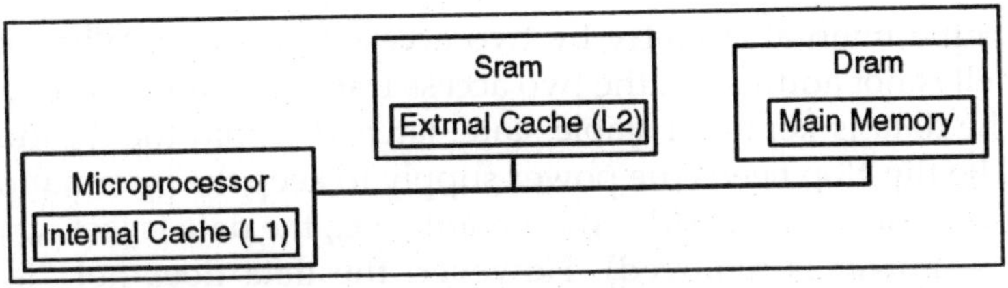

Fig. Typical Microprocessor Memory Configuration

SRAM is generally used for high-speed registers, caches and relatively small memory banks such as a frame buffer on a display adapter. In contrast, the main memory in a computer is typically dynamic RAM (DRAM, D-RAM).

An SRAM is designed to fill two needs: to provide a direct interface with the CPU at speeds not attainable by DRAMs and to replace DRAMs in systems that require very low power consumption. In the first role, the SRAM serves as cache memory, interfacing between DRAMs and the CPU.

The second driving force for SRAM technology is low power applications. In this case, SRAMs are used in most portable equipment because the DRAM refresh current is several orders of magnitude more than the low-power SRAM standby current. Many categories of industrial and scientific subsystems, automotive electronics, and similar, contains static RAM. Several megabytes of SRAM may be used in complex products such as digital cameras, cell phones, synthesizers, etc.

SRAM is also used in personal computers, workstations, routers and peripheral equipment: internal CPU caches and external burst mode SRAM caches, hard disk buffers, router buffers, etc. LCD screens and printers also normally employ SRAM to hold the image displayed or to be printed. Small SRAM buffers are also found in CDROM and CDRW drives to buffer track data, which is transferred in blocks instead of as single values. The same applies to cable modems and similar equipment connected to computers.

SRAM Cell

The SRAM cell consists of a bi-stable flip-flop connected

to the internal circuitry by two access transistors. When the cell is not addressed, the two access transistors are closed and the data is kept to a stable state, latched within the flip-flop. The flip-flop needs the power supply to keep the information. The data in an SRAM cell is volatile (i.e., the data is lost when the power is removed). However, the data does not "leak away" like in a DRAM, so the SRAM does not require a refresh cycle.

Static RAM is fast because the six-transistor configuration (shown in Fig 2) of its flip-flop circuits keeps current flowing in one direction or the other (0 or 1). The 0 or 1 state can be written and read instantly without waiting for a capacitor to fill up or drain (like in DRAM). However, the six transistors take more space than DRAM cells made of one transistor and one capacitor.When opposite voltages are applied to the column wires, the flip-flop is oriented in one of two directions for a 0 or 1. At that point, the flip-flop becomes a self-perpetuating storage cell as long as a constant voltage is applied.

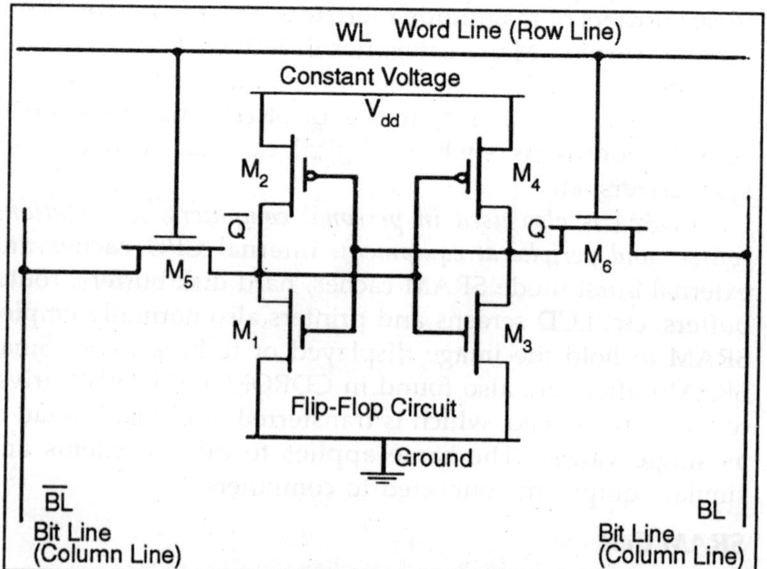

Fig. A Six-transistor CMOS SRAM cell

Random access means that locations in the memory can be written to or read from in any order, regardless of the memory location that was last accessed.

Earlier asynchronous static RAM chips performed read and write operations sequentially. Newer synchronous static RAM chips overlap reads and writes. Contrast with dynamic RAM.

SRAM Cells

The SRAM cells are categorized based on the type of load used in the elementary inverter of the flip-flop cell.

There are commonly three types of SRAM memory cells:

- 4T cell (four NMOS transistors plus two poly load resistors)
- 6T cell (six transistors-four NMOS transistors plus two PMOS transistors)
- TFT cell (four NMOS transistors plus two loads called TFTs)

4T (Four Transistor) Cell

This design consists of four NMOS transistors plus two poly-load resistors. Two NMOS transistors are pass-transistors.

These transistors have their gates tied to the word line and connect the cell to the columns. The two other NMOS transistors are the pull-downs of the flip-flop inverters. The loads of the inverters consist of a very high poly-silicon resistor.

The cell needs room only for the four NMOS transistors. The poly loads are stacked above these transistors.

Although the 4T SRAM cell may be smaller than the 6T cell, it is still about four times as large as the cell of a DRAM cell.

The complexity of the 4T cell is to make a resistor load high enough (in the range of giga-ohms) to minimize the current. However, this resistor must not be too high to guarantee good functionality. Despite its size advantage, the 4T cells have several limitations

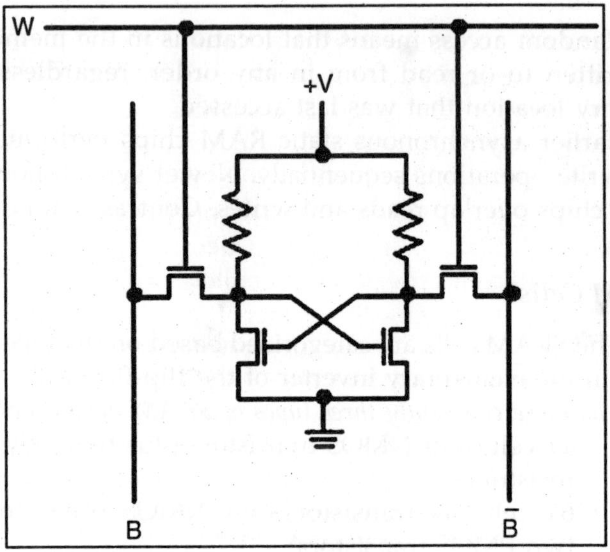

Fig. Transistor: Sram Cell

- Each cell has current flowing in one resistor. (i.e., the SRAM has a high standby current)
- The cell is sensitive to noise and soft error because the resistance is so high
- The cell is not as fast as the 6T cell.

6T (Six Transistor) Cell

A different cell design that eliminates the above limitations is the use of a CMOS flip-flop. In this case, the load is replaced by a PMOS transistor. This SRAM cell is composed of six transistors, one NMOS transistor and one PMOS transistor for each inverter, plus two NMOS transistors connected to the row line (as shown in fig 2). This configuration is called a 6T Cell. This cell offers better electrical performances (speed, noise immunity, standby current) than a 4T structure.

TFT (Thin Film Transistor) Cell

This new structure reduces the current flow through the resistor load of the old 4T cell. This change in electrical characteristics of the resistor load is done by controlling the channel of a transistor.

This resistor is configured as a PMOS transistor and is called a thin film transistor (TFT). It is formed by depositing several layers of polysilicon above the silicon surface. The source/channel/ drain is formed in the polysilicon load. The gate of this TFT is polysilicon and is tied to the gate of the opposite inverter as in the 6T cell architecture.

The oxide between this control gate and the TFT polysilicon channel must be thin enough to ensure the effectiveness of the transistor. The performance of the TFT PMOS transistor is not as good as a standard PMOS silicon transistor used in a 6T cell.

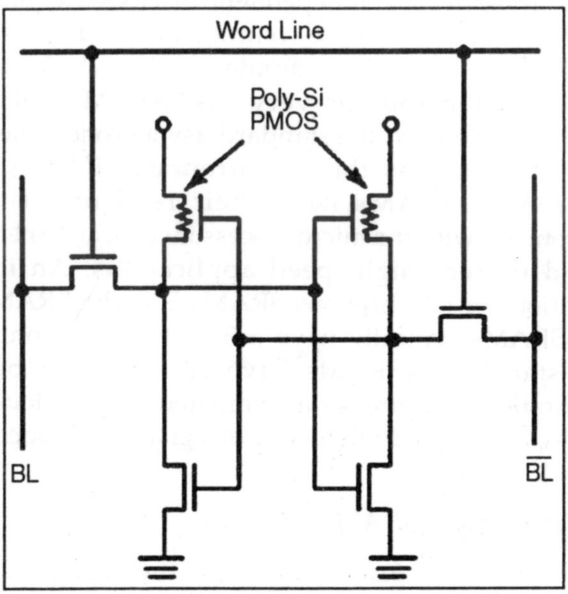

Fig. Thin Film Transistor (TFT) SRAM cell

This type of cell posses' complex technology compared to the 4T cell technology and poor TFT electrical characteristics compared to a PMOS transistor. In addition to such SRAM types, other kinds of SRAM chips use 8T, 10T, or more transistors per bit. This is sometimes used to implement more than one (read and/or write) port, which may be useful in certain types of video memory and register files implemented with multi ported SRAM circuitry. Memory cells that use fewer than 6 transistors such as 3T or 1T cells are DRAM, not SRAM.

Classification of SRAM by Transistor Type

- Bipolar junction transistor (used in TTL and ECL): very fast but consumes a lot of power
- MOSFET (used in CMOS): low power and very common today

Classification of SRAM by Function:

- *Asynchronous*: independent of clock frequency; data in and data out are controlled by address transition.
- *Synchronous*: As computer system clocks increased, the demand for very fast SRAMs necessitated variations on the standard asynchronous fast SRAM.

The result was the Synchronous SRAM (SSRAM). Synchronous SRAMs have their read or write cycles synchronized with the microprocessor clock and therefore can be used in very high-speed applications. An important application for synchronous SRAMs is cache SRAM used in PCs. SSRAMs typically have a 32 bit output configuration while standard ASRAMs have typically a 8 bit output configuration. All timings are initiated by the clock edge(s). Address, data in and other control signals are associated with the clock signals.

Classification of SRAM by feature

- *ZBT (zero bus turnaround)*: the turnaround is the number of clock cycles it takes to change access to the SRAM from write to read and vice versa. The turnaround for ZBT SRAMs or the latency between read and writes cycle is zero. In short the ZBT is designed to eliminate dead cycles when turning the bus around between read and writes and reads.
- *Sync-Burst (synchronous-burst SRAM)*: features

synchronous burst write access to the SRAM to increase write operation to the SRAM.

- *DDR SRAM*: Synchronous, single read/write port, double data rate IO. It increases the performance of the device by transferring data on both edges of the clock.
- *Quad Data Rate SRAM*: Synchronous, separate read & write ports, double data rate IO
- *Pipelined SRAM*: They (also called register to register mode SRAM) add a register between the memory array and the output. Pipelined SRAMs are less expensive than standard ASRAMs for equivalent electrical performance. The pipelined design does not require the aggressive manufacturing process of a standard ASRAM.
- *Late-Write SRAM*: Late-write SRAM requires the input data only at the end of the cycle.

SRAM-Cell Operation

Each bit in an SRAM is stored on four transistors that form two cross-coupled inverters (as shown in Fig 2). This storage cell has two stable states, which are used to denote 0 and 1. Two additional access transistors serve to control the access to a storage cell during read and write operations. A typical SRAM uses six MOSFETs to store each memory bit and the explanation here is based on the same.

Access to the cell is enabled by the word line which controls the two access transistors M5 and M6 which, in turn, control whether the cell should be connected to the bit lines: -BL and BL. They are used to transfer data for both read and write operations. Although it is not strictly necessary to have two bit lines, both the signal and its inverse are typically provided to improve noise margins.

During read accesses, the bit lines are actively driven high and low by the inverters in the SRAM cell. This improves SRAM bandwidth compared to DRAMs. In a DRAM, the bit line is connected to storage capacitors and charge sharing causes the bit-line to swing upwards or downwards. The symmetric structure of SRAMs also allows for differential signaling, which makes small voltage swings more easily detectable. Another difference with DRAM that contributes to making SRAM faster is that commercial chips accept all address bits at a time. By comparison, commodity DRAMs have the address multiplexed in two halves, i.e. higher bits followed by lower bits.

An SRAM cell has three different states it can be in:

- Standby where the circuit is idle
- Reading when the data has been requested
- Writing when updating the contents

Standby: If the word line is not asserted, the access transistors M5 and M6 disconnect the cell from the bit lines. The two cross-coupled inverters formed by M1 - M4 will continue to reinforce each other as long as they are disconnected from the outside world.

Read operation: Assume that the content of the memory is a 1, stored at Q. The read cycle is started by pre-charging both the bit lines to a logical 1, then asserting the word line WL, enabling both the access transistors. The second step occurs when the values stored in Q and -Q are transferred to the bit lines by leaving BL at its pre-charged value and discharging -BL through M1 and M5 to a logical 0. On the BL side, the transistors M4 and M6 pull the bit line toward VDD, a logical 1. If the content of the memory was a 0, the opposite would happen and -BL would be pulled toward 1 and BL toward 0.

Write operation: The value to be written is applied to the bit-lines to start the writing operation. To write a 0, we would apply a 0 to the bit lines, i.e. setting -BL to 1 and BL to 0. This is similar to applying a reset pulse to a SR-latch, which causes the flip-flop to change state. A 1 is written by inverting the values of the bit lines. WL is then asserted and the value that is to be stored is latched in. Note that the reason this works is that the bit line input-drivers are designed to be much stronger than the relatively weak transistors in the cell itself, so that they can easily override the previous state of the cross-coupled inverters. Careful sizing of the transistors in an SRAM cell is needed to ensure proper operation. To work properly and to ensure that the data in the cell will not be altered, the SRAM must be supplied by a Vdd (power supply) that will not fluctuate beyond plus or minus five or ten per cent of the main VCC. If the cell is not disturbed, a lower voltage level is acceptable to ensure that the cell will correctly keep the data. In that case, the SRAM is set to a retention mode where the power supply is lowered, and the part is no longer accessible. The power consumption of SRAM varies depending on how frequently it is accessed; it can be as power-hungry as dynamic RAM, when used at high frequencies. On the other hand, SRAM used at a somewhat slower pace, such as in applications with moderately clocked microprocessors, draw very little power and can have nearly negligible power consumption when sitting idle.

SRAM Interface

Basic Connection

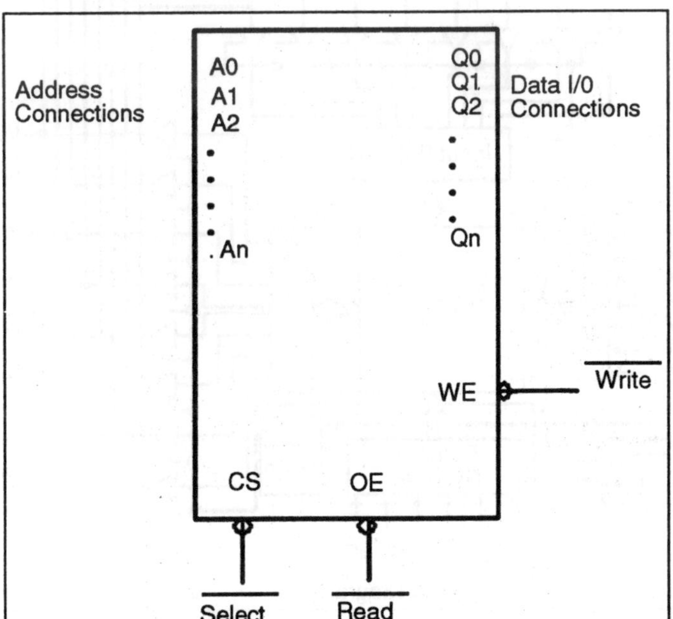

Fig. Basic Memory Component Connections

The pin connections common to all type of memory devices (including SRAM) are the address inputs, data I/O, some type of selection input and at least one control input used to select a read or write operation.

The address inputs are used to connect or select a memory location within the memory device. The memory device that has 10 address lines will be having its address pins labeled from A0 (Least Significant) to A9. The number of memory address pins found on a memory device is determined by the number of memory locations found within it. The data I/O connections are the points at which the data are entered for storage or extracted for reading. Today the memory devices are equipped with bi-directional common data I/O lines.

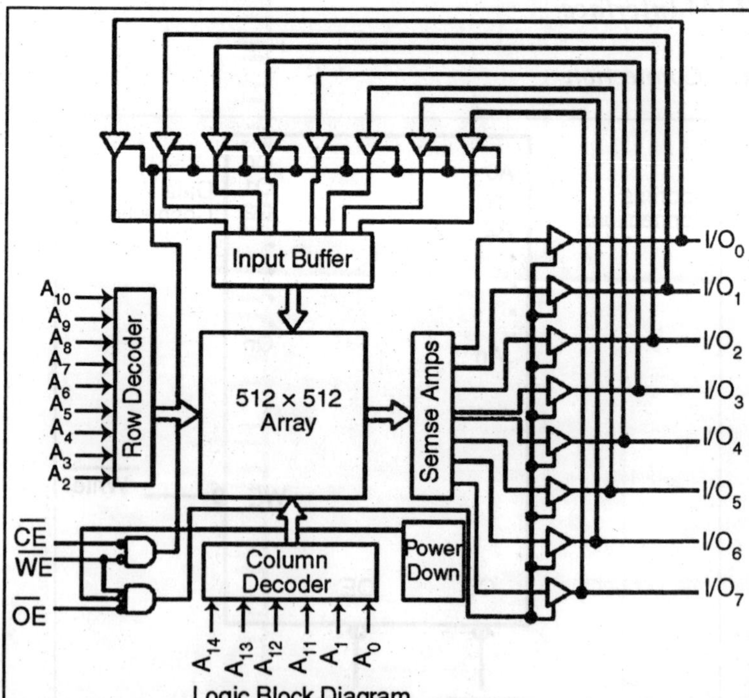

Logic Block Diagram

The SRAM has an input that selects or enables the memory device, called chip select (CS). If this pin is active (a logic 0 applied at this pin) the memory device performs a read or a write operation. The other two control inputs associated with SRAM are Write Enable (WE) and Output (also called read enable) Enable (OE).

Sometimes the (WE) is labeled as (W) and the (OE) is labeled as (G). The write enable pin must be made active (applying logic 0) to perform a memory write operation and the (OE) must be active to perform a read operation from the memory. But they must never both be active at the same time. Fig Above shows a typical functional block diagram and a typical pin configuration of an asynchronous SRAM (from cypress).

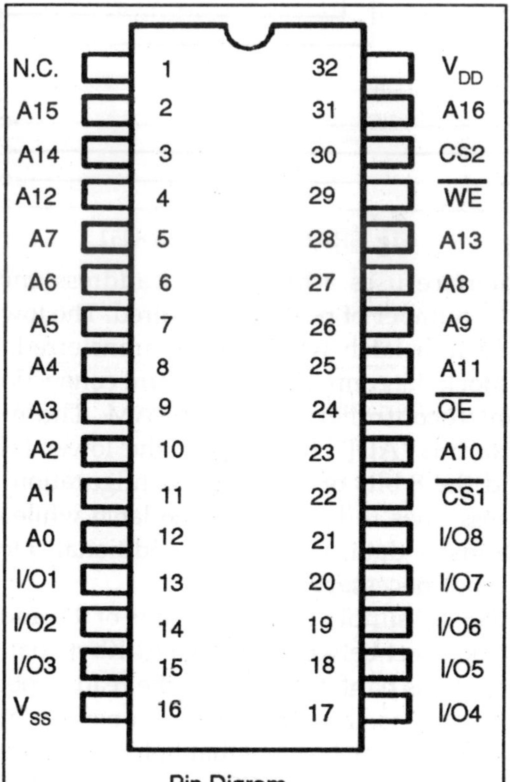

Pin Digram

Fig. Asynchronous SRAM- Logical & Pin Diagrams

Interfacing SRAM with 8051

Let us now try to understand how to Interface/interconnect an external static RAM (SRAM) to an 8051 microcontroller. It shows how to interface a generic SRAM to a C8051 device using standard GPIO port pins.

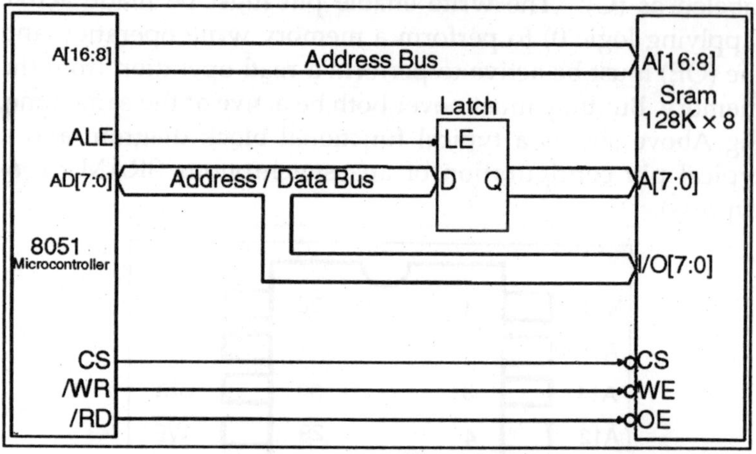

Fig. SRAM Interface to 8051

The interface uses a multiplexed address and data bus to reduce the number of port pins required. The lower address bits are held in a latch while data is transferred. Fig above shows the block diagram of the hardware connection between the 8051 microcontroller and the SRAM. The multiplexed address/data bus 'AD[7..0]' support the lower 8 bits of the address and the 8 bits of data. This configuration allows the lower address lines to be held by the latch while the SRAM and 8051 transfer data, such that 8 additional ports for data transfer are not necessary.

The 'A[15..8]' supply the upper 8 bits of the address. 'A16' acts as a bank select between the two 64 Kbyte banks. A '0' is bank one and '1' is bank two. 'RD' is the read strobe (operates active low). 'WR' is the write strobe (operates active low). 'ALE' is the address latch signal that holds the lower 8 address bits during data transfer. 'CS' is the SRAM chip select (operates active low). The following figures show the timing diagrams for a typical read and write operation.

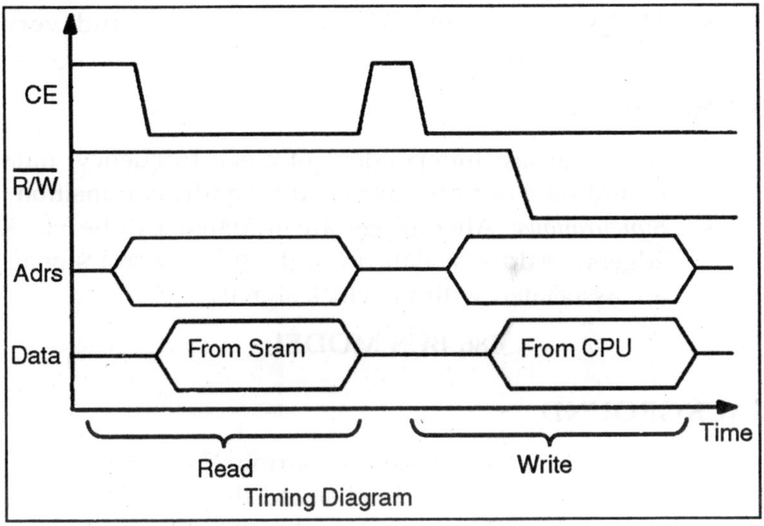

Fig. Start of Frame Packet Format

TYPES OF SRAM

Non Volatile SRAM

Non-volatile SRAMs have standard SRAM functionality, but they save the data when the power supply is lost, ensuring preservation of critical information. nvSRAMs are used in a wide range of situations — networking, aerospace,. and medical, among many others — where the preservation of data is critical and where batteries are impractical.

Asynchronous SRAM

Asynchronous SRAM are available from 4 Kb to 32 Mb. The fast access time of asynchronous SRAM makes it appropriate for networking equipment. They are used in various applications like switches and routers, IP-Phones, IC-Testers, DSLAM Cards, to Automotive Electronics.

By Transistor Type

- *Bipolar junction transistor (used in TTL and ECL)*: Very fast but consumes a lot of power

- *MOSFET (used in CMOS)*: Low power and very common today

By Function

- *Asynchronous*: Independent of clock frequency; data in and data out are controlled by address transition
- *Synchronous*: All timings are initiated by the clock edge(s). Address, data in and other control signals are associated with the clock signals

486 BUS MODEL

BACKGROUND

The 80486 was announced at Spring Comdex in April 1989. At the announcement, Intel stated that samples would be available in the third quarter of 1989 and production quantities would ship in the fourth quarter of 1989. The first 80486-based PCs were announced in late 1989, but some advised that people wait until 1990 to purchase an 80486 PC because there were early reports of bugs and software incompatibilities.

The instruction set of the i486 is very similar to its predecessor, the Intel 80386, with the addition of only a few extra instructions, such as CMPXCHG which executes the Compare-and-swap atomic operation and the XADD which executes the Fetch-and-add atomic operation.

Though many atomic test-and-set instructions have existed since the 8086/8088, they did not correspond to the atomic instructions implemented in certain RISC processors, which made it harder to port some applications from these processors.

From a performance point of view, the architecture of the i486 is a vast improvement over the 80386. It has an on-chip unified instruction and data cache, an on-chip floating-point unit (FPU), except in the SX and SL models, and an enhanced bus interface unit. Simple instructions (such as ALU reg, reg) execute in one clock cycle.

These improvements yield a rough doubling in ALU

performance over the 386 at the same clock rate. A 16-MHz 486 therefore has a performance similar to a 33–MHz 386 (or 286), and the older design has to reach 50 MHz to be comparable with a 25–MHz 486 part.

486 compatible processors have been produced by other companies such as IBM, Texas Instruments, AMD, Cyrix, UMC, and SGS Thompson. Some were clones (identical at the microarchitectural level), others were clean-room implementations of the Intel instruction-set. (IBM's multiple source requirement is one of the reasons behind its x86-manufacturing since the 80286.)

The 486 was, however, covered by many of Intel's patents covering new R&D as well as that of the prior 80386. Intel and IBM have broad cross-licenses of these patents, and AMD was granted rights to the relevant patents in the 1995 settlement of a lawsuit between the companies.

AMD produced several clones of the 486 using a 40 MHz bus (486DX–40, 486DX/2–80, and 486DX/4–120) which had no equivalent available from Intel, as well as a part specified for 90 MHz, using a 30 MHz external clock, that was sold only to OEMs.

The fastest running 486 CPU, the Am5x86, ran at 133 MHz and was released by AMD in 1995. 150 MHz and 160 MHz parts were planned but never officially released.

Cyrix made a variety of 486-compatible processors, positioned at the cost-sensitive desktop and low-power (laptop) markets. Unlike AMD's 486 clones, the Cyrix processors were the result of clean-room reverse-engineering. Cyrix's early offerings included the 486DLC and 486SLC, two hybrid chips which plugged into 386DX or SX sockets respectively, and offered 1 KB of cache (versus 8 KB for the then-current Intel/AMD parts).

Cyrix also made "real" 486 processors, which plugged into the i486's socket and offered 2 or 8 KB of cache. Clock-for-clock, the Cyrix-made chips were generally slower than their Intel/AMD equivalents, though later products with 8 KB caches were more competitive, if not late to market.

The Motorola 68040 (best known for its use in the

Macintosh Quadra series), while not compatible with the 486, was often positioned as the 486's equivalent in features and performance.

While the 68040 outperformed the 486 significantly on a clock for clock basis, the 486 had the ability to be clocked significantly faster and it did not suffer from overheating problems.

Until May 1994, Apple did not have any 68040-powered PowerBooks; prior to that, even Macworld reviewers conceded that the best choice for power users was the PC compatible Texas Instruments 486 notebook rather than Apple's top-of-the-line 68030-powered PowerBook 180.

Early 486 machines were equipped with several ISA slots (using an emulated PC/AT-bus) and sometimes one or two 8-bit-only slots (compatible with the PC/XT-bus). [6] Many motherboards enabled overclocking of these up from the default 6 or 8 MHz to perhaps 16.5 or 20 MHz (half the i486 bus clock) in a number of steps, often from within the BIOS setup.

Especially older peripheral cards normally worked well at such speeds as they often used standard MSI chips instead of slower (at the time) custom VLSI designs. This could give significant performance gains (such as for old video cards moved from a 386 or 286 computer, for example). However, operation beyond 8 or 10 MHz could sometimes lead to stability problems, at least in systems equipped with SCSI or sound cards.

Some motherboards came equipped with a 32-bit bus called EISA that was backward compatible with the ISA-standard. EISA offered a number of attractive features such as increased bandwidth, extended addressing, IRQ sharing, and card configuration through software (rather than through jumpers, DIP switches, etc) However, EISA cards were expensive and therefore mostly employed in servers and workstations.

Consumer desktops often used the simpler but faster VESA Local Bus, unfortunately somewhat prone to electrical and timing-based instability; typical consumer desktops had

ISA slots combined with a single VLB slot for a video card. VLB was gradually replaced by PCI during the final years of the 80486 period.

Few Pentium motherboards had VLB support as VLB was based directly on the i486 bus; it was no trivial matter adapting it to the quite different Pentium-bus. ISA persisted through the original Pentium generation and was not completely displaced by PCI until the Pentium III era.

Late 486 boards were normally equipped with both PCI- and ISA-slots, and sometimes a single VLB slot as well. In this configuration VLB or PCI thoughput suffered depending on how buses were bridged.

The VLB slot in these systems was usually only fully compatible with video cards (quite fitting as "VESA" stands for *Video Electronics Standards Association*); VLB-IDE, multi I/O, or SCSI cards could have problems on motherboards with PCI slots.

The VL-Bus operated at the same clock speed as the i486-bus (basically *being* a local 486-bus) while the PCI bus also usually depended on the i486 clock but sometimes had a divider setting available via the BIOS. This could be set to 1/1 or 1/2, sometimes even 2/3 (for 50 MHz CPU clocks).

Some motherboards limited the PCI clock to the specified maximum of 33 MHz and certain network cards depended on this frequency for correct bit-rates. The ISA clock was typically generated by a divider of the CPU/VLB/PCI clock (as implied above).

UART DESIGN

BACKGROUND

UART stands for "Universal Asynchronous Receiver Transmitter." For our purposes, it is a relatively simple device that illustrates the the nature of device controllers (DCs) in general.

A UART acts as the interface between an I/O bus and a serial device, such as a mouse or modem, which communicate with a computer one bit at a time. On a PC, there are two

UARTs that connect to the COM1 and COM2 ports on the back of the computer. The job of a UART is to accept bytes of data from the CPU 8 bits at a time (in parallel) and to transmit them one bit at a time (serially) to whatever device is plugged into its connector on the back of the computer.

At the same time, it receives data bits serially from the device, which it assembles into bytes that the CPU reads in parallel.

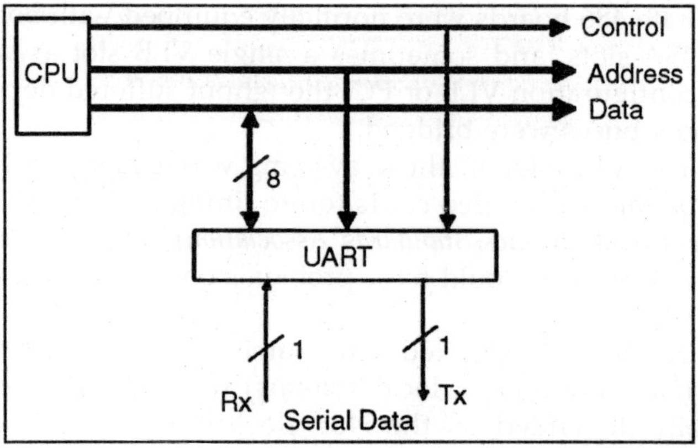

Internally, a UART has several different registers that the CPU can read and write. The following table lists just a few of them. The left column lists the addresses the CPU uses to access these registers for a UART being used for COM1 in a standard PC.

Address	**Name**	**Function**
0x3F8	RBR	Read Buffer Register. The CPU reads data bytes from this register.
0x3F8	THR	Transmitter Holding Register. The CPU writes data bytes to this register.
0x3F9	IER	Interrupt Enable Register. The CPU writes a byte to this register to tell the UART when to generate interrupts. Individual bits within the byte indicate whether to generate an interrupt when the RBR is full, when the THR is empty, or when an error condition is detected.
0x3FA	IIR	Interrupt Identification Register. The CPU reads

		this register to find out why the UART generated an interrupt.
0x3FB	LCR	Line Configuration Register. The CPU writes bytes to this register to configure parameters like baud rate (the speed at which bits are sent and received) and parity (error checking) options.
0x3FD	LSR	Line Status Register. The CPU reads from this register to find out whether the RBR is full, whether the THR is empty, or whether an error condition has been detected.

This table is far from complete, but it is accurate as far as it goes. The registers described here give us enough to work with so we can see how a Device Controller works.

To understand how a UART operates we also need to introduce two additional registers that are not in the table, and which the CPU cannot access directly. These are the shift registers connected to the R_x and T_x wires.

The R_x shift register (R_x SR) is an 8 bit register that receives incoming serial data. When 8 data bits have arrived, the R_x SR is transferred in parallel into the 8-bit RBR. While waiting for the CPU to read from the RBR, the R_x SR can start receiving bits from the next input byte on the R_x line. Likewise, there is a T_x shift register (T_x SR) that gets loaded from the THR in parallel, and then shifts the bits out over the T_x wire one at a time.

While the T_x SR is transmitting a byte, the CPU can write another data byte to the THR.

SOFTWARE LAYERS

The descriptions of the registers in the table above used phrases like, "the CPU reads ..." and "the CPU writes ...". Statements like this means that some software, called a Device Driver, executes the CPU's in and out ISA-level instructions.

For example, the Intel Architecture instruction inb 0x3F8 would read a byte from the RBR of the COM1 UART into the CPU's "AL" register.

Each Device Controller attached to the I/O Bus has its own Device Driver in the operating system. As the figure below indicates, the Device Driver is the lowest of several layers of software involved in I/O operations.

At the top of the figure, a programme (this could be a C or C++ programme) has set up an array of bytes named inBuf and calls a function to read a string of characters into the array.

We'll assume that the string the programme reads consists of characters a user types on a keyboard that is connected to the Rx input line of a UART.

The fgets() function is part of the C or C++ Runtime Library that gets linked to all C/C++ programs. The library functions manage their own buffer of data.

If there are enough data bytes available in the library buffer, the call to fgets() is just a quick function call that copies the requested string from the library buffer to inBuf, and the user's programme spends virtually no time at all making the function call.

But if there are not enough bytes in the library buffer to satisfy the call to fgets(), it calls read(), which is an Operating System Call that goes through several layers of software in the OS until finally some code extracts bytes from the Device Driver's "typeahead buffer" shown in the lower part of the figure.

When the device driver reads a byte from the RBR, it puts it into the tail of the typeahead buffer FIFO (first-in, first-out queue).

This buffer is called a "typeahead" buffer because the user can type characters before any programme tries to read them, and they will be kept here until a read() system call consumes them and passes them back up to the library's buffer.

But if the typeahead buffer doesn't have a complete string in it when the read() function is executed, the programme will be blocked until the user types enough characters for the Device Driver to put into the typeahead buffer for the read() function to complete.

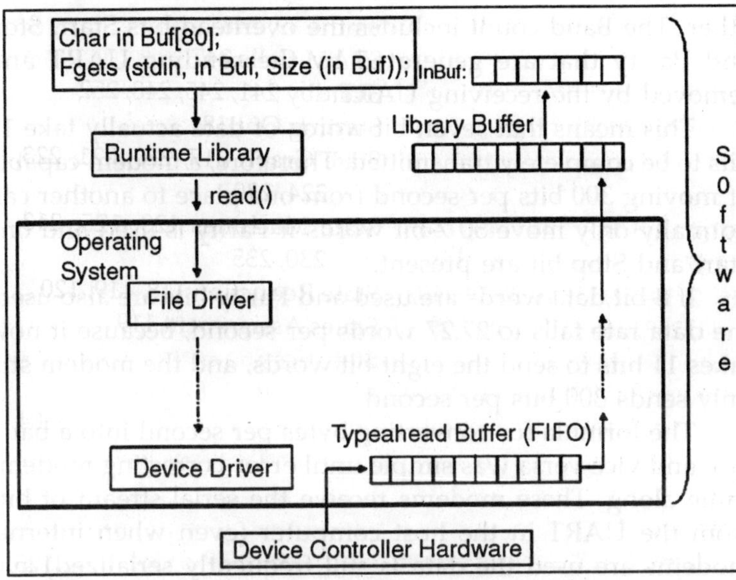

The boundary between the Runtime Library and the Operating System is an important one. The input and output instructions that Device Drivers execute are "privileged" instructions that will cause the CPU to generate a fault (a hardware-generated exception) if code in the library tries to execute them.

Switching the CPU from non-privileged to privileged mode is a very time-consuming operation compared to a simple function call, a topic (hopefully) covered in your Operating Systems course. The Runtime Library is designed to minimize the number of system calls a programme has to make as much as possible.

BITS, BAUD AND SYMBOLS

Baud is a measurement of transmission speed in asynchronous communication. Because of advances in modem communication technology, this term is frequently misused when describing the data rates in newer devices.

Traditionally, a Baud Rate represents the number of bits that are actually being sent over the media, not the amount of data that is actually moved from one DTE device to the other. The Baud count includes the overhead bits Start, Stop and Parity that are generated by the sending UART and removed by the receiving UART.

This means that seven-bit words of data actually take 10 bits to be completely transmitted. Therefore, a modem capable of moving 300 bits per second from one place to another can normally only move 30 7-bit words if Parity is used and one Start and Stop bit are present.

If 8-bit data words are used and Parity bits are also used, the data rate falls to 27.27 words per second, because it now takes 11 bits to send the eight-bit words, and the modem still only sends 300 bits per second.

The formula for converting bytes per second into a baud rate and vice versa was simple until error-correcting modems came along. These modems receive the serial stream of bits from the UART in the host computer (even when internal modems are used the data is still frequently serialized) and converts the bits back into bytes.

These bytes are then combined into packets and sent over the phone line using a Synchronous transmission method. This means that the Stop, Start, and Parity bits added by the UART in the DTE (the computer) were removed by the modem before transmission by the sending modem.

When these bytes are received by the remote modem, the remote modem adds Start, Stop and Parity bits to the words, converts them to a serial format and then sends them to the receiving UART in the remote computer, who then strips the Start, Stop and Parity bits.

The reason all these extra conversions are done is so that the two modems can perform error correction, which means that the receiving modem is able to ask the sending modem to resend a block of data that was not received with the correct checksum. This checking is handled by the modems, and the DTE devices are usually unaware that the process is occurring.

By striping the Start, Stop and Parity bits, the additional bits of data that the two modems must share between themselves to perform error-correction are mostly concealed from the effective transmission rate seen by the sending and receiving DTE equipment. For example, if a modem sends ten 7-bit words to another modem without including the Start, Stop and Parity bits, the sending modem will be able to add 30 bits of its own information that the receiving modem can use to do error-correction without impacting the transmission speed of the real data.

The use of the term Baud is further confused by modems that perform compression. A single 8-bit word passed over the telephone line might represent a dozen words that were transmitted to the sending modem. The receiving modem will expand the data back to its original content and pass that data to the receiving DTE.

Modern modems also include buffers that allow the rate that bits move across the phone line (DCE to DCE) to be a different speed than the speed that the bits move between the DTE and DCE on both ends of the conversation. Normally the speed between the DTE and DCE is higher than the DCE to DCE speed because of the use of compression by the modems.

Because the number of bits needed to describe a byte varied during the trip between the two machines plus the differing bits-per-seconds speeds that are used present on the DTE-DCE and DCE-DCE links, the usage of the term Baud to describe the overall communication speed causes problems and can misrepresent the true transmission speed.

So Bits Per Second (bps) is the correct term to use to describe the transmission rate seen at the DCE to DCE interface and Baud or Bits Per Second are acceptable terms to use when a connection is made between two systems with a wired connection, or if a modem is in use that is not performing error-correction or compression.

Modern high speed modems (2400, 9600, 14,400, and 19,200bps) in reality still operate at or below 2400 baud, or more accurately, 2400 Symbols per second.

High speed modem are able to encode more bits of data into each Symbol using a technique called Constellation Stuffing, which is why the effective bits per second rate of the modem is higher, but the modem continues to operate within the limited audio bandwidth that the telephone system provides. Modems operating at 28,800 and higher speeds have variable Symbol rates, but the technique is the same.

Asynchronous Serial Transmission

Asynchronous transmission allows data to be transmitted without the sender having to send a clock signal to the receiver. Instead, the sender and receiver must agree on timing parameters in advance and special bits are added to each word which are used to synchronize the sending and receiving units.

When a word is given to the UART for Asynchronous transmissions, a bit called the "Start Bit" is added to the beginning of each word that is to be transmitted. The Start Bit is used to alert the receiver that a word of data is about to be sent, and to force the clock in the receiver into synchronization with the clock in the transmitter. These two clocks must be accurate enough to not have the frequency drift by more than 10% during the transmission of the remaining bits in the word. (This requirement was set in the days of mechanical teleprinters and is easily met by modern electronic equipment.)

After the Start Bit, the individual bits of the word of data are sent, with the Least Significant Bit (LSB) being sent first. Each bit in the transmission is transmitted for exactly the same amount of time as all of the other bits, and the receiver "looks" at the wire at approximately halfway through the period assigned to each bit to determine if the bit is a 1 or a 0. For example, if it takes two seconds to send each bit, the receiver will examine the signal to determine if it is a 1 or a 0 after one second has passed, then it will wait two seconds and then examine the value of the next bit, and so on.

The sender does not know when the receiver has "looked" at the value of the bit. The sender only knows when the clock says to begin transmitting the next bit of the word. When the entire data word has been sent, the transmitter may add a Parity Bit that the transmitter generates.

The Parity Bit may be used by the receiver to perform

simple error checking. Then at least one Stop Bit is sent by the transmitter.

When the receiver has received all of the bits in the data word, it may check for the Parity Bits (both sender and receiver must agree on whether a Parity Bit is to be used), and then the receiver looks for a Stop Bit.

If the Stop Bit does not appear when it is supposed to, the UART considers the entire word to be garbled and will report a Framing Error to the host processor when the data word is read.

The usual cause of a Framing Error is that the sender and receiver clocks were not running at the same speed, or that the signal was interrupted.Regardless of whether the data was received correctly or not, the UART automatically discards the Start, Parity and Stop bits. If the sender and receiver are configured identically, these bits are not passed to the host.

Index